The Great Beer Trek

By **Stephen Morris**
Illustrations by Vance Smith

The Stephen Greene Press

Brattleboro, Vermont   *Lexington, Massachusetts*

To Laura and Jake. Next time we'll have air conditioning.

Richardson's Saccharometer is adapted from *One Hundred Years of Brewing* (1903: H.S. Rich & Co., reprinted by Arno Press) p. 24, and *Josiah Chowning, from his sign* from Bob Abel's *Book of Beer* (1976: Henry Regnery Co., Chicago), p. 175, with thanks.

First Edition

Copyright © 1984 by The Stephen Greene Press

This book is manufactured in the United States of America. It is designed by Vance Smith and published by The Stephen Greene Press, Fessenden Road, Brattleboro, Vermont 05301.

Distributed in the United States by E.P. Dutton, Inc.

Library of Congress Cataloging in Publication Data

Morris, Stephen, 1948–
  The great beer trek.

  1. Beer—United States. I. Title.
TP577.M67 1984   641.2'3'0973   83-25483
ISBN 0–8289–0525–8 (pbk.)

Contents

Preface

Moot Points and a Fluid Subject

Beer is a fluid subject. Moreover, it is a moving target. By the time the modern marketing man gets through with beer, the hapless beer drinker has a difficult time telling whether his affinity for a given brew comes from the contents of the bottle, the graphics on the label, or the peer group in the commercial.

Let's take a semi-hypothetical, and confusing, example. McSorley's Ale House in New York serves a libation which bears the establishment name. The widespread fame of the tavern results as much from this beer as the Liedercranz and onion sandwiches or the dusty wishbones strung over the chandeliers. Within the past two decades, however, McSorley's Ale has been brewed by three different brewers, Rheingold, Ortlieb, and Schmidt, in brewkettles from New Bedford, Massachusetts, to Orange, New Jersey. In tracing McSorley's lineage, in fact, one is hard pressed to find any consistent thread which distinguishes this brew from Coors or Old Milwaukee. Through the years brewers have changed, recipes have been altered, and equipment has evolved.

The murky pedigree matters not one iota to the beer drinker who rests his foot on the brass rail at McSorley's. So long as his brew retains a hoppier-than-thou aftertaste and provides the best possible accompaniment to a Liedercranz and onion sandwich, it will be forgiven transitory

moodiness. The man with the mug (or "woman," McSorley's having lost its status as an all-male sanctuary) will be indulgent so long as his brew maintains its basic integrity and continues to be served with love and care by a sympathetic barkeep. Where it is brewed and by whom are moot points.

My involvement with beer started typically enough. As a callow youth in college I began drinking the stuff, sometimes with discrimination, always with enthusiasm. My foam-filled horizons widened significantly several years after graduation when my wife, Laura, and I spent a year working in London. The clammy discomfort of a basement flat dictated spending many an evening toasting our buns by the coal fire in the neighborhood local, a friendly pub called the Queen's Elm. Over the course of a year, after quaffing countless pints of hand-drawn bitter, we learned:

1. The world of beer drinking is far more varied than a person reared on a diet of Pabst, Bud, and Miller Lite could believe.

2. An organization of fanatical British beer drinkers (called CAMRA) had formed to prevent the adulteration of their national brew by efficiency-minded beer manufacturers.

3. You can make your own beer! You can make it black, red, brown, or yellow with a taste range which extends from lemonade to coal tar.

Looking back now, a veteran of more than a hundred batches of home-brew, I am not sure why this last revelation so astonished me, but at the time the concept of making beer was as alien as the idea of making my own aspirin. Only when the image of "liquid bread" sank in could I grasp that my own creations—even when not the equal of the commercial brewers' — could infinitely enrich beer drinking pleasure.

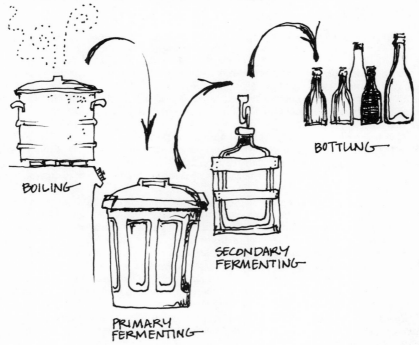

BOILING

BOTTLING

SECONDARY
FERMENTING

PRIMARY
FERMENTING

I can make my own beer!

Upon returning stateside, armed with a suitcase full of British brewing kits, I immediately set out to expose my friends to the wonders of home-brew only to discover that the pastime was illegal, moreover a felony (this was in the early 1970's). For the first time in a spoiled, middle-class life I actually felt my liberty threatened. The government of my fatherland would put me behind bars simply for mixing grain with water, adding

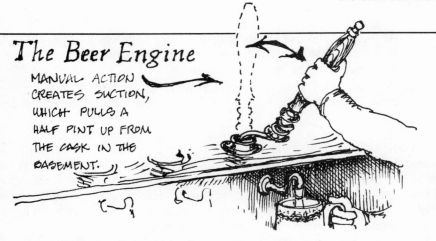

The Beer Engine

MANUAL ACTION
CREATES SUCTION,
WHICH PULLS A
HALF PINT UP FROM
THE CASK IN THE
BASEMENT.

The Campaign For Real Ale

In the early 1970's, British beer drinkers noticed a disturbing trend. Their unpasteurized, distinctive, traditional beers drawn from the wood were quickly being replaced by a cold, bland, gassy substitute. More alarmingly, the major brewers seemed caught in an acquisition frenzy which destined many fine local brews to oblivion. So the British beer drinker, in true God-Save-the-Queen spirit, did the only possible thing. He charged.

Thus was born the Campaign for Real Ale, known throughout beerdom as CAMRA. From the humblest of beginnings, its legions have swelled to include potent numbers of beer drinkers who feel that they have an inalienable right to a beverage which is neither adulterated with chemicals nor carbonated through the injection of gasses. In short, they have a right to real ale.

CAMRA has achieved its goals using a variety of weapons ranging from economic boycott to brewery picketing. It has outsmarted the brewing industry by effectively countering the brewers' claims that the proliferation of the pressurized keg beer was due to consumer demand rather than manufacturing convenience.

And the result? A resounding victory for the beer drinker. More than half of British pubs now serve real ale as opposed to a tiny fraction in the early 1970's when CAMRA was formed. Many small breweries have gained a new lease on life and even the larger brewers have seen the economic merits of producing hand-crafted, varietal beers to cater to the swelling ranks of real ale enthusiasts.

Could the Real Ale Revolt spread across the Atlantic? Unlikely, although the domestic beer drinker is no less a fanatic than his English counterpart. In the United States, the manufacturer has gained a stranglehold which will be hard to break. The poor suds swiller cannot truly lament the continuing disappearance of real ale because, chances are, he has never tasted the real thing. Unpasteurized, hand-drawn ales have not been readily available in this country since before Prohibition.

CAMRA—The Campaign for Real Ale   CAMRA—Canada
34 Alina Road   Unit 5
St. Albans, Herts   190 Booth Street
AL 1 3BW   Ottawa K1R 7J4
UK   CANADA

yeast purchased at the Stop 'n' Shop, waiting a few days, then drinking the concoction.

Now the die was cast. I felt a kindred spirit with colonial patriots who, back in 1773, dumped unfairly taxed tea into the waters of nearby Boston Harbor. (P.S. King George had levied a hefty tax on beer as well.) My patriotism had remained intact even through the Vietnam War, but no one was going to strip me of my God-given right to drink beer.

This affront to my liberties eventually motivated me to become more formally interested in the contemporary role of beer in America. A trip seemed the best way to learn. The Great Beer Trek is the chronicle of the resultant adventure. We hope our story can become your guide to an equally enlightening and lubricating journey into the nooks and crannies of beerdom.

Beer's newfound popularity has spawned a plethora of experts, each having his own framework of interpretation. Some use brewery ownership as the determining factor, others place of origin or brand name. Still others use taste as the demarcation line between beers.

We found the nuances of taste to be insignificant alongside the seemingly infinite ability of the beer drinker to create ritual around the act of consumption. So this book is not about beer and brewing so much as about beer drinking. And the best advice for the reader is to relax, don't worry, and have another. Forever beer.

The Great Beer Trek is intended either for reference or casual reading. While the narrative reflects the chronological growth of our knowledge, casual flipping is by no means inappropriate. But please, read this book with a beer by your side. That's the way it was written.

1 Beer Drinker Americanus

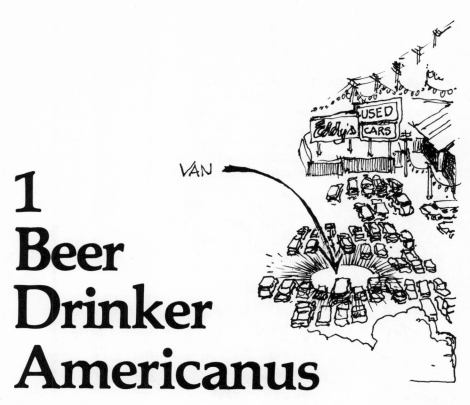

Scituate, Massachusetts

A Twilight of Darts

Old friends drift apart, rightfully so. If they meet again, the scars of passions, positions, wives, wars, children and success obscure once-familiar features. Behind a mask of the present each peers through the other's disguise. Not until the last bit of make-up is gone, the wigs and rubber noses discarded, do old friends become new.

So many of my friendships were formed over beer . . . over six-packs smuggled into football games, over sudsy water swilled from paper cups (one in each hand) at freshman mixers, over carefree pitchers at Rudy's Bar & Grill, over crisp pilsners on ceremonial weekends.

Now I manage to get together with old friends once or twice a year, whenever. The occasion may be a football game, fishing, a business trip, or, as in the instance about to be described, a Fourth of July weekend visit. But the occasion always involves beer.

In the morning there was a parade through town. We awoke to the off-key sound of a drum and bugle corps, followed by a twenty-one gun salute during which at least three guns misfired. The group that had gathered at odd hours in the night, stayed up too late, and drank too much, now arose to a morning buttered by holiday sunshine.

The day was designed especially for play, each of us having successfully left our shackles elsewhere. Implements of "war" were brought forth: tennis racquets, a croquet set, a canoe. The day was passed in frolic; Monday would be time enough to worry about sore muscles. By twilight the frenzy had passed and the tranquility of twilight was disturbed only by the soft thunk-thunk-thunk of darts slipping into a well-weathered

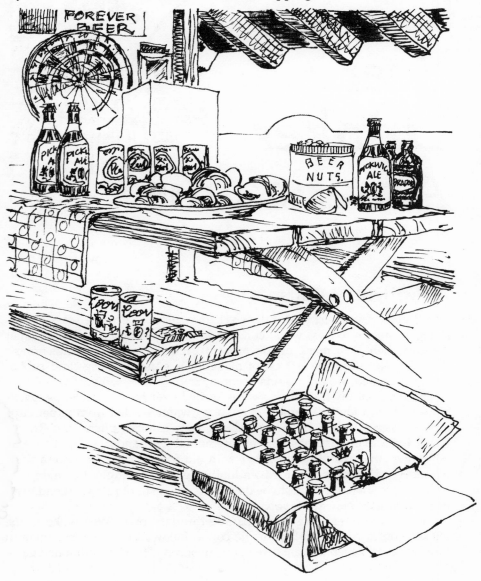

board, accented by the occasional PCHSSSST! The signs were unmistakable: Beer Drinker Americanus in his natural habitat.

Like a good host I had laid in ample provisions in anticipation of my old friends. Cherrystone clams, Pickwick Ale, beer nuts—the larder bulged with the essentials of the perfectly balanced holiday diet. Bob had driven from Baltimore with a case of National Premium beer and a box of boiled crabs slathered with a curry sauce so hot that the only effective antidote was more beer. Fen came from Montreal with a twelve-pack of Molson Brador, a potent, robust brew not exported to the United States. John, who has always identified with the common man, had taken an all-night Greyhound from St. Louis, his suitcase laden with Coors and Pearl. The man travels in style.

Darkness descended unnoticed on the back porch dart game until someone realized we could no longer see the board. Someone asked the score, and the rest of us groaned. No one cared. The night was warm, the crabs and clams delicious, the moon was yellow, and there was no conceivable way we could run out of beer. We could live forever in this twilight of darts.

The game eventually became incidental to the conversation. The obligatory catching-up had by now been dispensed with and the floor was given to a profound discussion of The Meaning of Life, a subject which had occupied untold hours in the term of our previous acquaintance. This time our pool of arrogant ease was not so brimming. We retreated into sentimentality, lamenting the absence of those who had shared our concerns, if not our fates. Remember Peter? What the hell do you think happened to Peter?

By midnight "The Meaning of Life" became "the meaning of our lives." We boasted of success, then shut up as we saw our accomplishments in light of the original goals. Not a single one of us had changed the world, and now, on a warm summer night, on a back porch, bathed by moonlight and gentle sea breezes, it did not seem so much in need of change. What was left to believe in?

The awkward silence was broken by John, master of timing and the well-turned phrase, who stood and repeated the litany which we realized had set the rhythm of the entire night: "When in doubt, have another beer. What can I get you: Molson, National, Pickwick, Coors, or Pearl?"

Aha. Perhaps we had been trying too hard. Why worry about cosmic issues beyond our control when we could be enjoying the simplest of pleasures—good food, good company, good beer.

The Great Beer Trek, thus, was born. The decision came easily once the alternatives were considered. On one hand was the life for which I had been raised—safe, secure, and plush enough to provide all the beer I could conceivably consume (although martinis or chablis were considered more appropriate). This component life, complete with optional extras such as Transcendental Meditation, est, TA, yoga, golf, Pyramid Power,

PTA, Jesus, valium, the VFW, or even my own shrink, featured a good job, a beautiful wife, a nice home, and a bleak future . . . The American Dream!

I began to perceive, not surprisingly, that the entire country, if not the world, revolved around beer. There was much to learn, but only so much to be learned where I lived. I felt compelled to go out to where the barley was grown. I had to see steelworkers and cowboys chugging. I had to taste the beers of the tiny breweries whose exotic names rang through my sodden brain—Leinenkugel, Yuengling, Anchor, Dixie. I had to learn the Secret of the Suds. I had to go on a Beer Trek.

The idea of a Beer Trek is not new. A popular entertainment in 17th-century Germany was "beer riding." A young noble loaded a cart with beer and left for the nearest duchy. After sharing the liquid refreshment with his host, he filled his barrels and headed for the next manor, taking with him any revelers who cared to come along. Their performance was repeated so long as people contributed beer and joined in the fun. The well-planned "beer ride" could last forever, the trip being over only when the beer ran out.

On an entirely unfrivolous level, I realized that by understanding a nation's beer drinking habits, one could understand the nation. The pieces slid into place. My wife, Laura, is, thankfully, a beer drinker who understands that civilizations rise and fall on their beer bellies. Our dog, Guinness (named for the world's finest stout), welcomed the chance to become the most beerwise dog in the annals of American canine history. Thus, it was settled. The three of us would cruise the land, learning about Beer Drinker Americanus, a noble and loftly goal. For a chariot we would ride in a well-used Chevy van with a mere 86,000 miles under its chassis.

If the Lord protects fools and tipplers, then surely The Great Beer Trek would be doubly blessed.

Explanation of the Trekker's Guide

The purpose of this book is to entertain and to inform. At the end of each regional section is an appendix of factual information to help the future or armchair beer trekker.

State Beer

Theoretically this represents the single brand most closely and uniquely identified with the state's personality. Utterly arbitrary and frivolous, but then how do you think state birds, flowers, and trees came to be?

Breweries

All known breweries and branch plants are listed. Tour information and breweriana availability are included. Brands are listed only once, with the parent company, except in cases where the subsidiary is clearly identified with specific brews. The transitory nature of brands must be stressed, as what is here today may well be gone tomorrow.

Kindred Spirits

At one time, beer fanatics were solitary figures in America, but now groups such as can collectors and home brewers have united. Members from either sector will likely be able to steer you to the best local brew.

Of Note

The people, places, and things which defy categorization but demand inclusion.

The Brews

THE ORDER OF THE TREK

Awarded to those brews which represent the region's highest expression of the brewing art. Taste is too personal to pass judgment on, but be assured that these brews are all drinkable. You can't go wrong with these beers.

WORTHY OF MENTION

A somewhat lesser category but still a mark of distinction, not always positive. Try these products, then form your own opinion.

Legend: ★ OF NOTE   🥛 KINDRED SPIRIT   DEFUNCT BREWERY   OPERATING BREWERY

2 The New World

Boston, Massachusetts, to Strafford, Vermont
7 days, 820 miles on the road

Where Have You Gone, King Gambrinus

New Bedford, Massachusetts

Thus was the garden tilled for the Fourth of July seed which would blossom into The Great Beer Trek. Another two years of preparation ensued; in fact, enough time elapsed that it became questionable whether or not the ship would ever set sail. Nonetheless, preparations began. I made up stationery and wrote letters to everyone in the beer business, from Augie Busch to Ed McMahon. I read every piece of beer-related literature I could find. I tasted every brew available locally. I bought a vehicle (a 1972 Chevrolet Beauville Sportsman with 86,000 miles) destined to become our noble steed, carrying us from beery highlight to lowlight. In short, I became like thousands of other beer fanatics across the country.

Eventually preparations were complete. The van was brewery-ready. The itinerary was finalized. Laura and Guinness reported for final inspection. Now came the hardest part—quitting the job and thus cutting the umbilical cord to reality. Reactions included incredulity, sympathy, and pity. Most of the world, it seems, is entangled in an ethic which defines a quest to learn the Secret of the Suds as an exercise in frivolity.

Nothing could be closer to the truth.

An unforeseen twist occurred when we discovered some two weeks prior to departure that Laura was pregnant, an occurence which would limit her consumption but not her enthusiasm. Oh well, at least there would always be a sober driver.

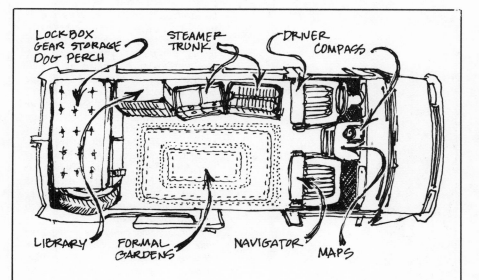

LOCKBOX
GEAR STORAGE
DOG PERCH

STEAMER
TRUNK

DRIVER
COMPASS

LIBRARY

FORMAL
GARDENS

NAVIGATOR

MAPS

Tactical Planning

An army travels on its stomach, a Beer Trek in its van, but for each the success of maneuvers will be directly dependent upon the thoroughness of the advance planning. Here are some tips learned through experience.

Indispensables

A Swiss Army knife, dash-mounted compass, Rand McNally Road Atlas with spiral binder, hardcover logbook, credit cards, BCCA (Beer Can Collectors of America) roster, NABA (National Association of Breweriana Advertising) roster, COOLER!

Clothing

A steamer trunk purchased for $5 at an auction proved to be a masterpiece of space-planning efficiency, as well-suited to a van as to a luxury liner stateroom. Bring exercise clothes, and, most importantly, a proper business suit. Often you will be overdressed, but people will

Mail and other communications

respect you for making the effort. You will be treated more seriously than if you appear in cutoffs and sneakers.

Your schedule must be flexible enough to accommodate sudden changes to meet a specific person or to attend a special event. Avoid making commitments too far in advance, and never make arrangements which depend on the other party getting in touch with you. In other words, don't say, "When would be a good time for you?" Instead say, "I will be in town on the 18th, and I will give you a call to arrange a meeting time." Arrange for someone to forward your personal mail to pre-arranged drop points. This is particularly important for your periodicals such as Brewer's Digest, Zymurgy, NABA Newsletter, All About Beer, *and* Beer Can Collectors' Monthly. *You need these to keep up-to-date. It is important to be able to establish your credentials through knowledgeable gossip.*

Library

Your basic homework must be done by the time you hit the road. There is no room for your collection of beer books, so plan to leave your classics at home. One Hundred Years of Brewing *(1903 H.S. Rich & Co., reprinted by Arno Press) is essential, as is the separate index prepared by William D. Ross.* Brewer's Digest's Annual Buyers' Guide *is indispensable as a who's who and source of addresses and phone numbers.* Goodfood, *by Jane and Michael Stern (Knopf), is a guide to the best in America's regional foods. Not surprisingly, there is a considerable overlap between the nation's best eating and beer drinking establishments.*

Forget anything? Of course, but chances are you can buy it at the next K-Mart. One is never far away.

The Great Beer Trek started with a simple theory—that beer is important, and therefore, learning about beer drinking customs and trends would reveal much about society. Minimally, we wanted to visit all existing independent breweries and to hit as many highlights as possible in between. We wanted to learn how beer is made and what role it has played historically in America. Then we wanted to put this information together to see if the original theory was correct. There comes a point, however, when the planning must be put aside and the key inserted into the ignition.

On Debarkation Day the first order of business seemed clear enough: let's have a beer. It seemed to be appropriate to make our first stop at one of our long-time favorite watering holes, Jacob Wirth's in Boston. Jake's has changed little since opening in 1868. The place still has the right counterbalance of elegance and grime which allows both the politicans from the State House and the local rummies to feel equally at home. The waiters still wear tuxedoes and starched aprons, and yet one need not feel guilty about spilling a few peanut shells from the elephant foot serving bowl. The fixtures are ancient, as are many of the waiters. Although other liquors are served, beer is the only suitable accompaniment for the fare at Jacob Wirth's. The menu relies heavily on unadorned and unmentionable parts of the pig.

I asked our waiter, a dignified old gent, about the beers served; one can choose between Jake's "Special Light" and "Special Dark." He was noncommital, saying that the manager did not want the brand of beer divulged, but he did reveal that it was a commercial brand locally available. The question obviously had piqued the interest of an employee who had spent many years serving a proud establishment, and he wanted to show off a little:

"Until a few years ago we served a beer specially brewed for us by Dawson. Now that was good beer."

I asked why they stopped serving Dawson.

"Why, they went out of business a few years ago."

I corrected him. I was an occasional Dawson drinker and had purchased a six-pack locally only a few weeks ago. The clouded look on the waiter's face foretold his confusion:

"I dunno, sir. I'm sure they went out of business five or six years ago."

I asked if he knew where the brewery was. Here was a perfect first adventure for the Beer Trek: to solve the mystery of the missing Dawson. We explained our mission to see, feel and hear nothing but suds for the immediate future. The import of being the first official participant in The Great Beer Trek escaped him, but nonetheless he was polite in his response:

"The brewery was somewhere around here, but I don't know just where. I know who would, though." He fetched another vintage gentleman from behind the bar and explained the Beer Trek to him in terms that were more flattering than I would dare to have used.

"Sure," said the bartender. "New Bedford. That's where Dawson was. But they're gone now." I explained my recent purchase, a phenomenon to which no one could provide an explanation. A silence ended the conversation. It was obviously time for the Beer Trek to set off for New Bedford.

I used the transit time from Boston to the old whaling port of New Bedford to try to find out more about Dawson. The only reference to be found in my mobile library was this short entry in *One Hundred Years of Brewing:* "Benjamin and Joseph Dawson, in 1899, founded this firm, and put their first brew of ale and porter upon the market in May, 1900."

The only mention of any brewery in New Bedford was in an outdated (1976) edition of *Brewer's Digest Annual Buyers' Guide* which listed a Forrest Brewery division of Rheingold.

Many passers-by and quizzical looks later we found the one-time site of Dawson's. It proved to be the same address as Forrest. Completely confused, we sought out a liquor store where we might find a six-pack of Dawson's. At the third stop we struck pay dirt, until we read the fine print on the label, Dawson Brewing Company, Hammonton, New Jersey! The Great Confused Beer Trek, some eight hours away from home, consoled itself with its purchase of a six-pack. The mystery of Dawson's, makers of Jake Wirth's Special, would for the moment remain.

No Matter Where I'm Going   *Cranston, Rhode Island*

The trip from New Bedford to Providence is pleasant in full bloom of spring. But when the brown has not yet turned to green only the bare essentials of life are visible from a passing Beer Trek van. The rivers— Nemasket, Agawam, Passumpsic, Weweantic—provide an historic and geographic orientation. They flow south through the bogs and marshes of southern Massachusetts toward Buzzards Bay. They are tidal rivers whose mud-polished banks glisten and smell at low tide like the wall of an intestine.

The van bounces over roads potholed by the blizzard of '78 and lovingly preserved by the Massachusetts Department of Public Works. The setting is unmistakably and dramatically New England. I am moved to song, spare and simple like the landscape, designed for the untrained voice:

No matter where I'm going
I remember where I've been
And I still like best
The things that seem like home.
Seacoast in the rain, take me there
Green fields from a train, take me there
Take me there.
I can see the sunlight shining
Over Narragansett Bay,
So lift a glass, my friend
And talk to me of home,
Of home.

I do not know if this song is an adaptation of an old whaling tune or the brainchild of an advertising copywriter, but for years this was the theme of Narragansett Beer, a brew which claims to be New England's own. Whether or not the song sold beer, it makes one love New England.

Exposure to Narragansett propaganda started at an early age for me. Curt Gowdy was the announcer for the Red Sox during the lean years of the late fifties/early sixties when the home team consistently failed to fulfill our expectations. After every rally-ending double play hit into by Jackie Jensen or two-base error by Don "Double Dribble" Buddin, Curt's reassuring voice would say, "Hi, Neighbor, Have a 'Gansett," and we would remember it was only a game. For all its faults, Narragansett, like the Red Sox, was the home team.

Sighting the brewery provided us with immediate relief. In an era of faceless industrial parks, the brewery is welcome brick, blood-red and teeming with vitality, a perfect location for the creation of frothy lagers and tart ales. King Gambrinus, patron saint of brewers, overlooks what was once an ice pond, the source of necessary refrigeration, to extend the brewing season. Somewhere along the line a master planner filled it in and converted it into a parking lot. A circular stained glass window over the front door states the company policy, "Made with honor, sold on merit."

On this day, however, the parking lot was empty. A truck driver standing idly by delivered the shocking news. The brewery was closed. Hopefully, temporarily. Production was coming out of the parent company Falstaff's more modern facility in Fort Wayne, Indiana. As to the fate of the Cranston brewery, the driver shrugged:

"They say they're going to reopen it . . ." His voice trailed off into the distance making his lack of confidence obvious.

The first barrels of Narragansett were released to the public in December, 1890. Twenty years later the company had become Rhode Island's largest brewer (225,000 barrels per year) with a thriving West Indies export business to supplement the New England trade. After repeal, theirs was the first beer back on the state market. Narragansett never looked back at local competition.

In the 1930's the firm was purchased by Carl and Rudolph Haffenreffer, prominent Boston brewers whose plans for an empire were cut short by Prohibition. Once in Cranston, they began producing their former brands. In succeeding decades, as other local firms succumbed to the pressure of competition, the Haffenreffers were always around to pick up the pieces. Hanley, Croft, Dugan . . . many of the most prominent names in New England brewing found their lease on life in the Narragansett kettles. Still no sign of Dawson, however.

Eventually and inevitably time caught up with Narragansett. Antiquated equipment needed modernizing, unions demanded higher wages, and television provided national breweries with the means to market to the masses. In 1966 the Haffenreffers joined the swelling ranks of ex-family brewers and sold out to Falstaff. At that time Falstaff was a success phenomenon in the brewing industry, a burgeoning company and the leading brand in each of the thirty-eight states where it was sold.

But time has been unkind to Falstaff. The company is now owned by the same people who own General Brewing, a company as faceless as its name. Their business strategy revolves around buying distressed brew-

The Falstaff Story

At one time this company was the embodiment of success in the beer industry—the first national brand. Falstaff was the leading seller in each of the thirty-eight states in which it was sold. Hell, it even outsold Bud in St. Louis.

The plan was Machiavellian in its simplicity. Buy faltering regional breweries, phase out the local brands in favor of inoffensive, bland Falstaff, especially formulated for the median taste. Lastly, use the efficiency of the mass media to deliver the message, "Your first one is never your last." Instead of a choice of a dry, hoppy ale or a spritzy pilsner, the beer drinker was offered a 12-oz. can, 12-oz. bottle, 16-oz. can, 16-oz. bottle, etc.

eries, reducing "frills" such as marketing expenses, and removing a fair amount of romance from the beer business. Is it any surprise that "New England's Own Beer" is now brewed in Indiana?

To General Brewing's credit, it is apparently more interested in selling beer than creating an empire. This means that Croft Ale, Narragansett Porter, Ballantine India Pale Ale, Haffenreffer Malt Liquor, and Pickwick Ale will be brewed so long as they can be sold. The beer drinker is richer for it, even if the native brews are coming from Fort Wayne rather than Cranston.

The Beer Trek van swung back onto Interstate 95, heading south. There was a prominent billboard greeting us with a hearty, "Hi, Neighbor, Have a 'Gansett," just as Curt Gowdy used to say it.

Someone should have told them the brewery was closed.

For a long time it seemed as if the Falstaff experiment would work. The brand originated at the Lemp Brewery in St. Louis, a mere stone's throw from the Anheuser-Busch cathedral. The Griesediecks, a long-time brewing family, took over the company and formulated the national strategy. Before long Falstaff was the third largest and fastest growing brewery in America.

What went wrong? Certainly the obstinate grit of the beer drinker was a factor. More probably, other brewers followed the Falstaff lead and did it a little better. Budweiser, Schlitz, and Pabst built regional facilities which enabled them to compete locally. The T.V. networks would sell time to anyone. Before long the other breweries developed the promotional techniques which enabled them to take advantage of the efficiencies of national advertising. Falstaff, the great consumer, became one of the consumed. But, for a while, they were indisputably the hottest show in town.

From Hull to Eternity   *New Haven, Connecticut*

The passions of an intimate relationship come bubbling to the surface when men consider their brews. As in any love affair, there is a courtship period after the initial meeting when a beer's wispy hoppiness or nutty richness is imprinted midway between the drinker's brain and throat. The period of devotion may be months, years, or a lifetime. Some beers are good wives, sharing equally times of exaltation and defeat, providing comfort and companionship, leaving us alone when we need to be left alone. Others are mercurial. They beguile us with tricks, and we become fast friends. As the dazzle fades, so does the marriage. Our eyes wander, we cheat. Soon we walk away, a new brand in hand.

We wear beers as badges. The Cape Verdean fisherman who operates a boat out of New Bedford may drink nothing but familiar 'Gansett on tap whether it is brewed in Cranston or Fort Wayne. His son who drives a sanitation truck for the city may order his wife to buy Bud or Schlitz so that his buddies will not think him a cheapskate when they come over to watch a Bruins' game. His son, a college freshman, buys the cheapo budget brand when away and Michelob at home (when Dad is paying.) The cycle is complete.

I returned to the land of Hull and my bright college years for selfish reasons. As the least expensive beer available, it was the natural first choice as the designated beverage on the mixer scene. Whenever social committees met, the question would be raised whether to serve premium beer or Hull's at college functions. The pros and cons would be brought forth in due parliamentary procedure and argued as strenuously as any debate before the political union. In the end would be left the inescapable fact that if we bought Hull's Export, we could buy much, much, much more beer. Case closed.

"Hull's Export Piss" it was called, but we drank it willingly, liberally, and enthusiastically. On a date, however, or at lunch with a professor we would snub these simple cans with their low-rent graphics in favor of beers more befitting our fledgling status in the world. We were young, vain, arrogant, mostly young. Now older, wiser, and more worldly, mostly older, I was in a position to make up for earlier thoughtless remonstrances on "Hull's Export Piss."

The early morning hours are arguably New Haven's finest. Thieves, pimps, junkies, and politicians rest in their lairs, while college students dreamily snooze away the excess of the night before. In four years I had seen New Haven in the cleansing stillness of dawn only in the bleary aftermath of an all-nighter. This morning, cruising once-familiar streets, I thought perhaps my memory had been unfair.

The Beer Trek pushed through the schizophrenic downtown looking for Congress Street and the Hull Brewery. Much of New Haven was leveled in the early sixties, decaying shops and storefronts replaced with cement fortress department stores and parking garages. The reconstruction, which enabled the suburbanite to commute or shop without encountering living beings (save through the windshield of an air-conditioned car), was initially hailed as a landmark of urban renewal. For the residents of New Haven, especially the black communities, the moat-like access roads and one-way streets of urban renewal neatly penned their neighborhoods into concentration camps.

We asked directions of a starched and pressed young black man well-prepared for another day of upward mobility. "Congress Street?" He sounded a suspicious note. "What part of Congress Street?" The brewery, we replied, confident of the prominence of this local landmark.

He nodded, told us to take a right, a left, and a right, cross over the access road, then proceed up Congress Street until we came to the brewery. "You can't miss it," he assured us. "It looks like it's been bombed." Bombed? Traffic was backing up, so we yelled a quick thanks over our shoulders. But the seed had been planted. Bombed?

Congress Street winds through a neighborhood known as The Hill. Originally an ethnic neighborhood (Italian?), "urban renewal" transformed it to exclusively poor and exclusively black. Even morning is not kind to

The Hill. No dew glistens. Children and winos people streets joylessly. The frivolity of The Great Beer Trek produced a flash of guilt, obscuring our nobility of purpose. Suddenly, a gigantic glass of beer loomed several hundred yards ahead. The billboard was attached to a large brick building which dominated the street for a city block. As we came nearer we read the line on the billboard, "Connecticut's only brewery."

Omigod.

The brewery had once been handsome. A noble Gambrinus, unmolested on a perch at the building's highest gable, preferred a toast to The Hill. Although the billboard was freshly painted, the building had experienced the equivalent of the bombing of Dresden. Windows were blown out, parking lots had become repositories for abandoned junk cars, doorways were boarded up, and the loading platforms gaped like open wounds, exposing brewery bowels to the entire world.

The air smelled faintly of malt and urine, a stale, dead odor well-suited to the surroundings. For hundreds of feet in either direction the streets were dusted with beer labels, testifying to a wild Friday night confetti party. I picked up a label: "Malta Caribe . . . pasteurizada. A carbonated cereal beverage brewed from water, malt, corn, corn and invert syrup, hops and caramel color." Not even beer. No self-respecting brewery brews a soft drink if they can brew beer. This is what Hull had been reduced to before succumbing. "Cerveceria Caribe, 820 Congress Street, New Haven, Ct. 06519." The venture did not warrant admission of the company name. This had been the final gasp of a terminally ill business.

The building was intact, yet beyond hope. Not long ago that production line had been humming, but the ensuing disintegration had been swift and lethal. I resisted the temptation to go through the open doors, a wise move when we were subsequently apprehended by three men in a city maintenance truck. Expecting a snarl in reply, I explained defensively that we were just harmless beer freaks taking pictures of the brewery exterior. "What's The Great Beer Trek?" asked the crew boss, a round, balding man of forty-five making a gesture toward the sign on our van. We explained and were rewarded by an unexpected outpouring of friendliness. "Wanna look around inside?" he asked. We did not need a second invitation. "I hope you like bottle caps," he said with a cryptic smirk.

Most of the bottling house equipment was intact, the components deemed of no value by human and animal scavengers. Labels blanketed every horizontal surface, with unthrown bundles waiting for the next party. Some harkened sadly to brews never again to be tasted—Hull's Export Lager, Hull's Bock, Hull's Cream Ale.

Beer experts have spoken highly of these brews. Michael Weiner in his *Taster's Guide to Beer* (Macmillan, 1977) calls Hull's Cream Ale "a real sleeper," while James Robertson's *The Great American Beer Book* (Warner Books, 1980) rates the export lager "one of the best lightly hopped American pilsners."

As for the bottle caps, the crew boss was right—there were passageways where the bottle caps were two feet deep. Footing was simultaneously treacherous and comic. The dim setting was perfect for a horror movie.

"My uncle worked here forty-two years, then just like that it's gone," said our tour guide, a young city worker in his late teens. He punctuated the observation by throwing a handful of caps across a room already knee deep. I asked if he had been a Hull's drinker. "Nah, My uncle said it was good beer, but no one around here drank it much. Said it gave you the shits." I flashed back to Sunday mornings after excessive Saturday nights of encounters of the Hull kind. I had made similar comments when it was the amount, not the quality of the beer, that was at fault.

Outside the boss was telling Laura his opinions on local government. Like any good city worker, he was not overly anxious to get down to work. "They're going to tear this down. You ask me, it doesn't make much sense. Look around here. This area's crap . . . just a bunch of crap. This brewery's the only decent thing left. They tear this down, sell off the brick, then put up one of these housing projects which won't be built half as good. It's a shame. This building's historical. They made beer here more 'n a hundred years." He looked at us for a reaction, but we were still too shell-shocked to register emotion.

"Been gone over pretty good in there, hasn't it?"

"Yeah."

"Yeah, Anything worth anything is long gone. Mazinni here's uncle worked forty-two years in this place."

"Lotta good it did him," piped in Mazinni.

The boss surveyed the surrounding neighborhood. Two little black kids played in the refuse of the labels. Most of the nearby homes were worse off than the brewery. The crew boss knew if he did not say something, it would be time to start work. "It doesn't make sense. This building's good for another hundred years . . ."

It was time for The Great Beer Trek to move on.

We bid adieu.

A Connecticut Cowboy in King Gambrinus's Court
Western Connecticut

From New Haven a stunned Beer Trek turned inland. The morning had soured, beer dregs from last night's party. No need to search deeply for the cause of Hull's ignominious demise. I confess, I murdered Hull. Who scorned the local beer in favor of the more prestigious national brands and imports? Who made jokes about Hull's "Export Piss?" Who assumed there would always be a local beer associated with old school days?

Who?

Me.

For a Beer Trek interpreting America in terms of its brews, so far we had encountered little booze for thought. Could the truth of this odyssey have come so quickly, so easily, and so depressingly? Perhaps there is no beer to trek for. Perhaps we would crisscross landscapes of plastic, neon, and parking lots, meeting only lobotomized swillers of Miller, Schlitz, and Bud.

We continued inland, watching Connecticut's personality change from megalopolis to New England. This diplomatic state maintains schizophrenic gentility in the face of torn loyalties. Is it a suburban and recreational adjunct of New York City or a bona fide rock and winter piece of Yankee real estate? In the town of Derby we stopped for a sandwich and a beer. Two men at the bar were vehemently arguing the relative merits of the Yankees and Red Sox, an ancient battle whose bloodiest field is Connecticut. The Yankee diehard drank Schaefer, the Red Sox booster Narragansett. Perhaps there was an order to the cosmos. We felt a little better.

Will Anderson's loyalties are worn on his forehead, sleeve, and bumper of his car. ("This is Red Sox Country!") Will Anderson is the dean of American beer writers. Protocol demanded the Beer Trek pay respect and homage.

Will Anderson's five beer books concern breweriana, a term invented to describe the realm of beer advertising collectibles—trays, calendars, lithographs, openers, bottles, cans, signs—anything on which the brewer has affixed his name. As much as anyone, Will Anderson's work has elevated and defined the field.

As one "paying homage," I felt entitled to a gray-haired statesman who could spin endless tales of brewing lore. On the trip from New Haven to western Connecticut I prepared a list of formal questions designed to provoke thoughtful answers from the contemplative person of my imagination. The list never got out of my notebook.

Will Anderson stands over six feet with brown curly hair, a mustache, and the build of an athlete ("You should see me on the tennis court or softball field.") He is not modest. He greeted us in baggy white cutoffs, a beer in one hand, a bowl of salad in the other, and French dressing dripping off his mustache. After a hard day on the job as marketing director for a New York publishing company, on top of commuting time, he was not about to put on airs, even for The Great Beer Trek. He made us feel right at home.

Will had a simple beer can collection when he first met his wife, Sonja. Then he graduated to the hard stuff—breweriana. Each new phase of collecting was entered with the uniquely Andersonian form and gusto. As a result they have one of the finest overall breweriana collections in the United States. Not surprisingly, Will's interests go beyond beer to such areas as baseball and rock and roll. In each case, his zeal for collecting is a testament to his passion.

Will's face mirrors the animation in his voice as he digresses long enough to tell us about the excitement of the early days of r[ock] roll. He never allows our beer mugs to fully empty. Although one o[f the] better known beer people in America, Will is not a beer snob. He serv[es] us Fort Schuyler, a budget product of the F.X. Matt Brewing Co., Utica, New York. "This is from one of my favorite breweries," he tells us. As the night wears on we find the list of Will's favorite breweries to be continually expanding. Fort Schuyler has a fruity taste, clean and not at all unpleasant. Will tells us that this beer can still be had for 99 cents a six-pack. Everyone's mug is topped off and the remainder of the bottle balanced precariously in the freezer. Sonja beings telling us about the perils of Life With Will.

"It can get embarrassing sometimes, especially in restaurants . . ."

Will interrupts. "I order the local beer wherever I am. I always order the local beer. If they don't have any, I ask why not."

"There have been times," continues an unruffled Sonja, "when we've walked out of the restaurant because all they have is Bud, Miller, or Schlitz."

"I'll be damned if I'm going to drink one of the national brands," Will begins stoking up. "I'm not going to support those companies. I'll drink a foreign beer before I'll drink a Miller or a Schlitz. I don't even like Heineken, but I'll order one before any of those others."

The phone rings, but before he answers it, Will directs a speech to me. "In your travels I hope you spend some time asking people why they don't drink the local beer. People with a great brewery right in their own town will drink bland fizzwater from the nationals, and pay more for it . . . Hello."

The conversation is swallowed by the phone, and the three of us in the kitchen eavesdrop on a one-way conversation which sounds like the hatching of some nefarious plot. "Just leave the boxes in back. I'll have the stuff by the weekend. Don't worry about the money. I'll hit you the next time I see you."

When Will rejoins us, I ask if perhaps he has another pastime about which he has not yet informed us. "Oh, that," he says with a laugh toward the phone. "My favorite beer is Stegmaier, made by the Lion Brewery down in Wilkes-Barre, Pennsylvania. I'm the unofficial distributor in this area. A lot of people around here have gotten hooked on it." Will tells about the time he was on the television show, "To Tell The Truth." At the end of the questioning he was asked the inevitable, "Which beer is best?" to which he answered Stegmaier. In the following week the brewery received more than two hundred requests for their beer. Will has done his part for local breweries.

More beer is brought out, the old poured atop the new, even though different brands are served. The same qualities which insure that no one will offer Will a waiter's job at the Ritz insure that he will never find himself out of place at a backyard barbeque, a post-softball get-together, or a can collector's convention. The second beer is Koehler from a brewery sched-

19

n Erie, Pennsylvania. "Don't bother," Will tells
heir doors. Another one bites the dust." I am
, but Will obscures the issue by splashing some
g.
derson house features breweriana, even the bath-
h of a stern-featured maiden stares down, pro-
e crowning glory of the house is a barn-like
ill and financed by the success of *The Beer Book.*
(The Pyne Press, 19..,. The vaulted ceilings and walls are obscured by
displays of bottles, cans, signs, trays, posters, and other beeraphernalia.
Most collectors of Will Anderson's magnitude store their treasures in a
warehouse for security reasons, but Will is adamant about enjoying his
collection. "When it gets to the point where I can't enjoy it," he states
simply, "I'll sell it."

"WHO WANTS THE HANDSOME WAITER"
SIGN. ALSO A TRAY.

HAMPDEN BREWING CO., 1934

DAWSON'S, ISSUED
SOON AFTER
REPEAL.

Breweriana, COLL. ANDERSON

Will shows us several trays acquired during a recent vacation to New
Bedford (the Andersons tend to choose vacation spots depending upon
the proximity to old brewery sites and Fenway Park). The trays are splendid
advertising pieces from defunct local breweries, including Dawson's. Each

acquisition has its own story of dusty back rooms and shady antique dealers. It is clearly the chase, not the kill, which motivates Will.

Between dashes to the kitchen for more beer, we hear about Will's
early days in the hobby. No organizations or publications had yet formed
to let practitioners know that other collectors shared a pursuit which normal people regarded as being beyond the lunatic fringe. Will started while
a student at Cornell. He and a roommate made weekend runs to different
brewing towns to procure new beer cans. Beer would be brought back
from Baltimore, Boston, or Philadelphia, and shared with fraternity brothers on the promise that all cans be bottom opened and returned. Ingenious,
even illegal ploys, were used to get new and more exotic cans. Once Will
and his roommate drafted a letter ("a masterpiece of commercial copy-
writing" he still calls it) to all fellow fraternity chapters around the country.
The letter explained that a local beer distributor was staging a contest to
see who could collect the greatest number of beer cans. The winner would
receive a stereo, an item desperately needed by dear old Phi Beta Delta,
or whomever.

The response was spectacular as fraternity chapters rallied to the assis-
tance of a music-deprived brother. Will and his roommate were awash in
beer cans from coast to coast. They had made one mistake, however. They
had requested only a single can of each type, and now there was no fair
way for the two collectors to divide the booty. Finally it was decided that
the only honorable way to settle was on the field of combat, specifically
a bowling alley. For each ten-point differential in score the winning bowler
could take a can from the pile.

"Being the better bowler I ended up with all the cans," Will chuckles
without a trace of humility. His roommate, now a prominent West Coast
breweriana collector, doubtless has his own version of the story.

Back in the kitchen, Will announces final call. Although he was still
going at 78 rpm, tomorrow would bring another long commute into the
city. We took our cue and invited the Andersons to stop by on their next
trip to Fenway Park. We said goodnight. As we walked into the night
Will's voice drifted after us: "Hey . . . you know the bricks on this walk
are from the old Ballantine Brewery."

Mountain Brew *Strafford, Vermont*

The fate of Dawson, we had learned from Will, was not unlike hundreds
of other local brewers. Prohibition had been survived and even World War
II, but the brewer in the post-war era found himself competing in an
entirely new world. The big brewers had successfully shipped their product
across the ocean to homesick and thirsty G.I.'s (Will had shown us some
of the specially designed olive-drab, camouflaged cans.) The prospect of
shipping across America was no longer imposing.

The country was suddenly more affluent, more cosmopolitan, more mobile. Every home had a refrigerator into which cans fit more easily than bottles. The bigger brewers were able to make the expensive packaging changes. With good, fresh beer available in the fridge, why go to the tavern?

Every household had an automobile. The corner grocer was displaced by the "super" market who could negotiate volume discounts from the big brewers. And eventually every home had a television. Now the national brewer could deliver his sales message into the intimacy of your own home with more effectiveness than the hometown concern. The fate of the local brewer was sealed. Dawson's lingered until 1966 when they ceased brewing. Their local and loyal consumership was gracelessly sold to a succession of other local brewers struggling to maintain volume levels by purchasing the hard-earned drinkership of less fortunate counterparts. Eastern Brewing in Hammonton, New Jersey, was merely the latest and perhaps last home of Dawson.

The sober reality of the brewery pogrom weighed heavily on The Great Beer Trek as we pulled into the visitors' parking lot of the gleaming steel and tile plant of Anheuser-Busch in Merrimack, New Hampshire. As often happens when one is in a bad mood, the resulting outburst is spontaneous and arbitrary. In this case the unwitting recipient of our abuse was the squeaky-clean, collegiate-looking wimp who was conducting our tour. He recited his script flawlessly, yet how was he to know that among the tourists in his group were beer trekkers unfairly blaming Anheuser-Busch for the ill fortune of hundreds of local brewers from coast to coast? His recitation of the brewing process was repeatedly interrupted by pointedly embarrassing questions. "Which of the 59 approved FDA additives are contained in Budweiser?" "Has Anheuser-Busch ever employed predatory pricing strategies in order to drive local brewers out of business?" "How much does Anheuser-Busch pay Ed McMahon to push their products on T.V.?" The guide responded with suitably innocuous gibberish.

After the tour we sat in the neo-Bavarian plastic splendor of the hospitality room. Acting petty never makes one feel good. And one feels even smaller when one accepts the hospitality and free beer of the recently abused host immediately afterward. It was a low, depressing moment for voyageurs who had set out to find the Secret of the Suds and who now apparently had found that there was no Secret left to find.

"Let's get out of here," I said to Laura.

We were now heading north into the Green Mountains and the hinterlands. Our next stop was in Strafford, Vermont, where we were scheduled to meet with Tim Matson, co-author of a simple tome on home brewing called *Mountain Brew* (1975, Miller Pond Books, Strafford, VT). Would we arrive only to find his rustic cabin to be in the same lame state as Hull or Narragansett?

The serenity of the passing scenery gave time to reflect on the recent stop in Merrimack. One had to give Anheuser-Busch their grudging due. First, the company did not have to give tours at all; that they chose to do so showed a laudable concern for the people who consume their products. Second, the tour was well-organized, educational, and professionally executed even if conducted by a callow, pimply tour guide rather than a ruddy-faced brewmaster. And lastly, the beer is good. One may not like the type of beer that Budweiser is, but for its type there is no better.

The tour depicted a brewery that takes no shortcuts in the brewing process, a series of steps which are finite in number but infinite in their variation. Grain, preferably barley, is harvested. The grain is allowed to germinate under controlled conditions, then roasted to arrest the process. The grain is steeped in water to extract the soluable sugars, flavored with hops, strained and cooled. Yeast, an organic mass of minute fungi, is added, and multiplies itself by feeding on the available starches and sugars, giving off carbon dioxide and alcohol as by-products. The resulting liquid is beer.

One can laugh at the homespun naïvté of *Mountain Brew*, but to do so is to misunderstand the intentions of this modest book. Once one has the proper orientation, or what Tim Matson would call "spirit," then one can laugh at *Mountain Brew*. Tim Matson confided that commercial wine- and beer-making supply shops hated his book and would not sell it. In his words, "They didn't like *Mountain Brew* because it was against all the bullshit. You know, I've been down the road with all those imported malts and fancy equipment, but here we were just getting loaded on Blue Ribbon Malt you could buy at the grocery store, making really sleazy beer, and having a great time. The beer wasn't great, but it was pretty good."

The book, or more accurately the booklet, was compiled and produced by Tim with no outside financing but lots of help from his friends. It was produced by a local women's collective who knew as much about graphics as Tim did about homebrew. The cover was adapted from a drawing by a nine-year-old girl. Tim describes the experience: "It was a very pure thing. No deals, no contracts, no calculations involved . . . everyone just grooved along with the idea."

To describe *Mountain Brew* as a guide to home brewing would be misleading. Rather it is a description of a life-style for which homebrew is a spiritual center. From the craftsman's standpoint, the book is oversimplified. A hydrometer, the instrument used to measure the unfermented sugars in the wort, is described as "made out of glass" with "numbers and lines on it." Some readers might object to a philosophy typified by statements like, "With food stamps I could make big batches of beer." And some passages in the book defy comprehension:

Technology is going down so fast you can't keep up with it. Or maybe it's the humidity. The greenhouse effect. Except rock. People try hard not to care about the rocks. Since rocks were there first, before the Indians. What do we do with rocks? Gouge them out and run highways through them. Those rocks never grow any corn or hops. And corn and hops make beer.

Its shortcomings should not keep one from enjoying the unique perspective of *Mountain Brew*. What the contributors lack in writing skill (in their defense it must be said that no pretensions of literary proficiency

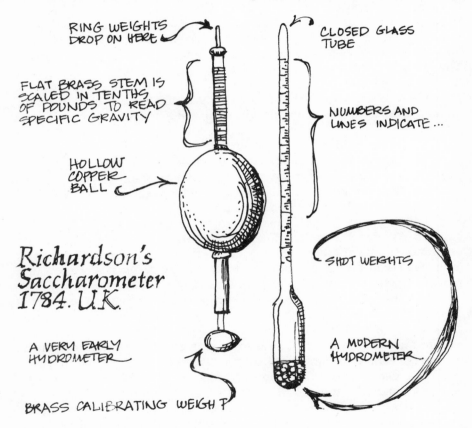

RING WEIGHTS DROP ON HERE

FLAT BRASS STEM IS SCALED IN TENTHS OF POUNDS TO READ SPECIFIC GRAVITY

HOLLOW COPPER BALL

Richardson's Saccharometer 1784. U.K.

A VERY EARLY HYDROMETER

CLOSED GLASS TUBE

NUMBERS AND LINES INDICATE ...

SHOT WEIGHTS

A MODERN HYDROMETER

BRASS CALIBRATING WEIGH?

were ever claimed), they make up for in ingenuity. Anyone discouraged with the blandness of American beers can look to *Mountain Brew* to learn about brewers who concoct experimental brews with Postum, wormwood, Maxim (to get a beer with caffeine), buckwheat groats, steak bones, chicken heads, maple syrup, and burdock root. There are no mysteries about beer to the Green Mountain brewers. A simple product results from a simple process which the brewer controls. Some experiments result in improved beers, some in swill, but all will be consumed in a society which cannot

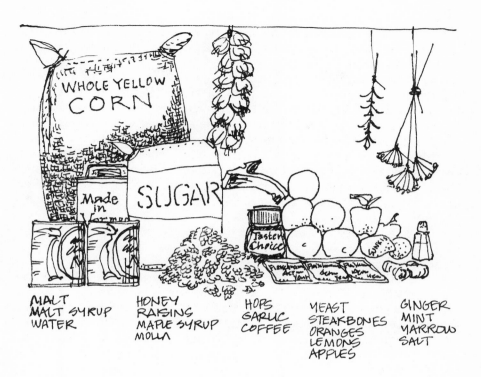

MALT
MALT SYRUP
WATER

HONEY
RAISINS
MAPLE SYRUP
MOLLA

HOPS
GARLIC
COFFEE

YEAST
STEAKBONES
ORANGES
LEMONS
APPLES

GINGER
MINT
YARROW
SALT

afford waste. In Vermont, where winters are harsh and money is scarce, homebrew plays the role of balm, nutrient, and sacrament. The role would not be understood by the president of Miller or Schlitz. One of the contributors to *Mountain Brew* comments on beer's elevation to the status of a luxury beverage by saying this about Budweiser:

> You know why everybody drinks Budweiser? Because they see the ads and they see the "King of Beers" and they think that if they can't have a little piece of the action at least they can drink the most expensive beer. They may never drive a Cadillac, but Budweiser!

Somewhere an advertising executive reads this, pours a second martini, and gloats over a job well done. In Vermont a flannel-shirted farmer sips on a second pint and feels the pain of a day of hard labor slipping away. Up there, they would say he is "blissed."

Tim Matson, author of *Mountain Brew*, is very much the mountain man on a smaller, more delicate scale. He wears the characteristic plaid wool shirt over a green jersey, blue jeans, and well worn boots. He has dark, medium length hair with a few strands of grey, the sign of the transition period between unadulterated youth and middle age. He is polite, friendly, and unpretentious, although initially wary of the Beer Trek. An old Vermont proverb says, "Beware of strangers in vans, particularly if their dog is black."

Tim offers tea, which we accept. His first batch of beer of the spring is just fermenting, so he had none to share. We sniff and taste the bubbling wort. It's going to be good. We talk about commercial beers. Tim's favorite is Narraganset Porter served on draft at the local roadhouse. He also likes Beck's and Busch, the latter not for its taste but for the claim of "no artificial anything." He is suspicious of any claims to purity made by commercial brewers and suggests that we make this a topic of Beer Trek investigation. "Mountain Brew was a purity trip, because we all realized how overdosed all the food was. We were trying to get away from all that, to have some control over our lives, some order."

Tim's first experience with home brewing was before he came to Vermont. He and some boarding school friends took cider, added raisins and Fleischmann's yeast, and stored the concoction in their closet. The inevitable explosion occured on Sunday morning, just before chapel. Tim and his friends had no choice but to show up reeking of homebrew. He laughs at the memory. "I think in my subconscious there had always been a feeling of rebellion associated with homebrew. Home brewing is rebellion. It is for people who like to get high and people who like to have ceremony. Two pints and you're blissed. The gratification of making homebrew is much different than, say, pottery."

Tim tells us about his early days in Vermont, when home brewing played as important a role in daily life as gardening or wood-cutting. He and his lady brewed batches of fifteen gallons at a time. Friends were pressed into service, especially at bottle washing time. They wound up drinking more than they helped, but that was part of the process. Homebrew was used as a form of barter, as no one in the country had any money. It also ranked as the #1 mountain folk house present. Working on the house, doing the garden, fixing the car; these were all passages of life accompanied by the ritual of beer. "Home brewing is like making bread. It's not a matter of knowing how. Many people try it once, then never again. You have to be into the kneading of the dough. Home brewing can be very boring. You have to be into your zen thing—hanging around the kitchen, washing bottles—it's work and you have to do it with the Spirit."

The tea is now gone, and Tim produces a six-pack of Beck's, that salty brew from the port town of Bremen, Germany, which we proceed to devour. The afternoon of the warmest day so far in the spring slips behind us. It becomes impossible to imagine how depressed we were on the morning of this very same day. The conversation turns philosophical, and then whimsical. The point to life, we somehow agree, is to drink good beer. Towards this end Tim draws up a map to a local roadhouse and promises to meet us later on. There, he promises, this truth will be self-evident.

Head and antlers above the rest.

North of the Border

In many ways Canadians suffer from a collective inferiority complex, the result of continually comparing themselves to their prominent neighbors to the south. In several arenas, however, "les habitants" take a back seat to no one, principally ice hockey and beer.

Somewhere the personalities of the North American nations diverged. In terms of beer, the Yanks turned bland while the Canadians retained their gusto, simple as that. True, many independent breweries have been consumed by the giants—Molson, Carling, O'Keefe, and Labatt—but the character and variety of individual brews has been preserved. Stouts, ales, and malt liquors still have meaning in Canada. Moreover, the ties to Her Majesty's realm mean that such U.K. standbys such as Guinness Stout (Labatt), Bass Ale (Carling), and McEwan's Export are readily available. Home brewing is legal and widespread, but a wholehearted brewing environment is short-circuited by restrictive provincial laws that regulate the sale of beer to such an extent as to convert the avid beer drinker to a teetotaler.

American beers eventually became bland enough to give the Canadians' appeal as exotic imports. Now they have descended en masse, a flannel-shirted brigade of bright-eyed machismo, situated midway between the working class ethic of Schlitz and the sophistication of St. Pauli Girl. Pricewise the Canadian brews are available as a suitable alternative for the drinker who balks at being either average or exceptional. Ah Wilderness, there is no doubt that the technique has worked and that the Moose is indeed Loose in America, fancy graphics and all.

The market niche discovered by Canadian beers is one which is bound to be further exploited in coming years. Popular brews such as Oland's Schooner, and Molson's Brador will inevitably find their way southward to the thirsty millions. But does it matter? One of the fastest growing brands north of the border is an import brewed by Labatt under license from a foreign brewery. It is called Budweiser.

Trekker's Guide to The New World

A Beer Trek of New England correctly begins in Boston, still the hub of the New World. The cosmopolitan population of transplanted collegiates is juxtaposed with parochial ethnic neighborhoods such as "Southie." The only common meeting ground is beer, in which both groups share rich traditions. The students may frequent trendy Cambridge bistros, while the locals prefer neighborhood taps with names like "Sully's," but both groups can enjoy a sunny afternoon in the Fenway Park bleachers where any animosities can be focused on whomever happens to be playing right field for the Yankees that year.

Head north or south from the Hub, and one is imbued in a nautical tradition. Style is paramount on the fantail, but the choice of brew is irrelevant so long as the accompaniment is the freshest seafood possible.

The east-west boundary is determined by beer and baseball loyalties. Natives root for the Red Sox and drink 'Gansett while intruders prefer the Yankees and Schaefer respectively. Both brews have slipped badly in recent years, depriving the New Englander of another precious bit of identity. Neither brand should be counted out yet, however, as regionality is returning to vogue.

There is also a north-south border which divides the upland from the flatland. Beerwise the change is marked by a preference for Canadian beers and homebrew which grows with each northward mile. The native cuisine is the potluck dinner, and everyone brings a six-pack. This is hardscrabble country. The winters are long, and beer helps them pass more pleasantly.

CONNECTICUT

State Beer   Black Horse Ale (Champale)
Kindred Spirits
  Nutmeg Chapter BCCA, Westport, CT
  Connecticut Red Fox Chapter BCCA, Southington, CT
  The Underground Brewer's Club, c/o Curt Hineline, Box 205, Ridgefield, CT 06877
Of Note
  (RIP) Hull Brewing Co., (1978), Congress St., New Haven, CT
    Recognition came too late to save them.
  Donald Bull, P.O. Box 106, Trumbull, CT 06611
    Prolific creator of materials of interest to collectors.
    Publications include *The Register of U.S. Brewers* (2 volumes, $8.95 each) and *A Price Guide to Beer Advertising Openers and Corkscrews* ($5.00 plus $1.00 postage).

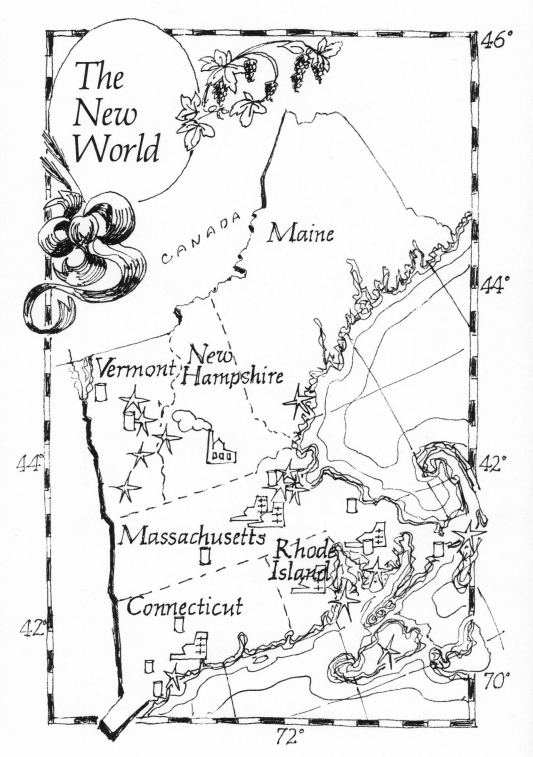

The New World

46°

CANADA

Maine

44°

Vermont New Hampshire

44°

42°

Massachusetts

Rhode Island

42°

Connecticut

70°

72°

29

MAINE

State Beer   Moosehead
Of Note
   Steve Bennett Enterprise Auctions, P.O. Box 375, York, ME 03909
   Mail-order breweriana auctions.

MASSACHUSETTS

State Beer   Pickwick Ale (Falstaff/General)
Kindred Spirits
   Pickwick Chapter, BCCA, Boston, MA
   Cape Cod Chapter, BCCA, Pembroke, MA 02359
   Cape Code Homebrewers Association, c/o Bierhaus, 68 Yarmouth Rd.,
     Hyannis, MA 02601
   South Yeast Massachusetts Brewers, c/o Peter Boss, 70 Pearse Rd.,
     Swansea, MA 02777
   Western Massachusetts Brewers Association, c/o William Santy, 291
     Prospect St., Chicopee, MA 01020

Of Note
   St. Patrick's Day Parade (March 17), South Boston
   The bleachers at Fenway Park anytime the Yankees are in town.
   The Elliott Lounge on Massachusetts Avenue in Boston. The place for
     gossip among beer drinking runners. Great place to speculate on
     the outcome of the Boston Marathon (April) or the Falmouth Road
     Race (August).
   Martha's Vineyard. RIP John Belushi, one of the greatest contemporary
     beer drinkers. Leave the site alone, but lift one in his memory.
   Cape Cod Brewers Supply Co., Box 1139, 126 Middle Rd., South
     Chatham, MA 02659. Mail-order homebrew suppliers.
   Winemakers Ltd., 999 Main Rd., Box C-406, Westport, MA 02790. Mail-
     order homebrew suppliers.
   (RIP) As a former brewing center, Boston is home to a number of
     standing breweries. The Haffenreffer Brewery in Jamaica Plain is
     being developed into light residential and commercial space.
     Dubbed simply "The Brewery," it will reputedly be the site of the
     Mariner Brewing Co., New England's first micro-brewery. Other
     prominent ex-brewing facilities include Dawson & Son (New Bed-
     ford), Hampden/Piels (Willimansett), and Carling (Natick). The lat-
     ter still stands on the shore of Lake Cochituate, just off Route 9, but
     now houses a high-tech computer firm.

NEW HAMPSHIRE

State Beer   Labatt's
Breweries
- Anheuser-Busch, Inc., 1000 Daniel Webster Hwy., Merrimack, NH 03054

    Tours (including Clydesdale Hamlet) available. Call for times (603) 889-6631. Extensive breweriana. Brands: see Anheuser-Busch, St. Louis, in The Great River Trekker's Guide.

Of Note
>   Dartmouth College Fraternity Row. Reputedly the model for the film *Animal House*. Ideal point to observe adolescent beer consumption habits on any Saturday night, but particularly during football season.

>   (RIP) Frank Jones Brewing Co. (Portsmouth). Little remains of the beer or buildings, but the legacy lives on in the form of the many development projects the Jones family undertook in downtown Portsmouth.

RHODE ISLAND

State Beer   Narragansett (Falstaff/General)
Of Note
>   Newport Cup Races, every fourth year in Newport. Quaff with the sporting set who definitely favor beer.

>   (RIP) Narragansett Brewing Co. (Cranston). A corpse so warm that cardio-pulmonary resuscitation appears possible. The owners still leave glimmers of hope, but meanwhile all New England brews are coming out of Indiana.

VERMONT

State Beer   Molson Golden
Kindred Spirits
>   Vermont Homebrewers Association, c/o Bill Hadsel-Mares, 429 So. Willard St., Burlington, VT 05401.

>   Cram Hill Brewers Association, c/o Stephen Morris, RD #2, Randolph, VT 05060

Of Note
>   National Repeal Day. April 7. Annual celebration of "the day they rolled out the barrels." Skyview Casino, Williamstown, VT

>   Vermont State Homebrew Championship. Labor Day. West Brookfield, VT

Tunbridge World's Fair. Third week in September. Tunbridge. Hardscrabble farmers and motorcycle gangs let off steam before a winter
of servitude to the wood stove.

Marlboro Morris Ale. Late May, various towns in Windham County.
Traditional dancers gather in southeastern Vermont to kick up heels,
then to quench thirsts.

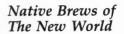

Native Brews of The New World

ORDER OF THE TREK

Pickwick Ale (Narragansett/General). The "poor man's whiskey" can
still be found, particularly in working class neighborhoods from
Boston to Providence. Reeks of hop oil, but tart and lively. Seems
to taste best in 16-oz. returnable bottles. The Inman Square Men's
Bar in Cambridge claims the dubious distinction of serving more
draft Pickwick than any other place in the world.

WORTHY OF MENTION

Busch (Anheuser-Busch). Specially formulated and distinctly different
from Busch Bavarian. Sweet and bland, geared to wean teeny-bop-
pers from soda pop. Head to the mountains, and bring your skate-
board.

Narragansett (Narragansett/General). Lots of memories associated with
"New England's own." Red Sox fans remember Curt Gowdy saying,
"Hi Neighbor, Have a 'Gansett," after each inning. The beer, alas,
is forgettable.

Haffenreffer Malt Liquor (Narragansett/General). Sole remaining
standard-bearer of the Haffenreffers, once among the most prominent of New England brewers. A potent, sweet brew which local
teenagers still drink on the rocks with a twist. A somewhat sad
testament to a great brewer.

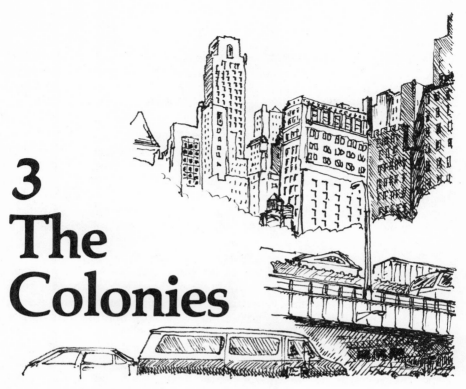

3 The Colonies

New York, New York, to Baltimore, Maryland
19 days, 3,130 miles on the road

A Lesson in Draft

New York, New York

A favorite American pastime is to knock New York, not just the city, but the state, its residents, and even its sports teams. From a beer drinker's standpoint, however, New York is a haven. There are plenty of breweries so the beer is fresh; prices are low; selection is unbeatable; and there is almost no time or place when the thirsty trekker cannot find a brew. The slogan "I love New York" could have been written by The Great Beer Trek.

An evening of pub crawling in Manhattan, however, was less than a resounding success. Beer is a beverage of the common man, and Manhattan is the city of bright lights and Broadway where everyone wants to be a star. No one, it appears, wants to be common.

We tried. We went to all the right places, spent a small fortune, but encountered beer drinking which could be described only as pretentious. Only McSorley's proved its reliable self. Finally we ran out of time as the bars closed.

Unwilling to give up, we ambled downtown to the Fulton Street Fish Market, where bars have special dispensation to stay open all night to serve the teamsters and stevedores who off-load the products of Maine, Cape Cod, the Chesapeake, and Florida, destined to become the Daily Catch in Manhattan's restaurants and markets. The market bars serve breakfast and beer to sleepy longshoremen, Mafia types, and the occasional uptowners out to experience the cacaphony of the fishy commerce. The crowd is the same every night, only the people change.

On nice nights like this, old Carmine sits on a folding chair in front of the bar which bears his name. The old lion surveying his domain, everyone says hello, more deferential than jocular. Occasionally someone approaches tentatively and mumbles something in his ear. For years Carmine has been a shop steward with the power to dole out jobs, equivalent to the power of life or death in the working class community.

"So and So said I should see you."

Depending on who So and So is, and when he last did a favor for Carmine, he nods, points, or waves his hand no. We watch the small drama over a mug of Schaefer, the only other choice being, appropriately enough, Rheingold. Twenty years ago Carmine might have offered Knick, Trommer White Label, and several other New York brands, but there is no point in crying over spilt beer.

We move on, fighting our way through throngs of dolly-pushing stevedores who vocalize a steady warning of "watch your back, watch your back." All Seven Ages of Man work in the bustle, each man threading his purposeful way through the stacked crates of hake, fluke, snapper, crab, flounder, mussels, and sea bass. Swordfish are neatly hacked into manageable chunks by men working machetes with the deftness of accountants swinging pencils. When dawn comes, the street will be returned to the day people. Razor-cut businessmen on nearby Wall Street will be oblivious to the nighttime hub-bub which takes place in the shadows of their citadels.

We enter the Paris Hotel, the city's oldest operating hostelry, although I am not sure who would want to stay there. The bar combines market functionalism with cut-glass cabinets from a day when the city's elite would meet the dawn in the bar of the Paris. Now a green formica breakfast counter takes up half the room. The bar is still elbow polished wood.

The craggy-faced blonde tending bar called constant greeting to passing workers. She had obviously been a market fixture for almost as long as the Paris.

"What will you have?" The voice matched the face perfectly, an edge of compassion which came from a thorough examination of both sides of life.

"What's good?"

"Scrambled eggs," she said disinterestedly.

"O.K., two scrambles."

"Coffee or beer?"

"Beer. Whaddya got?"

"Schaefer." The waitress was obviously into minimal effort as far as The Great Beer Trek was concerned. No matter, though, the surliness was appropriate for New York and the Fulton Fish Market where, at 4:30 A.M., you gotta be strong to survive. Scrambles and Schaefer. It tastes better than it sounds.

Before we had finished, the men of Fulton Street Fish Market were putting their meathooks into their back pockets and heading for the subway which would take them back to Brooklyn, maybe with the winey hoppiness of Schaefer at the backs of their throats. Across the river a few wispy fingers of gray were trying to pull aside the navy blue curtain of night. The Beer Trek had, at last, discovered good beer drinking in the Big Apple.

In blue collar Utica, it was quite another story. Good beer drinking found us in no time at all. We arrived on a suitably bleak Monday morning. The city's heyday has clearly passed. The businesses have moved south and west, as have the job-seeking sons and daughters. Utica is the home of the F.X. Matt Brewing Co., makers of Utica Club, Matt's Premium, and most recently, New Amsterdam beer. This firm is reknowned in the beer fanatic circles as a brewery which goes to great length to be hospitable to the beer drinker. They routinely host collector's conventions, sponsor road races, offer tours, create breweriana, and do countless other things to endear themselves to the consumer.

We anticipated with great pleasure getting to know the F.X. Matt people better. The plan of attack was to take the public tour anonymously in the afternoon, then to return the following morning to talk with company officials. For the time being, however, it was two hours until the first tour, and we had nothing to do.

As we strolled the streets of semi-deserted, downtown Utica, we passed a small bar on Bleeker Street named the Barn "In" Sider. I paused long enough to read a sign which said "Beer in Mason Jars." A patron spotted our hesitation and scurried outside. "C'mon in!" he bubbled enthusiastically. "This place has the best beer and popcorn in town!"

The man doing the exhorting wore a work uniform with the F.X. Matt logo. If brewery workers drank here, it had to be good. True, it was only 10:30 A.M., but this *was* the Beer Trek. Prejudices against drinking in the morning had to be overcome in the name of research.

We ordered a glass of Matt's Premium. Not that there was any choice— the Barn "In" Sider serves no hard liquor, no bottled beer, and no draft beers except Matt's. The promise of hospitality turned out to be somewhat misleading. Loyal patrons sat silently absorbed in a game show on T.V. Individuals would arrive, be served a beer, sit, stare, pay up, and leave with scarcely the exchange of a word. The decor evidenced a warped sense of humor. A handwritten sign on the wall read "Bleeker St.—the street of dreams." Nearby a pair of rubber ears were nailed to the wall. To say the Barn "In" Sider lacked coherent structure was to say that Utica had seen better days. Army recruiting posters adorned walls, while feedbags were draped over fake-Tudor rafters. A separate motif was lent by the shopping bags tacked to the walls.

Our presence had apparently made the regulars uncomfortable, judging from the concentrated television watching. I whispered to Laura to finish her beer so that we could chalk this up as a blind alley. The popcorn was fresh and good. Likewise the beer, served in mason jars, was fresh and lively. We finished our glasses and were immediately presented with two more which the bartender explained were compliments of the F.X. Matt worker who had originally asked us inside. We raised our glasses in silent salute, but the ice was now broken. The camaraderie of beer had taken over.

Our bartender and the owner of the Barn "In" Sider, Tony Sansoe, originated the idea of using mason jars for beer due to his dissatisfaction with the quality of beer service in competing establishments. The beer drinker, he believes, is entitled to clean hoses, clean glassware, and full measure. Mason jars, with associations of cleanliness and full measure, were chosen as the perfect beer vessels.

"You can be sure in a 16-ounce mason jar that you've got sixteen ounces of beer. With the false bottom in glass mugs you don't know whether you've got nine, ten, or twelve ounces of beer. Or take these bell-shaped pilsner glasses. They're supposed to contain eight ounces, but if you have one-half inch of head at the top where it's wide, you would be surprised at how much beer you're losing."

Tony proved equally fanatical about the proper cleaning of glassware: the slightest bit of grease or detergent, he explained, leaves a film on glass which is ruinous to the head on beer.

"Bartenders think something is wrong when their beer doesn't have any head. They call up the brewery and raise hell, but most of the time the problem is with their glasses. Or maybe the hoses are dirty. Or the beer is so cold it's practically frozen. You know how to tell a clean glass? Sprinkle salt on the inside of the glass. If it's really clean, the salt will stick to the glass."

Tony demonstrated on one of his mason jars. He uses a non-detergent cleaner not available commercially. He discovered the product while on duty in the National Guard and had to write directly to the manufacturer to get a supply.

Tony disappeared to take care of other customers. Upon returning he showed us his quart and half-gallon mason jars. They were big, they were full, and they were on the house. Laura and I gasped. So this is what the Beer Trek would be like—drunk by eleven each morning and dead before we reached the Mississippi. I had never faced a half-gallon of beer. Tony was confident I could handle it. The house record, he pointed out, was nine, held by a gentleman sitting several seats to my right. I turned and

SALT WILL STICK TO THE
SIDE OF <u>REALLY CLEAN</u>
GLASSWARE.

*" Clean Glassware and
Full Measure "*

– TONY SANSOE

asked for confirmation. He was a large man, but free of the belly to be expected from a prodigious drinker. He nodded, then spoke calmly, evenly, his reputation carried in the tone of his voice.

"I can do ten."

Tony's assurances not withstanding, we shared our beer bonanza as well as our mission with the other patrons. The television had been forgotten as the Uticans took advantage of an opportunity to strut their collective beer IQ. After all, this is a brewery town. The regulars of the Barn "In" Sider, hearing we were brewery-bound, had been full of who-to-see's and what-to-say's. The complaint nationwide may be that local populations do not support hometown breweries, but in Utica, Matt's (the brewery and the family) is an integral part of the community, a source of pride. Its employees and customers are roving ambassadors, not without senses of humor. We left with good-natured instructions to jab the well-placed needle:

"Ask them about Billy Beer. Ooo-oo, that stuff was awful."

"Hey, give them the business about cutting back to two free beers on the tour. Who can get drunk on two beers?"

"Ask them why they don't give out coasters to local businesses."

The jibes were in the spirit which comes after a couple of brews. Not a single malicious word was heard about the brewery or its products.

"See if you can get me fixed up with the babe on the Maximus Super poster."

It was noon and the lunchtime crowd was starting to arrive. We thanked Tony for the lesson on draft beer and for upholding the beer drinkers' bill of rights. I commented that he must be a beer drinker of repute, himself. "Oh, no," he replied. "I've never tasted the stuff. I'm a teetotaler. I've had people come in here, order two glasses of draft, and offer me as much as fifty dollars to drink one, but I never have."

We thanked him again, then fell off our stools and crawled to the van. We giggled our way to the Varick Street brewery. Utica's grayness had taken on a golden hue, casting the depressing reality of the city into a temporarily more flattering light. I began to understand why the girls get better looking at closing time.

Matt's is in the business of making friends, a fact self-evident in the obvious care and expense of their tour. The front reception area and hospitality room are furnished in the period decor of the 1890's. Antique advertising memorabilia is showcased on every wall.

Thanks to Tony Sansoe, the normal professionalism of The Great Beer Trek had been suspended. Today we would be sleazy, semi-drunk tourists, there for a free beer. We stumbled through the tour, but upon arrival in

BREWERY TOURS START HERE

AND MIGHT END AT THE BREWERY SHOP

THE HOSPITABLE *F. X. Matt Brewing Co.*

the hospitality room found ourselves greeted by West End's Publicity Director, Sales Manager, Vice President of Operations . . . and more free beer. Someone had detected the presence of The Great Beer Trek and decided to roll out a true F.X. Matt welcome. In classic brewery fashion, our mugs were never allowed to empty. We learned about brewing, beer, and the company, although at this point my memory becomes hazy. Apparently the arrival of The Great Beer Trek was an event of enough magnitude for most of the company to take the afternoon off and come by to say hi and to lift a mug.

That's all I can remember. The next morning I noticed the front bumper of the van covered with "Schultz and Dooley (Matt's well-known, talking beer mug spokesmen) Love NY" stickers. Will Anderson called this one of his favorite breweries, and now it was one of ours as well.

A Tale of Three Brewers   *Larchmont to Dunkirk*

After our overindulgence in Utica, the subsequent few days were long on research and short on beer drinking. In addition to Matt's we visited branch plants for Miller and Schlitz, Genesee in Rochester, and tiny Koch's Brewing Co. in Dunkirk. Additionally we met with Rudolph Schaefer, the legendary brewer whose name is almost synonymous with New York beer. Our knowledge had increased logarithmically, and we looked forward to consolidating conclusions.

RUDOLPH SCHAEFER, JR.

After a false start in which we first contacted Rudolph Schaefer the Fourth, then the Third, The Great Beer Trek finally succeeded in reaching the right number. We met in his well-appointed office across from the Larchmont railroad station. The decor is of dual motif, beer and sailing, with the latter more prominent, a clue to Mr. Schaefer's present priorities.

Discard stereotypes when thinking of Rudolph Schaefer; he is neither the affable, old world brewmaster nor the high-pressure executive. Even in his eighties, he is fit and perceptive, a testament to the salubrious effects of salt air and beer. His reputation in the beer business was as a straight-shooter, a tough, fair man who made inroads through industriousness and ingenuity. His reputation as a sailor is much the same. He is at once a renowned racer in New York yachting circles, and one of the driving forces behind the reconstruction of Old Mystic Seaport. In three generations the Schaefer family progressed from penniless immigrants to pillars of society. Theirs is the classic American success story, and they owe it all to beer.

Mr. Schaefer is retired now, an interested observer of the brewing industry, but no longer a participant. He is a rarity among family brewers in that he was not forced out of the beer business, but "escaped" on his own terms. It has been more than a decade since the family divested themselves of the Schaefer Brewing Co. by selling their shares to the public. Rudy Schaefer looked on the horizon of the sea of suds and saw more than

RUDY SCHAEFER'S
America

AN ALMOST EXACT REPLICA OF THE
1951 AMERICA'S CUP SCHOONER AMERICA

a squall looming. The captain put himself and his family in a lifeboat and headed into port. He could not save the ship, and unlike many brewers, he chose not to go down with it.

During 126 years (1842–1968) of sound family management, Rudy's grandfather Frederick Schaefer's original asset of one dollar was parlayed into New York's premier brewing operation, sixth largest in the nation. Since going public, Schaefer has dropped steadily in the national hierarchy and was recently taken over by Stroh of Detroit, as the relentless process of consolidation in the brewing industry continues.

Twenty-one-year-old Frederick Schaefer emigrated to the United States from Wetzlar, Germany, in 1838. He took a job with a New York brewer and wrote his brother, Maximilian, about life in the New World. The next year he, too, made the transatlantic leap, bringing with him a treasured recipe for lager beer, a type unknown in the United States where porters and English-style ales were still the norm.

The first American lager was brewed by John Wagner, a Philadelphian who had imported a special strain of lager yeast from his native Bavaria. The Schaefers, although not the first, now lay rightful claim to being the oldest brewers of lager beer in America. In 1844 the two brothers had prospered enough to buy out their employer. By 1848 their lager was perfected and introduced, gaining immediate acceptance. The following year the Schaefers had to move to more spacious facilities, setting a pattern of growth and expansion that continued until the 1960's.

Maximilian's son Rudolph assumed the presidency in 1912. Again expansion was called for, and Rudolph was equal to the task, although his timing could not have been worse. In 1916 in Brooklyn, he opened one of the grandest breweries in America only to see it emasculated by the Volstead Act less than four years later. The grand brewery was reduced to making near beer.

Rudolph I died in 1923. Control passed to his eldest son Maximilian whose tenure was cut short by health problems. In 1927, the same year that Jacob Ruppert's Bronx Bombers were making their owner as famous for baseball as beer, young Rudy Schaefer unexpectedly found himself the youngest brewery president in the United States.

There were growing pains, but Rudy found an unlikely ally in Colonel Jake Ruppert who had been executor of his father's will and his closest friend. The fraternal ties among brewers were obviously stronger than competitive threats. When Prohibition ended, Rudy Junior was ready and able to join the race to recapture America's beer drinkers. He atoned for his father's inability to anticipate the onset of Prohibition by anticipating its end. Before anyone knew for certain that Repeal was forthcoming, Rudy mounted an aggressive advertising campaign in the media which reminded the public that Schaefer's hand "had never lost its skill." Once the beer wagons started rolling, Schaefer left the competition in the starting gate. They had the further advantage of one of the finest manufacturing facilities in the nation. Obviously, no one had been about to build a new brewery

"—AND THAT HAND IS READY AND WAITING..." — RUDY SCHAEFER, 1933.

while Prohibition was in effect. While Schaefer had previously been one of several successful brewing companies in New York City, now it became the unquestioned toast of the town. By 1940 young Rudy had passed even his mentor, Colonel Ruppert, in sales.

Under the right circumstances, Rudy's sons William and Rudolph would now be the fourth generation to manufacture and sell beer to New Yorkers, but by 1960 the company was encountering problems in maintaining profitability. The nationals—Bud, Schlitz, Pabst, Falstaff, and, to a lesser extent, Miller—were now casting hungry eyes at the northeast market dominated by the "one beer to have when you're having more than one." Vicious price wars ensued. The regional brewers could maintain prices, knowing they would lose the cost-conscious segment of the consumership, or they could meet the unprofitable price, hoping their drinkers would not abandon them in droves once the prices returned to normal. The regionals who looked to the courts or government for defense against "selective" or "predatory" pricing were quickly disappointed, as no court or government agency wants to rule in favor of higher prices. The nationals' claim that price wars were an expression of free enterprise at its finest held sway. The issue will never be settled until the beer drinker has but a single beer to choose from. What will happen to prices then?

The Schaefers fought the battles and suffered many casualties. Serious family conferences were held to discuss strategy. Meanwhile, their peers— the Ballantines, the Kruegers, the Trommers—capitulated by closing their doors. At one point, the Schaefers took the first step toward going national themselves by buying an Ohio brewery (the one presently owned by C. Schmidt), but found it impossible to establish the Schaefer name in virgin territory. Rudy was a brewer, but beyond that he was a businessman. He could face the atrophy which had withered so many of his brewing contemporaries, or he could entrust the family namesake to others for a handsome sum. He chose the latter, and not for a single moment as he breathes the salt air on Long Island Sound is it a decision he regrets.

F.X. MATT II

F.X. Matt II speaks of the "mantle of the brewer" which is now his to wear. It was worn by his father, and will probably be worn by his son F.X. Matt III. The undisputed owner of the mantle, however, is, was, and will forever be his grandfather and namesake, known simply as "The First." He was born in 1859 in Ingelschlatt in Schichthal, Baden. When he died ninety-nine years later, he was chairman of the board. Until the day he died, he went to work every day and was actively involved in all phases of brewery management. More than twenty years after his death, his presence still dominates the brewery on Varick Street.

The F.X. Matt Brewing Co. is in the midst of a crisis, the third of their history. The first two, Prohibition and World War II (when raw materials and machine parts were impossible to procure), were survived through a combination of old-fashioned ingenuity and industry. F.X. Matt II feels the company will survive the crisis of competition from the nationals in the same way.

"My grandfather always said that a business is like a man—'You have to feed him to keep him alive.' We still believe that here. Our business is well-fed and healthy. We have to be more efficient than the nationals. Our equipment has been kept up-to-date. We have the flexibility of a private company, and we're small enough that management is integrally involved with all aspects of the product. You don't see that in a big company. Everyone is too specialized. There is no way the nationals can beat us in our own backyard."

In light of the uncertainties of the contemporary competitive environment, many regional brewers have been reluctant to make capital investments. Although the public image at the F.X. Matt Co. is that of turn-of-the-century hospitality, there is nothing anachronistic about the way they brew, package, and market their beer. But it is undisputedly a family affair: "During World War II materials were hard to come by. We would drive all over the state trying to convince farmers to grow hops. We would scavenge machine parts, then after church each Sunday the family would come into the plant to repair machinery."

F.X. Matt is proud of the number of technological innovations pioneered by his company. The question remains as to whether these weapons comprise enough of an arsenal to withstand the national onslaught. In a Beer War between titans, it is possible for a company like theirs to get caught in the crossfire.

F.X. Matt has the lean, Lincolnesque look of one accustomed to adversity. Certainly there is no fear. If the principles of industry and sound management set forth by the man whose portrait is on the wall are faithfully followed, everything should be all right. After all, F.X. III is standing in the wings, ready to inherit the mantle.

JOHN D. KOCH

Four hundred miles and one light-year from Larchmont, where Rudy Schaefer, Jr. rules his clan with patrician beneficence lies Dunkirk, New York. In Larchmont the sporting world in the form of the New York Yacht Club acknowledges its debt to the Schaefer legacy. In Dunkirk the sporting world acknowledges that John Koch of the Fred Koch Brewing Co. sponsored a bowling league or little league team. Perhaps he donated the keg for the annual softball banquet, but no one would refer to the Koch legacy.

The Fred Koch Brewery was founded in 1888, the same year F.X. Matt started his company in Utica. There the similarity ends. Whereas in Utica hope springs eternal, in Dunkirk it is realism. F.X. Matt II has the spare look of a Yankee farmer bracing for another winter. John Koch has been given a task he knows impossible to complete successfully. He has examined the statistics, balance sheets, and marketing surveys and knows he is fighting a losing battle. In no way, however, does this mean he will be less tenacious in the defense of his livelihood.

John Koch has the tall, powerful, graying at the temples look suited to an office overlooking a city skyline. Instead, he sits tailored and natty in a plain, unpretentious office where the only splashes of color come from an assortment of cans and bottles put out by his competitors. Mr. Koch is a pragmatist, not given to grasping at straws or lamenting his fate. A Beer Trek looks for the fun in beer, the magic of the suds, the off-beat, the obscure, the worthy, the legendary, the humorous, the buried treasure. Such pursuit is of passing concern to John Koch fighting for survival with an antique brewery in a day of megaplants. During our conversation I made the mistake of expressing passionate, yet naive, concern for the fate of small brewers. Mr. Koch listened patiently, then laid out the reasons why the days of the small independent brewer are numbered. By now the story was becoming familiar.

1. Government compliance regulations. Brewers small and large must comply with the dictates of OSHA (Occupational Safety and Health Administration), the EPA (Environmental Protection Agency), and other regulatory agencies. The ability to comply is not equal, however. The small brewer's profit must be plowed back into income-producing equipment to help him stay competitive. The cash for nonproductive expenditures is simply not available. Likewise in the case of a dispute, the small brewer does not have the legal or financial resources of a national to contend an issue.
2. Predatory or selective pricing.
3. Increasing importance of media, especially television.

Survival, explained Mr. Koch, is possible, but only under optimum circumstances. The brewer must be located in an out-of-the-way place which offers little market potential for the nationals. He must be protected by nondiscriminatory state licensing laws, or he must make a specialized product as does Anchor Steam in San Francisco. But, he sighed, even these strategies can be ultimately self-defeating. Any sizable growth will create a market profitable for the nationals to invade, and the successful small brewer will be David facing yet another Goliath.

I asked John Koch if he thought free enterprise was dead. He said no, but it was no longer available to the small guy. When government became big after the Depression, business became big to defend itself. The small guy could either crawl off and die or stand his ground, fighting bravely, and then die. His neighbor, the Erie Brewing Co., had closed its doors just weeks before. This was a good company run by smart, nice people who also made good beer. If there were a light at the end of his own company's tunnel, then John Koch could not yet see it. For the time being, however, he would keep making beer the best he could. And if I should come across any yellow brick roads in my travels, he said, be sure to give him a call.

Roots—The Origins of Beer   *Baltimore, Maryland*

From New York we penetrated the heart of Colonial America. From the highway much of the landscape is a blight of the country's insatiable thirst for growth. We tried our best to plot routes without numbers. This did not prove to be hard, given our suds-determined destinations. The back roads cast the mid-Atlantic states in a completely flattering light, making it easy to understand why this was the first settled section of America. We had also now grown comfortable with life in the van, Laura having discovered innumerable ways to make our rolling metal box a home. Some days our mileage figures were so low we could have covered the same distance in a covered wagon. No day, however, failed to supply an ample quotient of sudsy knowledge from the cradle of American civilization.

Soon after man learned to harvest wild grain, he tried to store it for consumption at a later date. The vessel in which he kept it was rained on, then contaminated by wild yeast. Fermentation began. When man discovered the goopy, bubbling mess, he slurped it down anyway. He became full and, at the same time, started thinking more kindly toward his neighbor. He belched and slurped down a little more. Thus, with this elementary grain porridge, was beer born.

Throughout history the only limitation on the ability of *Homo sapiens* to brew has been the availability of grain. This is as true of pygmies in Africa as the ancient Teutonic tribes.

Intoxicating beverages necessitate a framework for controlling their abuse, thus the development of brewing techniques is often paralleled by systems of collective control which we describe loosely as "civilization."

In time, history was recorded, man having invented the written word to catalog recipes, to document brewing technique, to extol the exhilaration of intoxication, and to damn the effects of excess. Early cradles of civilization from Egypt to China contain repeated references to the uses and abuses of fermented grain beverages.

The Britishers who first settled the shores of the New World were indisputably beer drinkers, possessing a genetic aversion to unembellished water. Christina Hole's *The English Housewife in the Seventeenth Century* describes the sudsy traditions of the original North American invaders:

> Our forfathers' drinks were as varied and plentiful as their food. In the country, home-brewed ale or beer was the normal drink at most meals, including breakfast, and the provision of a sufficient supply was one of the housewife's most important tasks. "Sufficient" in this case meant a good deal, for the daily consumption was heavy and hospitality was generous. Brewing took place once a month in many households and oftener if necessary, and every country bride expected to find her brew house adequately stocked with the barrels, firkins, tubs, coolers, ladles and other necessities for this complicated operation.

That the Pilgrims brewed immediately upon their arrival in America in 1620 is inarguable. Although there were no professional brewers among them (the first, John Jenny, arrived three years after the Mayflower landed), each citizen had a working knowledge of the principles of fermentation. Early inventories indicate they possessed the required "hogsheads, bucking tubs, payles, and firkins" for brewing. John Alden (of Priscilla fame) was by trade a cooper whose duties would have included maintenance of wood beer barrels. And finally, they possessed the necessary motivation as documented by this entry in the Mayflower log:

> That night we returned again to shipboard, with resolution the next morning to settle on some of these places: so in the morning, after we had called on God for direction, we came to this resolution: to go presently ashore again, and to take a better view of two places, which we thought most fitting for us, for we could not now take time for further search or consideration, our victuals being most spent, especially our beer, and it being now the 19th of December.

Not surprisingly, the voyagers chose Plymouth as the site for their settlement the next day. The trip is over when the beer runs out.

That first winter the Pilgrims had to slake their thirsts by brewing beers from transported stores of barley or, more probably, Indian maize (as had the Jamestown settlers earlier under the guidance of Captain John Smith). Barley was planted in the first summer's crop, and it is likely that the first Thanksgiving table featured the Pilgrims' finest brew.

Among the first legislative acts of the Massachusetts Bay Colony was a prohibition of the malting of wheat, an act which suggests that the thirst of the early settlers was more powerful than their need for bread. The creation of beer was a simple enough matter, then as now, and the Pilgrim's process makes an interesting comparison with the methods of prehistoric man or the contemporary brewer.

The first step was to steep the grain (barley, wheat, maize, rye, or any combination thereof) in a cistern for three days or until it was thoroughly soaked. Once germination began, the water was slowly drained and the husks allowed to aerate. For the next month the grain was turned four or five times daily until thoroughly dry. To test for starch to sugar conversion, the Pilgrims had none of the sophisticated methods available to the modern brewer. Instead they relied on taste, sight, smell and feel.

The malt was ground and boiled with water until a pudding-like consistency was achieved. Slowly, hot water was percolated through the liquor, or "wort," then drawn off, or "sparged," boiled with hops or whatever flavoring element was favored, then fermented through the addition of yeast.

Whether or not the beer of the settlers compared in quality to that of our modern, food-processing brewers, these early brewers must be given their due. Not only was their beer made without Kelcoloid 0, diatomites, Dinitropheny Chydrazine, or the many unpronounceable substances available to the Schlitz brewmaster, but also, prior to brewing, they malted their own grain (which only a handful of contemporary brewers do) and grew their own grain (which only Coors and Anheuser-Busch do today). Moreover, they cleared the land they stole from Indians, and they crossed the North Atlantic in a leaky wood vessel. Of such true beer-brewing grit is our ancestry.

Alice Morse Earle in her treatise *Colonial Days in Old New York* (Charles Scribner's Sons, 1896) confirms that virtually any occasion was considered important enough to toast with a drink. Farm hands, sailors, cobblers, tailors, and all other members of the working class would not work without drink provided by their employers. Even law-breakers subject to deprivation and confinement were still allowed small beer as a regular part of their diets. Comparing the New Yorkers to other colonists, Mrs. Earle says:

Of the drinking habits of the Dutch colonists I can say that they were those of all the colonies—excessive. Tempered in their tastes somewhat by the universal brewing and drinking of beer, they did not use as much rum as the Puritans of New England, nor drink as deeply as the Virginia planters, but the use of liquor was universal.

Indeed many of the most prominent names in colonial history were associated with the brewing trade. William Penn, both a good Quaker and lover of beer, opened the first commercial brewery in Pennsylvania in 1683, just several years after he had founded the colony.

Samuel Adams, the "Father of the Revolution," counted among his patriotic credits participation in the Boston Tea Party, signing the Declaration of Independence, a term as Governor of Massachusetts, and membership in the first Congress. He was a brewer by trade, as were other members of the Adams family.

General Israel Putnam left his tavern in Brooklyn, New York, to lead the Revolutionary Army to many victories. After the war, he returned to the tavern. George Washington brewed at Mt. Vernon, Thomas Jefferson at Monticello and James Oglethorpe at Jekyl Island. Alexander Hamilton, John Hancock, Patrick Henry, and James Madison worked actively to promote legislation to encourage the manufacture and consumption of a beverage widely regarded as a temperate alternative to hard liquor.

The English-style beers brewed by the early European settlers were probably similar to the homebrews of Tim Matson's Green Mountain men. In the mid-1840's something happened to change the course of American brewing. A Philadelphian, John Wagner, imported a special strain of yeast from his native Bavaria. This yeast fermented the beer wort from the bottom and required cooler temperatures to work correctly. The resulting beer was lighter and livelier than the prevalent types, and immediately won converts among the beer drinking consumership. Yet no one could have foreseen the extent of its eventual domination. With scant exception, the only beers available commercially in America are derivatives of John Wagner's lager. The introduction of this beer type coincided nicely with an influx of Germans, Dutch, Pole, and Lithuanians who came to mine coal from the hills. A brewer could not ask for more willing consumers. Of the hundreds of breweries that arose to serve, only the few strongest remain for the Beer Trekker.

Pennsylvania beers possess a taste characteristic which suggests evolution from a common ancestor. While these brews offer as much variety as is available in any state in the country, each bears the tattoo of its origin in the ferrous waters which have filtered down through the carbonacious hills. These are unabashedly coal miner beers, regardless of whether one is referring to Schmidt's quaffed in a Philadelphia men's club or Stoney's in the local union hall.

John Koch of the Fred Koch Brewing Co. in Dunkirk, New York, had cited the need for small brewers to have some measure of protection for their markets from incursions by the national brewers. While Pennsylvania has witnessed significant carnage in recent years (Ortlieb, Horlacher, Mt. Carbon, Erie), the passage of time had been kinder, beerwise, to this state than almost any other. Seven state-based brewers still sell their wares, offering the beer drinker an almost unthinkable variety by contemporary standards. They owe their existence to prohibitive distribution laws which limit sales to case lots from specially designated beer outlets. This, combined with the rugged topography and declining yet tenacious population, have made the nationals reluctant to invade the local strongholds of the Yuenglings, Stoneys, Straubs, Stegmaiers, Schmidts, Rolling Rocks, and Iron City's of Pennsylvania.

The Pennsylvania breweries came into and went out of The Great Beer Trek in quick sequence, each leaving an indelible footprint at the back of our throats, having its moment upon the stage, then being seen no more, stealing back into the green hills from whence it came. Of such memories are Beer Treks made.

STRAUB'S, ST. MARY'S, PENNSYLVANIA

We arrived at night, a fact which camouflaged the town's native blackness. We found no shortage of locals who were willing to tell about the local brew. Straub's has a sweet, pungent taste and an aroma which immediately fills up a room. It is a beer to be drunk in quantity, although locals brag about its strength (4% by weight) and after three, one begins to appreciate the subtle personality of St. Mary's. The next morning Gibby Straub himself took us around the brewery. The appearance of any rabid Straub fan (or a Great Beer Trek) is ample excuse to stop work for a few minutes. The archaic, labor-intensive operation is a joke by modern manufacturing standards, but not by anyone's beer drinking standards. Gibby confesses they close down for the first week of deer season. Could Anheuser-Busch afford that?

PITTSBURGH BREWING CO., PITTSBURGH

The business is definitely on the rebound. We tried to experience the magic of "Ahrn" by going to a few joints near the steel mills. One sits on the torn vinyl of a circular stool with tubular stainless legs and tries to appear inconspicuous in an environment as intimate as a stranger's living room. The patrons are veterans of the war between life's expectations and reality. They have fought and lost. Now there is nothing to do but grasp the comfort of Iron City and bide time until the next Steeler's game. As Joseph Lelyveld once said of Iron City in an article entitled "Small Beer" in the *New York Times Magazine* (May 22, 1977), "It's not for dreaming, for changing your lifestyle. It's for remaining the same. Between us it's for drinking. And one more won't hurt." Amen.

JONES BREWING CO., SMITHTON, PENNSYLVANIA

Stoney's is alive and well, thank you, and ruling a tiny corner of the beer world. President W.B. Jones III takes a no-nonsense approach to brewing which he will pass along to yet another generation.

Pittsburgh

ROLLING ROCK, LATROBE, PENNSYLVANIA

The beer is so squeaky clean that one can barely taste the coal dust. We caught the president, James Tito, Jr., just as he was preparing to fly to North Dakota to examine the year's barley crop. A connoisseur of the common man's drinking experience, he was looking forward to revisiting the Lakota Hotel which is distinguished by the fact that "it has not changed in the last fifty years." Latrobe has not changed in the last twenty-five.

SCHMIDT'S AND ORTLIEB'S, PHILADELPHIA

Ortlieb's was still independent when the Beer Trek passed through. We stopped in the brewery tavern which doubles as the hospitality room and worker's lunchroom. The kid sitting next to us was streaked with sweat, having done combat with a faulty pasteurizer all morning. The problem was acute, as a nonfunctioning pasteurizer could eventually bring all production to a halt. Joe Ortlieb, Jr., jammed the last of a sandwich in his mouth, mumbled an apology, and returned to work. Alas, "Joe's Beer," as Ortlieb's has long been known, will never be his beer, as the company has now succumbed to competitive pressures and sold out to nearby rival Schmidt.

D.G. YUENGLING AND SONS, POTTSVILLE, PENNSYLVANIA

Founded in 1829, the nation's oldest brewery, Dick Yuengling keeps one of the nation's most picturesque breweries in a town most notable for being the site of the nation's oldest brewery. Dick confesses that the "and Sons" part of the name is not accurate at the moment. His son used to work in the brewery, he says, but "It was terrible! I never knew where anything was." There is a twinkle in his eyes which belies the seriousness

BUILT ON A MOUNTAINSIDE "LIKE ALL OLD BREWERIES."

Yuengling's c.1844

of the conflict. "You know," confides Dick, "I was just the same at his age." We sampled first a Chesterfield Ale, then one of their reknowned porters, still bottled in the squat "Steinie" bottles which are obsolete in the rest of the world. Life in Pottsville, we conclude, is made bearable by the availability of Dick's beers.

THE LION, WILKES-BARRES, PENNSYLVANIA

En route to the Lion we passed the old Stegmaier plant, a magnificent building which stands in Gothic ruin by its railroad siding awaiting either restoration or the wrecker's ball. Just the slightest squint and one can recreate the might of the brewery during its red brick heyday.

Stegmaier's new home is just down the road at the Lion, a physical plant which has none of Steg's original grace and charm. This is a place to work. Brewmaster Don Mudrick and assistant Ed Siers greeted us in a crowded office on the fourth floor of the brewhouse. Like the beers brewed at the Lion, the office was unpretentious, a study in functionalism. Both men seemed glad to have us drop in to spice up what otherwise might have been just another day on the job. They were cordial, frank, and, with the wealth of experience between them, damn interesting.

Ed Siers graduated from the Siebel Institute and officially became a brewmaster in 1933, but clearly he had learned his craft during Prohibition. He told tales of brewing in toilet bowls where incriminating evidence could disappear faster than you could say "Elliott Ness." An Elks Club he knew of created a particularly effective deterrent—poisonous snakes on the floor surrounding the brew kettle. Don explained the two-way spigots—pull them toward you and you got near beer, push them the other way and you got "high test."

The Lion is a collecting point for some great beers whose breweries could not survive—Gibbons, Stegmaier, Bartels, Liebotschaner. Clearly its present existence is tenuous and depends on low overhead. Ed Siers recounted the breweries for which he had worked. None of them exist any more, yet none had expired because the beer wasn't good. A moment of silence is observed for the dearly departed, then the indomitable spirit overtakes Ed: "Hey, why don't you come to the Master Brewer's Crabfest in Baltimore?"

"Sure," says Don, his voice alive with animation, "If you want good stories, that's the place."

"Or fancy beer drinking," adds Ed, "but I tell you, no matter how much beer a brewer drinks you'll never see one get out of line. Not that we don't like to have a good time."

The phone rings. A minor emergency requires Don's attention and he leaves. Ed continued, "Sure, you should come to the Crabfest. Lots of food, lots of beer." He clouded suddenly. "But it's not like it used to be. The meetings used to be even more fun. But with Horlacher going out, and Erie, and who knows what's happening with Carling and Schaefer, this might be the last one. I don't know, there just aren't that many brewmasters any more. I guess this is the last of the romantic industries."

Research created for us a strong sense of beer's formative role in America's history, and yet our travels yielded scant evidence of even vestigial remnants of our English beer tradition. Just as Sherlock Holmes needed the pacification of several pipesful of shag tobacco from his Persian slipper to ruminate on a particularly vexing problem, a Beer Trek needs

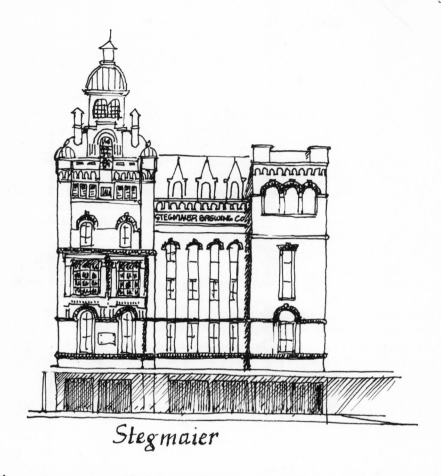

Stegmaier

the sustenance provided by experiencing the best that a local area can offer. Thus, we arrived in Baltimore determined to let actions speak louder than words. We are happy to report that good beer drinking is not hard to find in Baltimore.

First stop for the van was the Lexington Street market, where a bustling array of shops provided a suitably chaotic backdrop for Chesapeake Bay oysters to be washed down by National Premium. This inoffensive beer will never rank high on any connoisseur's list of favorites, but its blandness seems just right to allow the taste of seafood to bleed through. National is now owned by Heileman and brewed at the former Carling plant out by the Beltway. The original downtown plant stands fully equipped and idle, another red brick relic.

After the oyster bars of Lexington Street, we repaired to the restored harbor district of Fells Pt. for soft-shell crab sandwiches and more beer.

Then it was out to the Bromwell Inn in Fullerton for seafood chowder and crabcakes. Bromwell's is the type of place which has the Star-Spangled Banner on the jukebox and where patrons drink National Premium just because it is brewed in Baltimore. The evening was still young but we found ourselves too satiated to consider moving very far. The Bromwell seemed as good a place as any to contemplate what had happened to the English beer drinking tradition. Someone put on the national anthem. It had been written right here in Baltimore, hadn't it? And the tune was derived from an English tavern tune, right? We opted for another National Premium to help us consider the question.

The previous week had been brewery-intensive as we drove from New York to the western boundary of Pennsylvania and back again. We uncovered no evidence of the English beer tradition which comprises our sudsy national roots, but we did find abundant examples of the Bavarian tradition which replaced it.

We finish the pitcher, finish recounting our recent escapades in Pennsylvania and head for home, in this case the apartment of Bob, my college friend who had brought National Premium and boiled crabs to the Fourth of July festivity which spawned The Great Beer Trek. This was the first really steamy evening of the summer, and most of the town was out settin' on the stoop. Young and old, black and white, male and female, everyone in Baltimore sets on the stoop when the summer humidity sets in. All it takes is a transistor radio and a six-pack. The music changes by the block—rock, disco, schmaltz, soul. So does the beer. Pabst is very popular here, as is Miller, especially among blacks. No one seems to know why. National Premium holds its own in what is now a final stronghold.

Of course, none of the radios blare music if the Orioles are playing.

So this night we sat on a stoop in Baltimore, watching the cars stop at the traffic light. Da Boids were playing Boston, and there was a classic match-up, Palmer vs. Eckersley. Around the eighth, Earl Weaver took exception to one of the ump's decisions and got himself tossed. Then in the ninth, Murray belts a home run and da Boids win. On stoops throughout Baltimore, the crowd went crazy.

Trekker's Guide to The Colonies

The traditional brands from this section of the country—Rheingold, Ballantine, Schaefer, and Schmidt's—are distinguished by a pronounced hop character. Beer for the easterner must have its malty blandness counter-

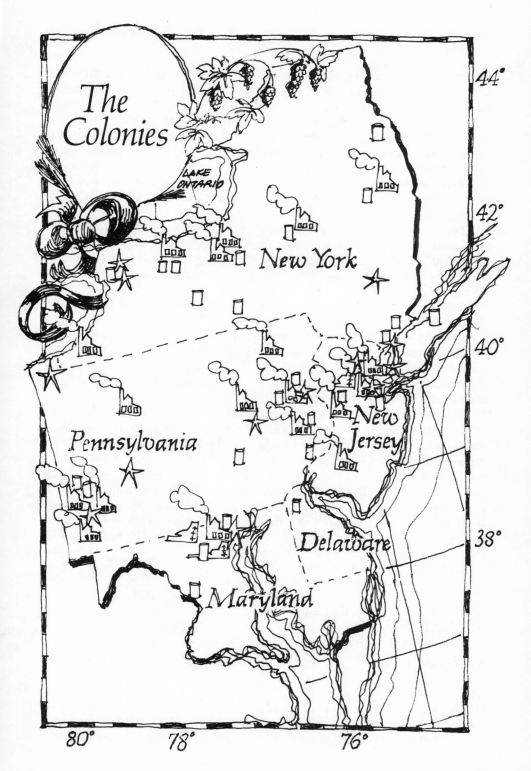

The Colonies

LAKE ONTARIO

New York

Pennsylvania

New Jersey

Delaware

Maryland

44°

42°

40°

38°

80°   78°   76°

balanced by a bitter bite. McSorley's Ale House in lower Manhattan is one of the few places remaining where the native taste preference can still be captured in a mug.

The present beer scene is fragmented and colored by signs of decay. New York's remaining brewers are the unlikely survivors in a brutal war of attrition. Who would have predicted that F.X. Matt's beer would survive Jake Ruppert's or Peter Ballantine's? Newcomers on the scene, Newman in Albany and Old New York in Manhattan are the forefront of a movement designed to restore some of the gusto from New York's English/Dutch heritage. More will come.

Pennsylvania offers the beer trekker a glimpse into yesteryear with seven independent brewers, including the nation's oldest (Yuengling), still plying their trade. Much of the state's population, however, seems to have fled to the Sun Belt, leaving Iron City (Arhh-n-n), Stoney's, Straub's, Gibbons, and Stegmaier as the brews in which unemployed steelworkers and coal miners can drown their sorrows. Rolling Rock and I.C. Light offer signs of hope.

New Jersey hosts several breweries, none of which can truly be called native, unless one wants to deem Champale "New Jersey's own." Delaware has Maryland and Maryland has the Chesapeake and National Premium, a great regional brew even though it has now become one of Heileman's stable of refugee beers.

Baltimore offers the best range and quality of beer drinking to be found in the mid-Atlantic states. Close-knit ethnic neighborhoods such as Camden Town and Fullerton remain faithful to the locals while debate among the stoop setters in other parts of town is as likely to concern the relative merits of Schlitz, Bud, and Pabst as the fate of "da beloved Boids." The places for drinking beer in Baltimore are varied, but the prime season is definitely late August, in the evening, when the temperature seems stuck at 90 degrees, the humidity the same, and the pennant race is entering its final phase. Bring the transistor out to the stoop, crack the first pop-top, and settle in for the full nine innings.

DELAWARE

State Beer   Miller High Life
Kindred Spirits
    Delaware Blue Hen Chapter, BCCA, Hockessin, DE

MARYLAND

State Beer   National Premium (G. Heileman)
Breweries
  • Carling National Breweries, Inc. (subsidiary of G. Heileman), 4501 Hollins Ferry Rd., Baltimore, MD 21202

No tours. No breweriana.

Brands: see G. Heileman, La Crosse, WI, in the Beer Belly Trekker's Guide

Kindred Spirits

Chesapeake Bay Chapter, BCCA, Baltimore

Brewers United for Real Potables (B.U.R.P.)

c/o Dan McCoubrey, 12301 Dalewood Dr., Wheaton, MD 20902

(Unnamed homebrewing club) c/o George Paytas, 5205 Lynngate Ct., Columbia, MD 21044

Of Note

Baltimore's ethnic neighborhoods, seafood, and local beer traditions make for one of the nation's richest beer drinking environments.

(RIP) American Brewing Co. (Baltimore), one of the nation's remaining treasures of brewery architecture. National Brewing Co. (Baltimore), original home of National Premium, is still intact and awaiting the right person to come along to flip the "on" switch. He may never come.

NEW YORK

State Beer   Genesee

Breweries

- Anheuser-Busch, Inc., 2885 Belgium Rd., P.O. Box 200, Baldwinsville, NY 13027

  No tours. No breweriana. Former Schlitz plant.

  Brands: see Anheuser-Busch, St. Louis, in the Great River Trekker's Guide

- Genesee Brewing Co., Inc., 445 St. Paul St., Rochester, NY 14605

  No tours. No breweriana. "Our one brewery makes it best." One of the few breweries to do their own malting.

  Brands: Genesee Beer, Genesee Cream Ale, Genesee Light Beer, Genesee 12 Horse Ale, Genesee Light Cream Ale.

- Fred Koch Brewing, Inc., 15-25 W. Courtney St., Dunkirk, NY 14048

  No tours. T-shirts, hats, glasses, posters, and patches sold at the brewery.

  Brands: Golden Anniversary Beer, Holiday Beer, Black Horse Ale, Black Horse Beer. Final repository for Simon Pure, last vestige of Buffalo's once mighty brewing industry.

- F.X. Matt Brewing Co., 811 Edward St., Utica, NY 13502

  Tours available (for time, call (315) 732-0762). Extensive breweriana shop, including everything from etched glasses to hop pillows.

  Brands: Matt's Premium, Matt's Light, Maximus Super, Utica Club Beer, Utica Club Cream Ale, Utica Club Light, Porter (draft only), New Amsterdam Amber (for Old New York Beer Co.).

- Miller Brewing Co., P.O. Box 200, Fulton, NY 13069
  No tours. No breweriana.
  Brands: see Miller Brewing Co., Milwaukee, WI, in the Beer Belly
     Trekker's Guide.
- William S. Newman Brewing Co., Inc., 32 Leonard St., Albany, NY
  12207
  Tours Saturday at 11:00 A.M. T-shirts and stickers sold at the brewery.
  Brands: Newman's Pale Ale, Newman's Albany Amber, Newman's
     Winter Ale (available November–March). Note: Newman's products
     are currently available only on draught and are sold at the brewery
     in 1-gallon and 2½-gallon refillable containers.

Kindred Spirits
BCAA chapters:

Congress, Syracuse
Knickerbocker, New York
Genessee Valley, Rochester
Long Island, Floral Park
Officer Suds, Utica
Schultz and Dooley, Schenectady
Simon Pure, Buffalo
Southern Tier, Johnson City
Yankee, Glens Falls

Upstate New York Homebrewers Association, c/o Gordy Association,
   Wine Press, 7 Schoen Pl., Pittsford, NY 14534
Yankee Bubblers, c/o Joe Becker, Box 761, Ithaca, NY 14850
Amber Waves of Grain, c/o Lisa Lane Hickey, 69 Gleneida Ave., Car-
   mel, NY 10512

Of Note
Hunter Mountain Beer Festival, mid-summer, near Woodstock, NY,
   lots of different brews to sample in a pastoral setting.
Buffalo Chicken Wings. Get 'em mild, medium, hot, or blast furnace.
   A unique local style, deep fried and served with celery sticks and
   blue cheese dressing. Available anywhere but created by Frank and
   Teressa at the Anchor Lounge, 1047 Main St., Buffalo, NY.
Herb Ashendorf Antiques, 21 Montclair Rd., Yonkers, NY 10710. The
   shop of one of the nation's largest collectors of breweriana.
Paul K. Michel, 1152 Kensington Ave., Buffalo, NY 14215.
   Mail-order, breweriana auctioneer.
Old New York Beer Co. (Manhattan). Beer is presently brewed at
   Matt's, but the eventual plan is to start a new city brewing tradition,
   just like the old one.

NEW JERSEY

State Beer   Champale

Breweries
- Anheuser-Busch, Inc., 200 U.S. Hwy. 1, Newark, NJ 07101
  No tours. No breweriana.
  Brands: see Anheuser-Busch, St. Louis, MO, in The Great River Trekker's Guide.
- Champale, Inc., P.O. Box 2230/1024 Lamberton St., Trenton, NJ 08607
  No tours. No breweriana.
  Brands: Pink Champale, Extra Dry Champale, Golden Champale, Black Horse Ale, Metbrau (near beer).
- Eastern Brewing Corp., 334 No. Washington St., Hammonton, NJ 08037
  No tours. No breweriana.
  Brands: Canadian Ale, Milwaukee Premium, Fox Head, Old Bohemian, Nude Beer, and a million others.
- Pabst Brewing Co., 400 Grove St., Newark, NJ 07106
  No tours. No breweriana.
  Brands: see Pabst Brewing Co. in The Beer Belly Trekker's Guide.

Kindred Spirits
Jersey Shore Chapter, BCCA, Holmdel, NJ
Garden State Chapter, BCCA, Cranford, NJ
The Christian Ferment League, c/o John McClure, 207 Loetscher Place 6B, Princeton, NJ 08540

Of Note
(RIP) P. Ballantine & Sons., Christian Feiganspan, Gottfried Kreuger Brewing Co. (Newark). The latter still stands, notable as the first brewer to package beer in cans.

U.S. Beer Coaster Guide, c/o Tom Byrne, P.O. Box 173, East Hanover, NJ 07936 ($7.95 plus $1 postage).

Who's Who in Brew, c/o Edward W. Scott, P.O. Box 2771, Paterson, NJ 07509 ($7.50 plus 75¢ postage), a complete listing of post-Prohibition brewers and brands.

PENNSYLVANIA

State Beer   Iron City
Breweries
- Jones Brewing Co., Smithton, PA 15479
  No tours. No breweriana.
  Brands: Stoney's Gold Crown, Esquire, Fort Pitt, Old Shay, Old Shay Golden Ale.
- The Lion, Inc., Gibbons/Stegmaier Brewery, 700 No. Pennsylvania Ave., Wilkes-Barre, PA 18705
  Tours by appointment. No breweriana.
  Brands: Stegmaier Gold Medal, Steg Light, Esslinger, Bartels, Crystal, Gibbons Light Lager, Stegmaier Porter, Liebotschaner Cream Ale, Liebotschaner Special.

- Latrobe Brewing Co., Box 350, Latrobe, PA 15650
  No tours. Some breweriana sold on premises.
  Brands: Rolling Rock Premium, Rolling Rock "Light."
- Pittsburgh Brewing Co., 3340 Liberty Ave., Pittsburgh, PA 15201
  Tours Tuesday and Thursday, 11:00 A.M. and 1:00 P.M. T-shirts, mugs,
    signs, and other items sold at the brewery. Brands: Iron City, I.C.
    Light, Old German, Old Dutch, Olde Frothingslosh.
- F&M Schaefer Brewing (division of Stroh), P.O. Box 2568, Allentown,
    PA 18001
  Tours available, call for schedule (215) 395-6811.
  Breweriana sold.
  Brands: Schaefer, Piels, Malta Schaefer, Schaefer Light, (Stroh coming
    soon, once direct-fired brew kettles are installed).
- Christian Schmidt Brewing Co., 127 Edward St., Philadelphia, PA
    19123
  No tours. Some breweriana available.
  Brands: Schmidts of Philadelphia, Schmidt's Light, Tiger Head Brand
    Ale, Valley Forge Beer, Prior Preferred Golden Light, Prior Preferred
    Double Dark, Duke, POC, Bavarian, Brew 96, Rheingold, Knick-
    erbocker, McSorley's Cream Ale, Ortlieb's.
- Straub Brewery, 303 Sorg St., St. Mary's, PA 15857
  Tours Monday–Saturday, 9:00 A.M.–noon. No breweriana.
  Brands: Straub.
- D.G. Yuengling & Son, Inc., 5th & Manhantongo St., Pottsville, PA
    17901
  Tours Monday–Thursday, 10:00 A.M and 1:30 P.M. Mugs, shirts, hats,
    posters, tap knobs available.
  Brands: Yuengling Premium, Old German, Chesterfield Ale, Bavarian,
    Yuengling Porter, Mt. Carbon.

Kindred Spirits
  BCCA Chapters:
  Brews Brothers—Allentown
  Coalcracker—Wilkes-Barre
  Delaware Valley—Philadelphia
  Fort Pitt—Pittsburgh
  Horlacher—Allentown
  Keystone—Harrisburg
  Olde Frothingslosh—Pittsburgh
  Presque Isle—Erie
  Must Makers, c/o R.C. Byloff, 3750 E. Market St., York, PA 17402
  Brew It Yourself, c/o Ed Krug, Rt. 1, Box 131 E, Loretto, PA 15940

Of Note
  Barnesville Oktoberfest in July. Unlimited beer and oom-pah bands.
  Pittsburgh on Sundays during football season. Pre-game tailgate par-

ties and post-game trips to the favorite local. These people know how to drink beer.

A Beer Drinker's Guide to the Bars of Reading, available from D. Wardrop, Box 405, RD #1, Temple, PA 19560. Reading's 132 Bars are described and rated. ($2 plus 54¢ postage).

Mail-order homebrew supplies:

Bierhaus International, Inc., 3721 West 12th St., Erie, PA 16505.

Wine & Brew Hobby U.S.A., P.O. Box 1866, Allentown, PA 18105.

Beer can be purchased for take-out in taverns or by the case from specially designated beer outlets, a system which has worked to the advantage of Pennsylvania's small brewers.

Native Brews of The Colonies

ORDER OF THE TREK

Black Horse Ale (Champale and Koch). Brewed under license by two breweries, the Champale version seems to be truer to its English roots. Hop/malt balance seems about right, meaning you can actually taste the hops. Originally a Canadian product.

Genesee Cream Ale (Genesee). An ultimate American ale, slightly more body than average, but utterly devoid of either taste or aftertaste. Exceptional in its inoffensiveness.

Straub (Straub's). The aroma carries across the room. This beer's character comes not from imported malts and fancy hops, but rather from the practiced hands which work the sulfurous water which bubbles up from the coal-veined hills surrounding St. Mary's.

WORTHY OF MENTION

Schaefer (Schaefer/Stroh). A brand on the rebound. Has the sassy bite of hops to cut through the surrounding pollution. Welcome back.

Schaefer-Malta (Schaefer/Stroh). A specialty brew for the Caribbean trade. It's very difficult to understand how anyone could mistake this for beer.

Newman's Pale Ale (William S. Newman). English-style ale brewed by New York's newest and smallest brewer who, unfortunately, is learning that Americans don't like warm, flat beer, no matter how good it is. Now served cold.

Milwaukee Premium (Eastern). One of the least pretentious beers in America, and one of the worst. Still, it is drinkable and for most palates the equal of Bud.

Ballantine XXX Ale (Falstaff). One of the few beers still brewed in the English tradition. If you like the taste of hop oil, this is for you. A completely different product than the bland beer of the same name brewed in Falstaff's Omaha plant and available in Western states.

Ballantine India Pale Ale (Falstaff). One of the most unusual beers in America, reputedly aged in wood for the length of time it takes a clipper ship to sail from Southhampton to Calcutta. Definitely puts hair on your chest.

Matt's Premium (F.X. Matt). Utica's finest. Distinct fruity flavor and a sparkling liveliness. Forgive F.X. Matt his T.V. commercials featuring himself and buy it whenever you find it.

Rolling Rock (Rolling Rock). A good example of a top-quality product from a small brewer. Rolling Rock is light and bland, but consistent and unflawed, winning many devotees.

Schmidt's (Schmidt's, Philadelphia). Schmidt's has become a mortuary for defunct eastern brands. Their flagship brand, like all their products, is hoppy and well-brewed.

Prior Preferred Double Dark (Schmidt's, Philadelphia). Dark, malty, and almost chalky. Keep a six-pack around for when your palate needs a break. Originally brewed under license from Czechoslavakia.

Iron City Light (Pittsburgh). Widely praised light beer which has helped restore Pittsburgh Brewing Co. to the black. The average Steeler fan can down a twelve-pack per game.

Stegmaier (The Lion). An archtypical Pennsylvania beer once voted the state's worst by an incompetent panel from Philadelphia Magazine. Steg's biggest sin is its lack of pretention. For the price you can't beat it.

Yuengling Porter (Yuengling). "It's getting darker all the time," claims Dick Yuengling. Notable primarily as one of the few remaining porters produced by a United States brewer. Still bottled in returnable "Steinie" bottles. A beer worth buying for its nostalgia value more than its flavor.

4
The
Wasteland

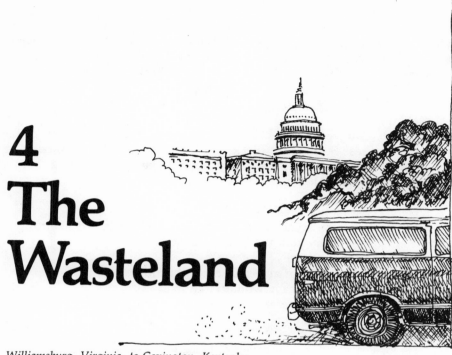

Williamsburg, Virginia, to Covington, Kentucky
28 days, 6,930 miles on the road

Give Me Liberty Or Give Me Beer

Washington, D.C.

It was worth a try. After all, we were in Washington, D.C. and would not have a better opportunity to call the White House. This was a task for Laura, fair maiden of The Great Beer Trek and first lady of the van:
Ring . . . Ring . . . Ring.

"Hello, The White House."
"Hello, this is The Great Beer Trek, and I would like to get some information on what beers are served at the White House, either informally or at State functions."
"Beer . . . OK, one moment."
Ring . . . Ring . . . Ring.
"Hello, Press Office, may I help you?"
"Yes, I'd like to know what beers are served at the White House, either informally or at State functions."
"What beer is served?

"Umm (snicker). Just a moment. (aside) Bob . . . I have someone here who wants to know about beer at the White House (chuckle). No . . . what kinds are served. Who could I connect her to? Grace (chuckle), there's a person calling who wants to know what kind of beer is served at the White House . . . I think so. Ask Charlie, does he know?"

(Back into the receiver). "One moment please, we're working on it."

"Thank you."

(Aside) "Can we connect her to the kitchen? OK, then, how about the First Lady's Press Secretary?" (Back into the receiver.) Hello, I'll connect you to the First Lady's Press Secretary. Sorry to keep you waiting."

"That's OK. Thank You."

Ring . . . Ring . . . Ring.

"Hello, First Lady's Press Secretary's office."

"Hello, I'm doing some research on beer in America. I'd like to find out what beers are served at the White House."

"You mean to the family? (Snicker)"

"Either to the family or at official State functions."

"Oh . . .(chuckle), I really wouldn't know."

"Could you connect me to someone who might know?"

"Umm . . . one moment."

Ring . . . Ring . . . Ring.

"Hello, Press Office." (A different voice.)

"Hello, I think I've been here. I'm doing research on American beer, and I would like to find out what beers are served at the White House either informally or at official functions."

"Beer?"

"Yes."

"Well . . . (sigh) Let me think who'd be able to help you. May I ask what organization you are representing?"

"This is The Great Beer Trek."

"The . . . Great . . . Beer . . . Trek."

"Yes."

"OK, one moment." (put on hold.)

"Hello? I really can't get you that information."

"Well, could you have someone check the refrigerator?"

"Hm-m-m. That would be the easiest route. What's your number? I'll call you back."

But they never did call back, a fact which demonstrates both a lack of follow-through on the part of national government and a disorientation of priorities. Oh, well.

Having not been invited to the White House to share a cold one, The Great Beer Trek visited the United States Brewers Association, the industry's biggest lobbying group. The Association was founded in 1862 to help the Union cause at a time when the Confederacy was threatening to dominate the conflict. Exactly what the USBA accomplished for the war effort has long since been forgotten, but the diehard beer drinker cannot help but notice the date of the organization's inception coincides exactly with the time the tide began to turn favorably for the Union.

The people we met at the USBA were polite and helpful, but they made it entirely clear that they were concerned with the Big Issues, those factors which can affect the nation's overall consumption. The Big Issues include topics such as litter, teenage alcoholism, and drunk driving, not beer treks. Beneath the apparent altruism of the trade organization is the very calculated desire to keep the trading environment as open as possible for its membership. The industry must keep a small step ahead of its critics if it hopes to avoid restrictive regulation which will make operating a brewery less profitable. The brewing industry lobbies hard, for instance, against bottle bills which increase the price of goods and the nuisance factor of doing business. As an alternative, the USBA developed an educational anti-litter campaign called "Pitch-In" which encourages proper disposal of non-returnable containers. The question remains as to whether the brewers can mount an effective campaign before being subjected to a bewildering variety of state-passed bottle bills. Probably not.

Positive Litter Reduction
FROM THE U.S.B.A.

Lurking in the deep recesses of the association's mind is the fact that for thirteen years their membership was subjected to the most rigorous restrictions imaginable in the form of Prohibition. The brewers of the time, who were aware of beer's historical reputation as the beverage of moderation, never anticipated that their product would be caught in the tangled net of temperance along with hard spirits. It could happen again, the USBA reminds us, but for their constant diligence. Let us hope they are wrong.

As for the Big Issues from the perspective of The Great Beer Trek, the USBA's explanations followed predictable party lines. Beer in the United States is not bland or faceless, they say. There is no lack of choice. The

Prohibition 1919 ~ 1933
COULD THIS HAPPEN AGAIN?

brewers give the beer drinker what he wants and he wants what he gets. Otherwise, he would not buy it, and the brewers would go out of business, but instead beer consumption has been on the rise over the past decade. The American consumer gets what he wants.

The industry position is inarguable, and equally irrelevent to the beer drinker. Consumption may be rising, but it is still low compared to other countries, notably England and Germany, where a wider range of malted products is available. Behind their professional smiles and expressions of encouragement, the industry association was stonewalling our efforts to learn about beer drinking in America. It was time to take the case back to the people. Luckily we found a proper place to do so, not far from the USBA, on 22nd Street, NW.

The Brickskeller is a mecca for the homesick, the curious, the jaded, the can collector, or the beer trekker. The bar is downstairs in a brownstone. The walls are lined with all manner and description of beer cans, a display which can entertain for hours. A not uncommon sight at the Brickskeller is people drifting sideways, face to the wall, mesmerized by the variety of design and color. I began to whimper as I surveyed the beer list. By the time I had reached the end, tears were streaming down my cheeks, and I was throwing money at the bartender, a redoubtable lad named Jack Blush. The Brickskeller stocks over three hundred American beers and an almost equal number of imports. They were all there. I could complete our itinerary without moving from this one bar. From Billy to Blitz, from Lucky to Leinenkugel. I had found a home.

The Brickskeller's own truck travels the nation to acquire local brews which in Washington become the exotic. The business is supported by can collectors and pure beer drinkers. On any given night 90% of the sane people of Washington can be found in the Brickskeller trying to undo the effects of trying to run the country for another day. The establishment is an umbilical attaching an entire city to reality. I asked Jack Blush, who is as honest as he is knowledgeable about beer, why such a haven had no draft beer available.

"Because draft beer doesn't come in cans."

Selling beer is just a single facet of the Brickskeller business. Cans are bottom opened. Those not kept by customers are sold via mail-order to collectors nationwide. A private-label beer, Brickskeller Saloon Style, brewed by Pittsburgh Brewing Co., is sold across the bar, as are Brickskeller t-shirts. Jack introduced us to his boss, Maurice Coja, the mastermind behind this frothy empire. He has been a publican most of his life and has owned the present operation since 1957. The burgeoning interest in beer cans gave him the idea of creating a place where a collector could personally supervise the expansion of his collection.

There was more empire to see. The upstairs of the Brickskeller is a cavernous room bedecked with breweriana and a battery of dart boards. This is the dart capital of the nation's capital. The Brickskeller sponsors not one dart team, but twenty-six. As a setting for darts, it is inspirational. Combined with a beer selection which borders on the infinite, this is a place where a beer drinker could spend the rest of his days. I pinched myself to be sure I had not died and gone to heaven.

And still the empire stretched on. There is a dart pro shop to satisfy the whimsy of even the most serious chucker. Then there is the import business. Mr. Coja is the sole importer of Le Gueuze, a weiss beer (brewed with wheat, not barley malt) from the Payottenland district of Belgium. This is one of the famous lambic beers, fermented without the addition of yeast, but rather by the controlled contamination of wild micro-organisms, an unthinkable procedure for the antiseptic-minded modern brewer. [An excellent description of lambic beers appears in Michael Jackson's *The World Guide to Beer* (Running Press, 1982).] We were treated to a taste. The beer is fresh, winey, alive, and unlike anything made in this country.

Although the sun almost never sets on Maurice Coja's beer conglomerate, he is still gazing out toward the horizon. He would not be insulted to hear himself described as a wheeler-dealer. He has hustled a business from beer; now there appears to be no limit to what can be done. The secret is to not think small. Shortly after Miller began to brew Löwenbräu domestically, he began making inquiries into acquiring import rights to the real Löwenbräu. After a healthy dose of bureaucratic shuffling, the government turned down his application, giving the reason for their denial that importing the real Löwenbräu would tend to confuse the public.

Maurice Coja shook his head slowly as he told the story. Taking no for an answer is not one of his strong suits. Some night while sitting in his throne at the Brickskeller he would figure out a way . . .

THE REAL
Löwenbräu..?

He asked about the Beer Trek, and we told him how we had encountered great interest in beer, but a hopeless outlook for all but the largest breweries. The consensus listed the remaining breweries by 1990 at less than ten.

"Don't be too sure," he said with the confidence of someone who knows that his four-of-a-kind beats your straight. "I think there will be *more* breweries in 1990 than there are now."

He deliberately left the bait dangling, and I willingly swallowed. "How do you figure that?"

"Look around," he said with an expanse of the hand. "People are willing to pay good money for good beer. Now grain is cheap, water is cheap, hops are cheap, and you don't have to be a genius to brew a barrel of beer."

I pressed him for details, wondering if future batches of Brickskeller might originate from the house brewery.

"Like I said," Maurice Coja shrugged and made eye contact to lend emphasis to the enigma, "grain is cheap, water is cheap, and you don't have to be a genius to brew a barrel of beer."

Blood, Sweat, and Beers   *Williamsburg, Virginia*

In 1766 Josiah Chowning heralded the opening of his business by advertising an establishment "where all who please to favor me with their custom may depend upon the best of entertainment for themselves, servants and horses." His tavern was an "ordinary," a notch below The Kings Arms, Wetherburn's, and The Raleigh Tavern in appointments and service. It was, very likely, the liveliest place in Williamsburg. It still is.

Today Chowning's Tavern, as with all the restorations of Williamsburg, achieves the proper balance of historical authenticity and 20th century functionalism. The tavern is crowded every night, just as it might have been during "Publick Times," a twice yearly event in the Colonies when General Court was in session and the local populace flocked to the capital to join in the general merriment which accompanied horse races and fairs.

Today costumed waitresses wedge tourists into rough hewn tables where they munch peanuts and sip on bland approximations of colonial drinks while a troubadour serenades with period folk songs. Period games of skill and chance (mostly the latter) are distributed to the willing, and

Josiah Chowning

FROM THE SIGN OUTSIDE HIS TAVERN.

tourists participate with an enthusiasm that supercedes formal introduction. It is perhaps the closest approximation of the colonial tavern experience available to the denizen of the 20th century, and yet not the least pretension is made of preserving the historical accuracy of the beverages.

At Chowning's they serve, albeit in a stoneware mug, a dark lager made by Miller and light lager made by Schmidt's. Although this choice is to be commended in terms of its variety compared to the average contemporary hostelry, the blandness becomes obvious when compared to the creative concoctions which might have been offered in the same tavern several hundred years ago.

History graces us with rose-colored glasses which make the world look blurrily cheerful as if viewed through the bottom of an empty mug. We forget Thomas Jefferson's pimples, George Washington's wooden teeth, and Daniel Boone's body odor. We correctly remember colonial taverns as being lively social centers where the pillars of society met, over beer, to discuss the principles which were to become the foundation of America.

With such properly motivated founding fathers, is it any surprise that these United States have gone on to become the mightiest nation on the face of the earth and, not coincidentally, its largest beer producer? And yet, is it not an indication of the country's current predicament that our

The Conceptualist's View of Beer History

(Prehistory–1640) North American native beverage pulque (fermented juice of maguey cactus) is augmented by the brewing of Spaniards (1544) and English (1607). Pilgrims, especially, bring with them an affinity for malted beverages. Homebrewing becomes a way of life.

(1640–1760—Pre-Colonial) Advances in mercantile trade make imported beers more readily available. Domestic industry lags, except in mid-Atlantic states where William Penn helps establish Philadelphia as the nation's brewing center, building the region's first commercial brewery in 1683.

(1760–1800—Revolutionary) War effort demonstrates vulnerability of beer supply. Founding fathers (Washington, Jefferson, Adams, Madison) promote legislation to encourage domestic brewing industry.

(1800–1840—English Tradition) Rooted in the traditions of our English forebears, commercial brewing industry attains regional viability. D.G. Yuengling Co., founded in 1829, is oldest United States brewer still in operation.

(1840–1880—The Bavarian Influx) Our greatest contemporary breweries all date from this era. The United States Brewers Association forms during the Civil War. If there was a Golden Age of Brewing in the United States, this was it.

(1880–1920—The Precipice) Technological advances in the late 19th century barely overshadow the growing racial and social backlash to the burgeoning Germanic communities. World War I gives the "Dry" contingent the outside stimulus needed to pass Prohibition.

(1920–1960—The Martini Era) The nation finally returns to its senses long enough to repeal Prohibition, but the sudsy recovery is hindered by yet another World War. Beer languishes during the fatuous fifties, a decade most notable for its staggering number of brewery closings.

(1960–2000—The Renaissance) The raising of consciousness in the sixties opens people's eyes to the bleakness of their sudsy surroundings. The Coors Mystique returns beer to respectability and paves the way for the enlightenment of the Beer Drinker. The direction for the balance of the century appears assured.

leaders no longer gather at the tavern for a fraternal tankard? The alcohol-tinged portrait of the current political leader is likely to be closer to the vodka-swilling senator in the arms of his floozie at the Silver Slipper or the lonely, depressed First Lady washing down her valium with gin.

That this nation was founded on the blood, sweat, and beers of great men is immediately apparent upon visiting Williamsburg. The Raleigh Tavern became the capital of Virginia when in 1774 the House of Burgesses

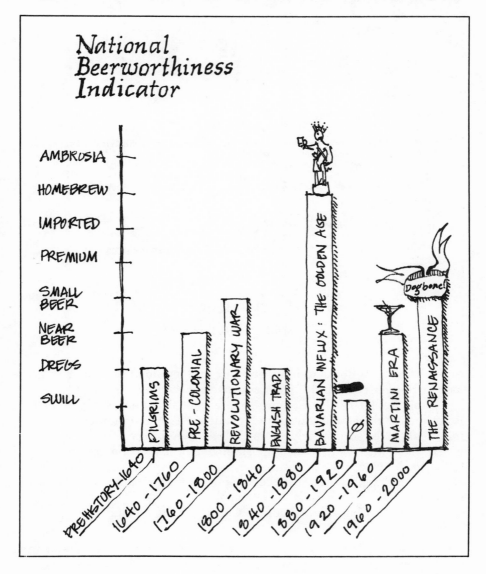

National Beerworthiness Indicator

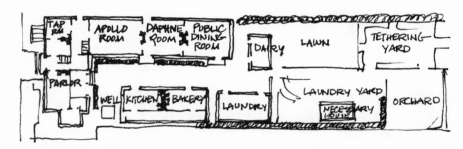

Raleigh Tavern
COLONIAL WILLIAMSBURG

met in its Apollo Room to unify support for blockaded Boston. Yes, it all happened over beer, and, in some respects, because of beer.

Until the 1760's the Colonies had accepted a role as a part of the Empire. The movement toward independence gathered momentum in the mid-1760's. Not surprisingly, from the beer's-eye view of a besotted historian, this coincides with the imposition of a British tax on imported beer. Hitherto the colonists had consumed the readily available English beers and ales. Suddenly, they faced being shut off without a domestic product to fill the void. A revolution was inevitable.

The Williamsburg guidebook tells us about the Raleigh:

The Raleigh was a center of social activity . . . planters and merchants gathered at the bar. Sturdy tavern tables were scarred by dice-boxes.

Tobacco smoke from long clay pipes filled the air, together with heated political discussions. Good fellowship was sealed by a toast of Madeira or a hot rum punch, or by a pint of ale drunk from a pewter tankard.

But what about the beers? Were they as quenching to the thirst as the image of the Raleigh is to the memory? Or were those brews as appealing as George Washington's wooden smile?

The eighteenth-century American sought the same things at his local tavern as we do today—comfort, camaraderie, and booze. Although coffee and tea were popular beverages in the Colonies, they did not appear as features on the tavern bill of fare. Principal liquors sold were domestic and imported wines, fortified wines (brandy, claret, and Madeira), rum, gin, hard cider, and, of course, beer. Exotic punches involving combinations of the aforementioned spirits carried colorful names such as Kill Divil, Ockuby, Rumbullion, Stonewall, Blackstrap, Tiff, Sillibub, Sampson, Hotch Potch, Caudel, Arrack, Athol Brose, and Swinglingtow and undoubtedly packed the same impact as the modern day depth charge or stump-lifter. Later in this chapter it will be shown how creatively beer was used as a base for the colonial punch.

An average tavern offered small beer, domestic ale, imported strong beers and ales, and porter. As opposed to today's selection of brews where differentiation is achieved more through packaging than taste, beers at the colonial tavern had distinct characteristics:

Strong Beer and Ale—Imported brews, then as now, were more respected than domestic products. Commercial brewing did not thrive in the New World until the 1760's when the British increased the tax on beer as part of the Stamp Act. Although barley was abundant in America, there were few commercial malt houses, and existing breweries depended on imported malt. Even worse, there was no bottle manufacturing industry. Until the 1800's most beer and ale was brewed in the tavern or home. Legislative acts initiated by Thomas Jefferson and James Madison encouraged brewing and established the fledgling industry.

The distinction between ale and beer was as unclear in colonial times as it is today. Some sources (and some early recipes) are consistent with sixteenth-century English custom defining ale to be a drink made without hops. Other sources differentiated beer and ale along the lines currently used in British brewing, the former being darker and more heavily bodied, the result of using more highly roasted malts. Neither definition bears much resemblance to contemporary American usage where "ale" is regarded as having double the macho quotient of a similarly branded beer.

Taste was highly variable depending on ingredients, regional taste, and local water supply (even New World brewers corrected water for hardness but could not remove minerals as does a modern brewery). Comparisons with present-day, top-fermented English imports (Whitbread,

Watney's Red Barrel, MacEwan's or Newcastle Brown Ale) would not be unreasonable, although clarity and stability were inferior to the contemporary product. Some of the popular imports in Williamsburg included London Ale, Scotch Ale, Bristol Beer, and Welsh Ale.

Small Beer—This was the common beverage of working classes and country people. Both sexes and all age groups consumed small beer with every meal, especially in cities where the public water supplies were suspect. Small beer is made from a second infusion of the grain after the initial wort has been drawn off to make strong beer or ale. This second brewing produces a weak beverage which must be drunk fresh. It is the original light beer. Because of its low alcoholic strength (approximately 2.5% by weight, variable by brewer) which gave it a low preservative value and high perishability, it was never transported far from the brewing site. In Williamsburg small beer was known as "Virginia Middling Beer" and cost one-half the price of domestic beer which in turn cost one-half of imported beer or ale. No equivalent of small beer exists on the market today. An approximation of the taste can be had by mixing Bass Ale, or perhaps homebrew, with an equal part water.

Porter—Some versions of this beer are highly hopped, while others tend toward sweetness; some are both. Porter is brewed from dark, highly caramelized malts that give it a mahogany color similar to bock. The name derives from the popularity of this beverage with the porters in the London markets where it originated.

Varietal Beers—These domestically brewed beers were limited in variety only by the imagination of the brewers making them. Each recipe combined regionally available items according to the whim of an individual. Varietal types included spruce beer, maple beer, lemon beer, hop beer, nettle beer, ginger beer, and corn beer. These beers live only in the memories of the contemporary home brewers whose imaginations know no restraints.

But were the Colonial beverages any good? The modern American commercial brewer would say emphatically, "NO!" Without the advantages of mechanical refrigeration and modern methods of achieving sanitation and quality control, these beverages must have seemed neanderthal compared to the clean, crisp, consistently sparkling product available today. On the other hand, the more adventurous home brewer, whose quest for gustatorial adventure will tolerate the flat cloudiness of occasional contamination, would counter with an equally resounding "YES!" Particularly when drunk fresh, there is no reason these beverages could not slake the thirst as well as homemade bread satisfies the palate.

But after all, it's a free country where we can worship the brew of our choice. That is what the Revolution was all about.

HMM... EYE OF BAT, WING OF NEWT, 2 KEGS ALE...

A Colonial Sampler

In addition to the various beers and ales available, the frequenter of the colonial tavern might have had colorful and exotic sudsy concoctions prepared, and perhaps invented, by his friendly purveyor of spirits. Many recipes survive which provide insight to the good humored wit of the creators as well as the capacity of the imbibers. What would you call a mixture of half old and half bitter ale? Why, "Mother-In-Law," of course. Rum plus beer was "Calibogus," while "Lamb's Wool," "Rumfustian," "Bellowstop," and "Colonel Byrd's Nightcap" each describe unique colonial beer-based cocktails. To read through these recipes is to appreciate the versatility of beer for the adventuresome palate. Not only were many brews served hot instead of cold, but they featured ingredients ranging from ground ginger, to egg yolks, to spiced toast, to a cucumber garnish. In honor of our visit to Williamsburg we created our ale punch, guaranteed to slake the thirst of any traveler. Ask for it the next time you stay at a Holiday Inn. If the bartender gives you a blank stare, you can tell him how to make it:

Beer Trekker's Bellyache—Pour two quarts strong ale into a cast iron caldron. Warm gently with lemon peel and enough crumbled brown bread to make a pudding-like consistency. With a mortar and pestle crush one quarter ounce ginger together with twelve cloves, and one large pinch bruised cinnamon and grated nutmeg. Into a separate bowl crack a dozen eggs. Add spices along with one gill brandy, one gill gin and bitters, and one bottle of sherry. Mix contents, add to caldron. Stir vigorously with a glowing poker until the mixture starts frothing over. Strain through a tammy. Garnish with a slice of cucumber.
Go to bed.

Where Have You Gone, Billy
Boy, Billy Boy
Plains, Georgia

All good Yankees have been conditioned to fear the South. Its residents have been portrayed as bombers of innocent black children, blasters of defenseless hippies, and aboriginal rapists of defenseless canoeists. Thus, it was with some trepidation that The Great Beer Trek hitched up its pants and plunged into a land which, in terms of its sudsy offerings, was as hospitable as a moonscape.

We were spoiled by this time. The initial shock of the recent carnage of independent breweries was now behind us. Any disappointment had been long since overcome by our positive reception at the remaining breweries, and by meeting such a wide variety of likable and well-informed beer drinkers. The original hypothesis of the Trek—that almost any situation is improved through the addition of beer—had gained ample support. Despite some early setbacks we were clearly gaining momentum, momentum we would need to survive the Wasteland.

There are no independent breweries left in the Southeast. The regional beverages extend to the extremes—from Coke, Pepsi, and Dr. Pepper to sour mash, moonshine, and bourbon. The middle remains neglected. Beer prices are high, while liquor is relatively cheap. Dry counties dot the map, reviving the spectre of a beerless society.

Why?

From Williamsburg the van plunged South as far as Auburndale, Florida, site of the nondescript Duncan Brewing Co., makers of Dunk's Beer, a former independent now operating under the Heileman corporate umbrella. This is the closest the Wasteland comes to having a native brewery. The nationals all have strategic outposts in the South, manufacturing dreadnoughts of minimal interest to us. Decent taverns are few and far between. In fact, the most popular watering hole in most southern towns is likely as not to be associated with a national chain, and we did not pack up in our van to drink beer in the Macon, Georgia, Pizza Hut.

And yet, if the brewers have plants here, obviously beer is consumed, but where and by whom? Not until we visited Plains, Georgia, did we learn about the southern beer drinking subculture.

Plains is as southern a town as exists. It has neither the mystery of the Piedmont, the allure of the Okefenokee, nor the lonely desolation of the Georgia coast; but it is a nice place where people tend to business and strive in their quiet ways for the comforts of 20th century life—a new pickup, a bass boat, a modern kitchen, and enough money for beer. At least, it *was* a nice place until one of its sons became President, catapulting the town into the national limelight.

On Route 280 is a huge parking lot asleep in a dusty field where the Welcome Center was built to handle the flood of tourists who never came. We went in and had forced upon us an unwanted armful of brochures touting the tourist attractions of Plains. The pamphlets were dutifully transported several hundred feet to a trash barrel half-filled with the things. Someone, in fact many people, had over-estimated the appeal of Plains. Our goals were simple. When Jimmy Carter was elected President in 1976, a key factor in his victory was his appeal to the common man. Plains played a part in the image, as did his colorful family, especially brother Billy. Billy was a jewel whom the media discovered, polished, and eventually discarded.

Billy Carter ran for mayor of Plains on a noncommercial platform, vowing, if elected, to do everything in his power to keep Plains the simple, friendly town it has always been. He lost, and soon town residents were falling all over each other to make a buck off the expected tourist bonanza. The town dressed in the gaudy clothes of an amusement park to suit equally tasteless tourists who wandered about the simple town to break up the drive from Bayonne to Disneyworld. Tours of Plains were initiated to show visitors points of interest such as the softball field where Jimmy played, Billy's wife's old home, Amy's school, and Jimmy's Uncle Alton's home.

If indeed it was inevitable that tourists would be coming to Plains and throwing money in the streets, then Billy, who more than anyone was in a position to pick up the money, was not too proud to bend. He formed his own tour to leave from his already famous gas station. If people wanted to pay $2.50 to look foolish sitting in a wagon pulled by a little choo-choo past the simple church, ranch homes, and softball fields of a backwoods Georgia town, Billy would oblige them.

We pulled into Billy Carter's gas station, swallowed an obligatory beer, and watched dust settle on Main Street, Plains. It was the kind of afternoon when Huck Finn would play hooky or Stanley Kowalski would come home drinking. There was nary a tourist in sight. We sat on the hard bench,

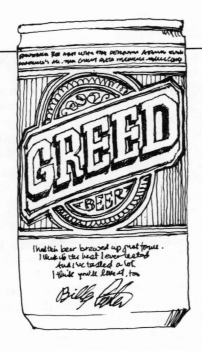

The Saga Of Billy Beer

"Greed?" Billy Carter was once quoted in Newsweek *(November 14, 1977), "I know him. He's a good ol' sonovabitch." He also proved to be the undoing of a laudable plan to save America's small breweries by creating a national brand which could be produced locally.*

Those involved tried hard to make sure this was not a one shot rip-off of cans filled with swill. Falls City brewmaster John Brown formulated several prototypes from which Billy selected his favorite. The Falls City people insist that Billy's qualifications as a beer drinker were well-documented by his ability to pick out the same sample in repeated tests. At this point Billy Carter's involvement effectively ended. He bears no responsibility for the fiasco which ensued.

With the advantages of centralized purchasing and the ability to use the mass media for promotion, the theory was that the little guy might finally stand a chance against the nationals. It was with such lofty hopes that Falls City licensed manufacturing rights to F.X. Matt (Utica, New York), Cold Spring (Cold Spring, Minnesota), and Pearl (San Antonio, Texas). Billy's wife Sybil picked out a can design, and Billy Beer was off to the races.

A tremendous amount of free publicity was received, and initial orders were much heavier than anticipated. Success unraveled the plan, and the air became filled with mud and arrows. Some say that Falls City lacked the expertise to manage a coherent national program. Falls City accused its licensees of filling their Billy cans with cheap swill to exploit a short-lived phenomenon. Before long accusations became as common as unsold cases, and one by one the participating breweries ceased production. The plan to save the local breweries became an interesting footnote in the history of the suds.

Billy Beer continues to be controversial. Reports of fabulous sums being paid for cans keep surfacing, although discounted by serious collectors. Even in repose, it seems that the old sonovabitch Greed wants to be associated with Billy.

swatted flies, and discussed what to do next. Plains was apparently a blind alley; time to move our lazy bones back into the van.

As we were pulling out of Billy's station, a young man with dark hair flagged us: "What's The Great Beer Trek?" (One does not drive around in a van with "The Great Beer Trek" plastered all over it unless one expects a few questions like this.) I explained our quest and about our loosely defined mission in Plains, i.e., to add another brush stroke to the national beer drinking portrait.

"Y'all looking for Billy?" The young man shielded his eyes from the late afternoon sun.

My reply carried at least a tinge of sarcasm. "I'm willing to bet he hasn't been here since the election."

The man replied slowly, without reacting to the sarcasm. "He was just here a few minutes ago. He's probably still around, or maybe up at the Country Club. Told me he had to get home because he has to go to Nashville tomorrow. You're interested in beer? You been up to the Country Club? It's the best place to drink beer in these parts. Maybe I'll meet you there later." He gave us directions. We decided it was worth the risk; our travels wouldn't be bringing us to Plains again.

The "Country Club" is a misnomer. This modest road house, located on Route 280 a mile west of Plains, is described on its menu as "old and rustic." It is neither, although it is made of wood and has no furnishings more elaborate than a napkin dispenser. No one else had seen fit to grace the Country Club with their presence this day, not even any dumb tourists. We sat at the counter in awkward silence and sipped on another beer waiting for something to happen. The beers (Pabst, Schlitz, or Billy) were served ice cold and in the can. We asked the bartender, our voices again oozing with Yankee sarcasm, if Billy had been seen recently.

"Y'all just missed him. He couldn't have left more'n ten minutes ago. Y'all musta passed him on your way out of town," came the laconic reply. I began to get the feeling that this was the official party-line response around Plains to inquiries as to Billy's whereabouts.

The bartender and the cook at the Country Club, Gene Bacon, serves a mean, cold beer and makes a more-than-passable barbeque. He likes people, but will not speak unless spoken to. Initially we thought him taciturn with strangers, but later understood his silence as a form of acceptance. Had he not liked us, he would have busied himself in the kitchen. We asked, but Gene had no strong opinions about the transformation of Plains or the celebrity of Billy. Everyone else in town worried about such things. Gene concerned himself with barbeque, where his expertise could be documented by taste, not words. His barbeque sauce, containing 1001 ingredients, is his legacy. A man needs something of his own, something of his own creation which will live on when he dies. Gene may not be slick or glib, but neither is he gullible or dumb. If you want to recreate his sauce, he will give you the ingredients, and you are welcome to spend your life experimenting as he has. We started to copy down the ingredients, but gave up somewhere between the grapefruit and tabasco. We were again preparing to leave when our friend from town showed up. "I've been waiting for you. What are you doing up here?" Our puzzlement showed in our lack of response, so he continued. "This front part is for tourists. The good beer drinking's out back."

The entrance to the back section of the Plains Country Club is through a slightly askew door with a scrawled sign "Good Ol' Boys." The inside is rough and spare, proudly so. By comparison, the back makes the front seem as plush as any lounge in Atlanta's Peachtree Plaza. There is a jukebox and a pinball machine, both of which operate constantly, lending the scene a veneer of reality. Out here in the sticks, miles from the nearest Cuisinart or St. Pauli Girl, it is fitting that one should be able to listen to the ties which bind hillbillies nationwide—Willie Nelson, Ol' Waylon, Jerry Jeff Walker, and Dolly. Beyond the noise there is a rough wood floor, rough wood tables, and rough wood chairs. As in all the finest beer drinking places, there is nothing to distract one from the other people.

Introductions were accomplished easily. The people we met were Sam, Walter, Ed . . . all good 'uns who accepted us immediately since we were guests of one of their own. The lack of amenities was a patch worn on every sleeve, as if the Good Ol' Boys were clinging to a rough hewn ethic that changing times and the community's notoriety threatened to strip them of. These were rednecks in a small world where the redneck was king. We were flattered that they welcomed us into their temple.

They liked the idea of a Beer Trek, and pumped us with suggestions, opinions, and questions. Their own sense of style was unique. Bartenders and customers were one. Proper etiquette was to get a beer in the most expeditious way, usually to walk back to the cooler and grab one. At the end of the night everyone pushed through beer-fuzzed brains to reconstruct tabs. We were treated to a house specialty, a deep-fat-fried porkskin. This delicacy appears on the menu whenever so-and-so feels like cooking and what's-his-name has just slaughtered a hog. Pabst is widely the preferred brand of the good ol' boys, with Schlitz a close second. Everyone agreed that Billy beer tasted all right, but a hillbilly is too independent to identify with any man's beer, even Billy's. Quality is synonymous with temperature: the colder the better.

A favorite pastime of the Good Ol' Boys of Plains is to make fools of tourists. We were challenged to several raucous pinball games which accomplished just that. Tall tales began coming out by the third or fourth beer. Billy's celebrity was regarded as a perfect example of cracker cunning. They giggled hilariously at some of the famous and pretentious people he had dragged into the back room. Reporters, country singers, politicians— many had faced the acid test of the Country Club regulars and many had failed. Typically they would endure the coarse surroundings and even coarser language for only so long before bolting to the Holiday Inn from which they came. "Good riddance," sniggered the good 'uns, another unworthy stranger driven from their midst.

"Used to be," a wild-eyed, bearded man at the pinball machine told Laura, "this room was where the nigguhs drank. But when the tourists came, us old ol' boys got pushed back here." He watched her reactions carefully, hoping she would blanch. She held fast. "Don't know where the nigguhs drink anymore. Most go up to the motel in Americus." The test finished, our points scored, the pinball game merrily continued. Like most of the regulars, he had come directly from work in the fields, just hopped in the truck or on the cycle and come down to the club for a few cold ones, the chance to guffaw with the guys, and, tonight, to gawk at a few strange Yankees. I obligingly provided the biggest laugh of the night when I asked for directions to the men's room.

"Hell, we got the biggest men's room in the whole wide world," said the bearded man. With that I was directed to a propane tank in back of the Country Club. I pissed long and hard into the Georgia dusk, experiencing a sense of freedom along with bladder relief. To my right, sharing the planet of a men's room was a tall man with dark hair flecked with gray.

"Like our men's room?" he asked.

"I feel honored. I mean, I'm really pissing where Billy Carter has pissed."

"Billy, hell. You'd be surprised who's pissed out here. You think we build a men's room when Jimmy comes?"

"You mean the President has pissed here?"

"Sure," the man said over his shoulder as he headed back to fill his bladder again. The import overwhelmed me. I looked around for some kind of confirmation, an historic plaque on the propane tank, something. The machinations of the cosmos had me reeling. When the Beer Trek left Massachusetts it was beyond my wildest dreams to think I would urinate on the same patch of real estate as a President. Ironically, there was no way to document the historic occasion. A picture would be fruitless, and a handful of soil would not impress anyone who had not shared the experience. I would have nothing to show my grandchildren.

The Country Club closes around 9 P.M., mercifully. At the accelerated rate of beer consumption, by midnight there would have been one large pile of drunk hillbillies and Beer Trekkers. Gene Bacon had long since abandoned his post in the tourist part of the Country Club and quietly joined in the clamor. Every so often he would shake his head slowly and complain how his wife would kill him when he came home to their trailer, but for now he was having a good ol' time. And all the while Willie, Waylon, and Dolly played on.

At nine everyone piled out into the parking lot for a final farewell. These people truly believed in the nobility of our odyssey and were proud to have participated. On our part we had met enough good beer drinkers to have made meeting Billy superfluous. The vehicles—motorcycles, pickups, and even a pink 1969 Lincoln Continental—peeled onto the two-lane blacktop into Plains, roaring engines punctuated by rebel whoops. The Great Beer Trek, slightly rougher at the edges but happy to have pierced the armor of the Wasteland, made a quick trip back to the propane tanks before heading north.

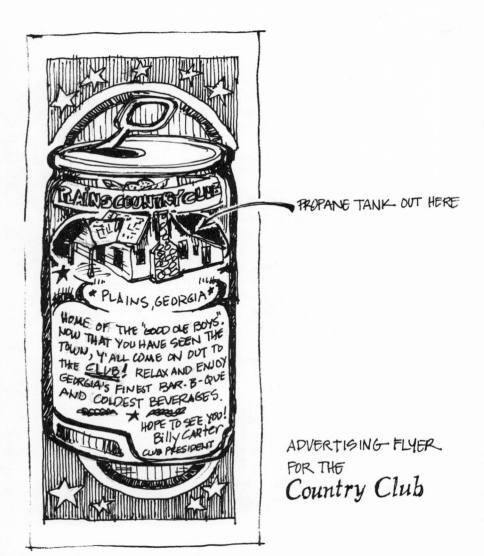

ADVERTISING FLYER
FOR THE
Country Club

- ROLL BAR
- CIBIE SUPER OSCAR
   LIZARD BURNERS
- GUN RACK
- HAT RACK

Good Ol' Style

The Good Ol' Boy can be a Gulf Coast cowboy or a Georgia hillbilly. There are subtle differences, but, even more important, striking similiarities. A pickup, for instance, is required, although style, color, and make are left to choice. Also required:

1. *A pretty girl who knows what she is getting into.*
2. *A cooler.*
3. *Tapes of Waylon, Willie, and "The Killer" (don't ask, or you'll show your ignorance).*

And, of course, beer. Currently in favor are the seven- and eight-ounce midgies introduced by the brewers for diet-conscious women, but appreciated by good 'uns for their ability to preserve the maximum chill and carbonation of the brew. (The mania for coldness was best demonstrated for us at a Florida oyster bar where the waitress floated a glass of ice in our unfinished pitcher to keep it frosty.) The floor of the pickup cab is properly a clanking sea of these containers which fall out whenever the door is opened.

Hats are required, although the choice is a personal affair. Gulf Coasters will opt for lacquered, straw cowboy hats which rise a foot above the head and then dip precipitously below the chin. The hillbilly prefers the adjustable baseball cap emblazoned with the emblem of his favorite macho product. Cowboy boots and jeans complete the uniform.

The final requirement is the CB radio, and the language which accompanies it. To make your twang suitably indecipherable, practice such phrases as:

"Eyowjow rahjah thassa beeg tenfoah yar yar whass yer twenny? Kamoan-n-n."

Your vocabulary will need to be expanded. For instance, the word for "beer" in CB'ese can be selected from among the following:

Bevo	*Rocky Mountain Kool Aid (Coors)*	*Super cola*
Barley pop	*Honey*	*Little pony*
Brown bottle	*Red, White & Blue (Pabst)*	*8-0-7*
Buttermilk	*7-0-8's*	*Forty-eight*
Cold coffee	*Spring water*	

Now train yourself to live on a diet of Slim Jims, biscuits and gravy, and barbeque. You're almost there.

When You're Out Of Schlitz   *Southern Roads*

The Good Ol' Boys of Plains, enthusiastic as they were regarding beer consumption, were very inarticulate on the subject. Beer was, to them, a yellow, highly carbonated beverage meant to be drunk at near-freezing temperatures. End of discussion. Choice meant beer in 7-, 12-, 16- or 32-oz. containers.

These were the limits of their sudsy horizons. Through no fault of their own they had not been exposed to the vagueries of homebrew, the spectrum of imported beers, or even the regional subtleties of local breweries à la Pennsylvania. In a way we envied their innocence. They have so much to look forward to.

Ironically, it is the unsophisticated tastes of the Good Ol' Boys which are the targets of the marketing efforts of the major brewers, and rightly so. The big national brewers brew 99 percent of the beer in the United States, and the Good Ol' Boys drink 99 percent of that. It is natural they should get together.

When we visited the United States Brewer's Association in Washington, we asked if they had any suggestions for future stops. "Yes," came the reply. "St. Petersburg, Florida. There is more brewing experience collected there than anywhere else in the country." Although the van never made it to St. Pete, several days before our visit to Plains we encountered a man on tiny Captiva Island just off Ft. Myers who raised our IQ's substantially regarding what it takes to bring buyer and seller together in the world of big brewing.

DeWitt Jones had for many years been in charge of the Schlitz account while a vice president of the Leo Burnett Advertising Agency in Chicago. During his tenure, Schlitz maintained the number two position in the national volume sweepstakes, riding the backs of such memorable lines as, "Real Gusto in a Great, Light Beer" and "When You're Out of Schlitz, You're Out of Beer." Now they have fallen substantially and have even lost their status as an independent concern, having been acquired by Stroh of Detroit. The Great Beer Trek hoped to find out, from the perspective of someone whose orientation was product identity and media strategy rather than malt and hops, why Schlitz's fortunes changed.

DeWitt Jones spends more time these days fighting condominium developments and photographing roseate spoonbills than wondering about the ebbs and flows of the beer wars. He broke from these pursuits long enough to educate us. He serves Schlitz to his guests, and we shared one as we talked:

Beer Trek: Did everyone at Leo Burnett know immediately that "Real gusto in a great, light beer" was a great line?
DeWitt Jones: We knew it was a good line. It felt good. It had all the right

strengths and none of the negatives. It wasn't hard to understand. It was executable. You could do something with it.

Beer Trek: Did the line have a secret ingredient?

DeWitt Jones: It was simple, and simplicity is the soul of good advertising. Also we discovered that there were absolutely no negative connotations to the word "gusto."

Beer Trek: Who were the gusto ads directed toward?

DeWitt Jones: Everyone. The beer people always want to reach the heavy beer drinker, the guy who drinks twenty-seven six-packs a minute. Problem is, there aren't that many heavy beer drinkers and they are hard to identify, so it is hard to target your advertising toward this group. We worked on the theory that if we could get more people to drink a little bit, we'd be better off. At the same time, we felt it important that we not turn off the heavy beer drinker.

Beer Trek: Other ad campaigns, such as Schaefer's "One beer to have when you're having more than one," have been successful because they reached the heavy beer drinker. What is the difference?

DeWitt Jones: With Schaefer you are dealing with a regional product where you can reach your entire market. With a national product like Schlitz this is impossible. You can't afford to fractionate your advertising or your appeal.

Beer Trek: That the "gusto" campaign had unprecedented success was proved by increased sales. Why was it changed?

DeWitt Jones: Most good ad campaigns are changed long before they outlive their usefulness.

Beer Trek: Why?

DeWitt Jones: Because the client lives with the advertising more than the customer. The customer sees an ad maybe once a week, but the client sees it every day. He gets sick of it.

Beer Trek: How does an agency keep a client from changing a campaign they know to be doing a good job?

DeWitt Jones: You have to keep good advertising fresh—change the picture, change the scenery—just don't change the message, if it's good.

Beer Trek: What has happened with the most recent "gusto" advertising?

DeWitt Jones: In an attempt to keep the advertising fresh the simplicity was covered up by foolishness and frippery.

Beer Trek: Are the changes in the advertising the cause of Schlitz's current problems?

DeWitt Jones: Advertising alone can't be held responsible for that, nor can it take sole credit for Schlitz's success in the sixties. Advertising is one part of a total effort. It is more than one magical phrase like the "gusto" line. It's the execution of the line, the execution of the marketing plan, the enthusiasm of the sales force, the enthusiasm of the management. You can't get by with just good advertising. You need good beer.

DeWitt related a story about how the line, "When You're Out of Schlitz, You're Out of Beer," came to be. An agency person was having a beer in his favorite tavern when the man next to him ordered a Budweiser. When informed by the bartender that their supply was exhausted and offered a second choice, the customer shook his head and stood to leave. "Nope," he said. "when you're out of Bud, you're out of beer."

The executives at the advertising agency were so taken by the musical simplicity that they used it for their own beer, lest it fall into enemy hands, a purely defensive maneuver.

Later, when I related the story to a Good Ol' Boy at a local roadhouse, he put another perspective to the situation: "Shee-it! That ain't the way the line should go. It's "When you're out of beer, you're out of beer!" The logic was inarguable.

When you're out of beer, you're out of beer.

The Schlitz fall from grace has an important factor which DeWitt Jones did not discuss. At the height of their popularity, Schlitz management changed their manufacturing to achieve greater efficiency, reasoning that the indiscriminate beer drinker would never notice or care. He did notice and he did care. As Jones said, you need good beer, and Schlitz did not have it. As important as good advertising is, it is worthless without the beer.

Northward, and northward still. Despite the interlude in Plains, the beeriness of the northern climes attracted us. We pushed harder and drove longer. We stopped in Nashville, hoping to experience the associations between beer and life so frequently celebrated in country songs. No such luck. Nashville is simply the place where the experiences of elsewhere are recorded. We did find the Gerst House, however, which made up for any disappointment.

The Gerst House is the former lunchroom for the workers at the William Gerst Brewing Co. The brewery is no more, but the restaurant provides the best glimpse of Bavariana this side of the Mason-Dixon line. The pace is frantic, the beer plentiful (they feature Andeker, Pabst's superb premium brand served in bowl-like goblets), and mittwurst. It is the service, however, which sets the Gerst House apart from the Ground Rounds and Bonanza Steak Houses which sprout like weeds along southern roadways, for the service is, in a word, abusive. The waitresses, chefs, and kitchen help are one at this establishment, and while the food is unquestionably excellent, the moods of the staff cover the range of human emotions. In a world where scrub-faced, beaming faces of uniformed (and uninformed) help in the fast-food chain now proliferate, it is a relief to encounter real humanity. At the Gerst House the surliness of the help is definitely made tolerable by the excellence of the fare.

And northward still. By now one could sense Bavaria in the air. Louisville even had the warm corpse of a brewery, Falls City, creators of the renowned Billy Beer. (Alas, the concern ceased operation soon after we passed through.) We found a friendly neighborhood tavern, Chek's Cafe, on Burnett Street which served a splendid array of regional delicacies, both solid and liquid. The gentlemanly owner, Joe Munroe, gave us beers on the house simply because we were new faces and he wanted us to remember him kindly. He made us promise to send postcards and whenever we did, he always replied with a polite note. At lunchtime, Chek's runs

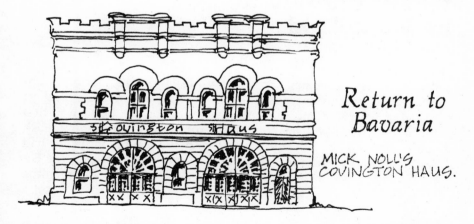

Return to Bavaria

MICK NOLL'S COVINGTON HAUS.

on the honor system. Eat as much as you want, then settle up as you leave. The crowds are so heavy he often spreads tablecloths on the pinball machines to accommodate them; yet no one would dare cheat someone with as much class as Joe Munroe. He claims that no one has. We believed him.

That evening we spent in Covington, Kentucky. By now the stirrings were unmistakable, and Covington confirmed it. This town is so sudsy that it is hard to believe one is still south of the Ohio River. The crowded streets are dotted with tiny locals where the entire block gathers, kids and all, to share the latest gossip while sipping a local beer, either Wiedemann's from nearby Newport or Burger, brewed by Hudepohl just across the river in Cincinnati. After visiting five or six friendly joints we found a comfortable roosting place on the roof of Mick Noll's converted firehouse. The muffled grunt and moan of an oom-pah band could be heard beneath us. The locals were clearly going crazy, as it was a Saturday night. For once, however, we did not join in. We sipped at our Christian Moerlein, a super-premium made by Hudepohl, and gazed through the budding trees beyond to the Ohio River, which separated us from Cincinnati and the heart of Bavaria. Lewis and Clark must have felt the same when they gazed onto the Pacific.

"We made it," said Laura, her sigh of relief superfluous. The maltiness of the Christian Moerlein, which has a characteristic husky taste of grain, was now imprinting itself on my brain, making the statement seem profound. A lot of miles, many of them beerless, were now fading peacefully away, leaving the highlights of good ol' boys and mittwurst. She offered a toast.

"To the Wasteland, and to survival." We drank. And the beer tasted very good.

Trekker's Guide to The Wasteland

The Wasteland refers neither to a territory nor its people, but to an unfortunate set of circumstances which has resulted in America's bleakest beer drinking environment. The pedigree is fine, as can be seen from a visit to the taverns of Williamsburg. The South is steeped in the English tradition of brewing, and nearly every respectable plantation owner had his brewhouse and favorite recipe. After the Civil War, however, the Bavarian influence never went south of the Mason-Dixon line. Between the venerable Old Ebbitt in D.C. and Nashville's Gerst House, there is not a lot.

A Beer Trek of the South is now a bleak affair. There are no local breweries to speak of, only the strategically placed manufacturing outposts of the nationals. Thus, there is no regional pride tied to brand selection. The southern beer drinker is willing enough, but he has been relegated to outlaw status, condemned to backroads and sleazy bars. The southern gentleman has found his need for ritualistic male bonding in the drinking of bourbon.

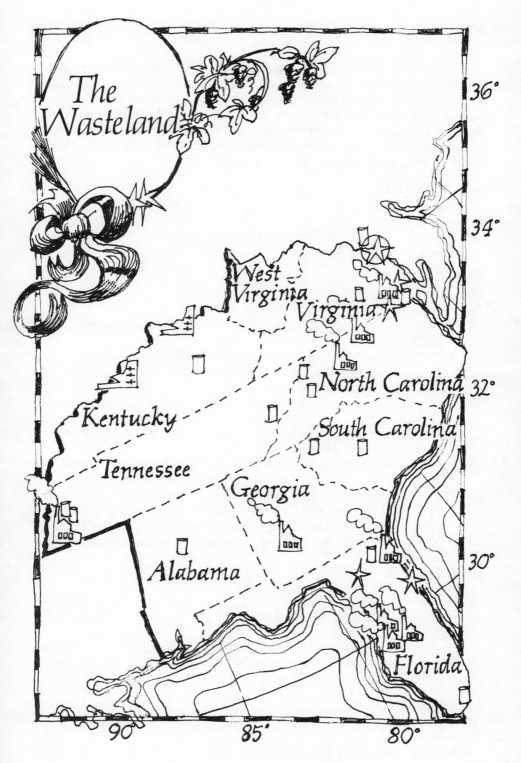

The Wasteland

West
Virginia

Virginia

North Carolina 32°

Kentucky

South Carolina

Tennessee

Georgia

Alabama

Florida

36°

34°

30°

90°   85°   80°

To call the southern beer drinker ignorant would be unfair. Let's settle for "unexposed," unexposed to beer types other than lager, and unexposed to the beneficial effects of temperate beer consumption on society. These factors combine to give the South one of the most desirable traits of all Beer Trek regions—an unlimited potential. The scene is set for the Wasteland. The land is rich, the beer drinkers enthusiastic, the spirit willing. Have no fear that the South shall rise again.

ALABAMA
State Beer   Miller Lite
Kindred Spirits
> The Dixie Dregs, c/o Beck (Sludgemaster) Bryant, 1821 16th Ave. South, Apt. G., Birmingham, AL 35205

FLORIDA
State Beer   Michelob
Breweries
- Anheuser-Busch, Inc., 111 Busch Dr., P.O. Box 18017, Jacksonville, FL 32229. No tours.
  3000 Busch Blvd., P.O. Box 9245, Tampa, FL 33674. Tours, breweriana, and theme park. Brands: see Anheuser-Busch, St. Louis, MO. in The Great River Trekker's Guide.
- Florida Brewing Co. (division Heileman) 202 Gandy Rd., Auburnville, FL 33823
  No tours. No breweriana. Brands: Hatvey Malta, Regal Malta, Fisher Beer, Fisher Ale, Dunk's Beer.
- Joseph Schlitz Brewing Co., (division Stroh), 111 30th St., Tampa, FL 33604
  Tours available. Breweriana available. Brands: see Stroh Brewing, Detroit, in the Beer Belly Trekker's Guide. This brewery will be reportedly exchanged in a straight player swap for the former Hamm's plant in Minneapolis, presently part of the Pabst/Olympia amalgamation.

Kindred Spirits
> Jax Chapter BCCA, Jacksonville, FL
> Les Amis du Suds, c/o Sandy Morgan, Wine & Brew By You, 5760 Bird Rd., South Miami, FL 33155

Of Note
> Daytona 500, Spring Break, Daytona Beach. Get rowdy on the beach.
> *Beer Drinker's Guide*, 4 South Main St., Gainesville, FL. A local guide to beers and bars produced by Will Nally.

GEORGIA
State Beer   Pabst
Breweries
- Miller Brewing Co., 405 Cordele Rd., Albany, GA 31702

No tours. No breweriana. Brands: see Miller Brewing Co., Milwaukee, WI, in the Beer Belly Trekker's Guide.

- Heileman Brewing Co., P.O. Box 1013, Pabst, GA 31069

No tours. No breweriana. See Heileman Brewing Co., La Crosse, Wisconsin, in the Beer Belly Trekker's Guide. Originally built as a Pabst plant (check the address), and still producing Pabst under license.

Of Note

(RIP) An historical plaque marks the remnants of Georgia's first brewery on Sea Island, built by James Oglethorpe to quench the thirst of his soldiers.

KENTUCKY

State Beer   Falls City (Heileman)
Breweries

- George Wiedemann Brewing Co. (division Heileman), 601 Columbia St., Newport, KY 41972

No tours. No breweriana. Brands: see G. Heileman, La Crosse, Wisconsin. Catch it while it lasts, for this brewery is about to brew its final batch. (Whoops, too late. Closed April, 1983.)

Kindred Spirits

Lone Wolf Brewers, c/o Michael Berhide, 100 Morningside Dr., Berca, KY 40403

(RIP) Falls City Brewing Co. (Louisville). Brand still available from Heileman's Sterling plant in Indiana.

NORTH CAROLINA

State Beer   Miller High Life
Breweries

- Miller Brewing Co., 863 E. Meadow Rd., P.O. Box 3327, Eden, NC 27288

No tours. No breweriana.

Brands: see Miller Brewing Co., Milwaukee, WI, in the Beer Belly Trekker's Guide.

- Joseph Schlitz Brewing Co. (division Stroh), 4791 Schlitz Ave., P.O. Drawer T, Salem Sta., Winston-Salem, NC 27107

No tours. No breweriana.

Brands: see Stroh Brewing Co., Detroit, MI, in the Beer Belly Trekker's Guide.

Kindred Spirits

Blue Ridge Brewers Club, c/o Thomas Keating, 32 Spring Forest, Asheville, NC 28803

High Country Brewers, c/o Scott Gladden, Rt. 3, Box 652, Boone, NC 28607

SOUTH CAROLINA

State Beer   Bud Light
Kindred Spirits
    Atlantic Chapter, BCCA, Columbia, SC
    Greenville Homebrewers Club, c/o Janice Gaunt, 17 Circle Dr., Green-
    ville, SC 29609

TENNESSEE

State Beer   Red, White, and Blue
Breweries
  • Joseph Schlitz Brewing Co. (division Stroh), 5151 E. Raines, Memphis,
    TN 38118
    No tours. No breweriana.
    Brands: see Stroh Brewing Co., Detroit, MI, in the Beer Belly Trekker's
    Guide
Kindred Spirits
    River City Chapter BCCA, Memphis, TN
    Bluff City Brewers, c/o Jill Jemison, 60 So. Cooper St., Memphis, TN
    38104
    East Tennessee Brewers Guild, c/o Don Lee, Rt. 5, Box 351-C, Lenoir
    City, TN 37771

VIRGINIA (including Washington, D.C.)

State Beer   National Bohemian (Heileman)
Breweries
  • Anheuser-Busch, Inc., P.O. Box Drawer U, 2000 Pocahantas Trail,
    Williamsburg, VA 23185
    Tours, breweriana, theme park available.
    Brands: see Anheuser-Busch, St. Louis, MO, in the Great River Trek-
    ker's Guide.
Kindred Spirits
    Capitol City Chapter, BCCA, Washington, D.C.
    Richbrau Chapter, BCCA, Richmond, VA
    Tidewater Beer Can Collectors, Virginia Beach, VA
Of Note
    A pending brewery—Chesapeake Bay Brewing Co., Virginia Beach,
    VA
    Brands: Chesbay Light, Chesbay Dark
    (RIP) Champale (Norfolk). Closed in 1982.

WEST VIRGINIA

State Beer   I.C. Light (Iron City)

**Native Brews of
The Wasteland**

ORDER OF THE TREK

Alas, none.

WORTHY OF MENTION

Dunk's (Duncan/Heileman). Slightly dark, slightly sour. Maybe it is an accident, but this beer is better than one would expect from a brewery whose forte is brewing generic beer for supermarkets.

Wiedemann's (Heileman). Low-rent, but an honest workingman's beer. Bland and watery, but well-balanced with a taste that invites another. Future cloudy since the closing of the home brewery.

Country Club Malt Liquor (Pearl/General). Brewed in Texas, but as southern as Dr. Pepper. Could be renamed "First Date Malt Liquor." Never consumed by anyone who has reached legal drinking age.

5 The Beer Belly

Cincinnati, Ohio, to La Crosse, Wisconsin
40 days, 8,120 miles on the road

The Ghost of Geyer   *Frankenmuth, Michigan*

Cincinnati is populated with stout Bavarian stock for whom the brewing tradition is cherished. Two independent breweries survive, even prosper, while a third (Wiedemann's across the river in Newport, Kentucky) turns out, at least for the present, a solid working-man's brew for an affordable price.

On Friday we spent the morning at the Schoenling Brewery, a company started in 1937 by two fellows so aggravated by the long wait for their weekend's quarter keg that they decided the town needed another brewery. Now a second generation of Schoenlings are finding success by carving a niche among brewing giants, not so much through the taste of their beer as by packaging in ways that the major brewers would not find economical. Little King's Ale, a full-flavored cream ale, is available only in eight-packs of distinctive 7-ounce bottles, while Schoenling Lager can be had in giant 64-ounce party-size bottles known affectionately as Big Jugs. Dick Schoenling plays a tape of a radio commercial which advises us to "snuggle up to a couple of big jugs." Budweiser could never get away with that, he snickers. Even more important, the "old man" said it would never work. The original brewing Schoenlings built a successful business, watched it wither, and now, thanks in part to the infusion of new blood, are weathering the storm waters just fine, thank you.

The brewery which kept the Schoenling brothers waiting for their quarter keg in 1937 was Hudepohl, for years the undisputed kingpin of the Cincinnati brewing scene. In recent years this company has appeared destined for the statistical graveyard, another victim of antiquated equipment and the economics of scale. The inevitable, however, has apparently been postponed by the strategy of specializing in whatever the big breweries cannot. The most recent success has been the introduction of Christian Moerlein, a beer named for the most famous brewer in Cincinnati's sudsy history. Here is a beer designed not for the casual beer drinker but for the quaffer who values personality, not blandness, in his mug.

After visiting both breweries The Great Beer Trek, infused with enthusiasm and with the huskiness of Christian Moerlein at the back of our throats, set out for a weekend of visiting places our brewing hosts had suggested as personifying the quintessential Cincinnati beer drinking experience. As always with trekkers, blind alleys outnumbered good leads. The "great, raunchy, little bar" in Newport turned out to be only raunchy and little. The Oar House and Sleep Out Louis's had potential, but did not fulfill it during our visit. At the University of Cincinnati we watched a chugging contest where contestants sucked brew from baby bottles. Sacrilege! And a waste of good beer to boot. Total satisfaction came finally by accident when we stopped in one of Cincinnati's myriad chili parlors. The first fiery spoonful had hardly been doused by a slug of Hudepohl when we realized we had been trying too hard. The unique delights of the Queen City of the Ohio were now literally within our grasp. (One mystery we were never able to answer: Why is chili more popular here than in any city north of Laredo?)

On Sunday afternoon it was back to work. We pushed hard and north, flogging the van along Interstate 75. For once we eschewed the back roads, because the next day would feature a rare triple-header—visits to all three of Michigan's remaining breweries: Stroh, Carling, and Geyer Brothers.

The Stroh Brewing company is conveniently located within sight of the interstate that bypasses the downtown area. Rubble-filled lots offer unimpaired vistas of highway overpasses, distant tenements, and the mammoth brewery. The neighborhood causes one to instinctively roll up the windows and lock the doors. Against the horizon, skyscrapers of Motor City rise like the Grand Tetons against a sky streaked with industrial excess, as unlikely and as unappetizing a location for ambrosial suds as could be imagined.

Stroh, as a company and as a beer, is universally well thought of. Everywhere, ironically, but its hometown. Detroiters mouth the same mumbo-jumbo as beer drinkers everywhere to describe their prejudices against the local product: "Taste doesn't hold up . . . taste is still with you the next day . . . they're not making it the way they used to . . . gives you diarrhea . . . has a bad head . . . company hires too many blacks . . . company doesn't hire enough blacks." Rarely is there truth to any of the claims, certainly not in this case. Stroh stands for Detroit, and most Detroiters want to be associated with anything and anywhere but Detroit. When one lives in the Motor City, where there is not much of anything green, the grass is greener in the Rockies, in the desert, wherever there are jobs. Stroh's cannot claim the magic of mountain spring water or even an association with God's Country. An exotic image is far-fetched when your plant is in the middle of a Detroit ghetto.

Stroh is a clean beer, free of warts, moles, and beauty marks, undeserving of either extravagant praise or condemnation. A good beer for most of the time, it provides the beer drinker with no hooks on which to hang his hat. Stroh's is "fire-brewed," a process where the brew kettle is heated directly by oil flame rather than via a steam coil within the kettle. The higher heat reportedly precipitates unwanted solids, resulting in longer shelf life and more durable taste. As Stroh's literature points out, the other famous brewery in the world to employ this technique is the reknowned Pilsner Urquell plant in Czechoslovakia, a fact of inconclusive coincidence.

The personnel of Stroh were uniformly courteous and professional in their treatment of The Great Beer Trek. Survival for this company, unlike Schoenling or Hudepohl, will not be dependent upon carving a niche in beerdom so much as surviving as an equal among the combatants in the Beer Wars. As a family and a company the Stroh's are determined to survive. Their recent acquisitions of Schaefer and Schlitz show that Stroh's posture will be active and aggressive.

Following a tour of the brewery, beer was sampled in the Stroh hospitality room. Maybe it was the early hour or perhaps the Bavarian-plastique surroundings, more akin to McDonald's than a true rathskeller, but it was time to move on. One down, two to go.

North of Detroit giant factories flatten, first into endless parking lots, then into endless suburbs. Unions, churches, and fraternal groups add three more influences to an already over-governed life. Television, tempered by beer, provides narcotic relief. It is a way of life seemingly mired in despair, yet defended with such vigor that one must assume its beauty to be hidden from the passing van.

Frankenmuth is centered on the most fertile farmland in Michigan. Founded in 1845 by Lutheran missionaries who hoped to Christianize the Chippewa Indians, the German settlers until recently still spoke a unique form of pidgin German, called Bi-rish. Now the ethnic heritage has been converted into old world quaint, and Frankenmuth is Michigan's largest tourist attraction.

There are two breweries along Main Street. The more prominent, and the first visited by The Great Beer Trek, is a Carling-National plant, now owned by Heileman. It is known locally as the Frankenmuth "Dog" Brewery, a description applying not to the beer, but to the mascot—a dachshund. The company in its heyday maintained a kennel for public relations purposes. Now the brewery, the original home of Mel-O-Dry beer, produces a range of Heileman products—including Tuborg, Black Label, and Colt 45. Altes Golden Lager, a long-standing Michigan brand, is also made here. This brew is supposedly reminiscent of Fassbier, an archaic type of German draft beer. Since no one has tasted real Fassbier for several hundred years, the claim is safe. Beer, remember, is a fluid subject. With such a diverse roster of products it is unrealistic to think that any difference between the brews goes deeper than the packaging. Although Heileman is to be commended for maintaining some of the diversity once available to the beer drinker, it is questionable how meaningful the differences are. After a forgettable tour we passed up the hospitality room in favor of continuing on, our throats growing increasingly parched.

Thus far the day had produced fascinating insight to the plight and dilemma facing the contemporary brewer but precious little in the way of good beer drinking. What was this, we mused, a Beer Trek or field study for an MBA program?

It was just past 5:00 P.M. when we arrived at the brick Geyer Brothers plant. As opposed to our two previous stops, there was no clearly marked visitors' entrance, and the office was locked. Fearful of having missed our chance to see the brewery we poked our heads in an open door hoping to see a sign of humanity. There was one fellow visible, a swarthy guy with a two-day stubble and a sweat-drenched t-shirt. We introduced ourselves and apologized for the late arrival. He countered with a simple: "Hi, want a beer?"

He gestured to a single spigot protruding from the brick wall. Only a simple sign reading "Free beer today, free peanuts tomorrow" designated this as the brewery hospitality room. He drew three glasses of Frankenmuth Dark—a tart, husky brew which instantly compensated for the overdose of blandness which had characterized the day thus far. One could think of many words to describe this bierstube environment of painted brick, cement floor, and hissing pipes, but pretentious would not be one.

Our host drained his glass, drew another, and did the same for us, simultaneously motioning us to a wooden bench. We thanked him and made a polite inquiry as to his role at the brewery.

"Oh, me?" he said off-handedly. "I'm the janitor." We nodded politely as he continued. "and the bottler, and the accountant, and the public relations man, and the truck driver . . ." We marvelled at his versatility, but now realized that we were being set up. "and the maintenance man, and the president." He laughed at the punchline, a booming laugh which filled the empty brewery and instantly transformed an eerie setting into one of conviviality.

Dick Brozovic's belly attests to sharing a few too many beers with customers, tourists, and Beer Treks. The sweat and the grime are real. He is a working man.

Brozovic and his wife, Jeannie, were thrust into the brewing business by the unexpected death of a brother who had been attempting to revive the tiny Frankenmuth brewery. His own experience with beer consisted of sampling brews at various enlisted-men's clubs as a career army man. Had he known what he does today, Brozovic asserts, he would never have undertaken the kamikaze mission of maintaining an antiquated brewery in a world of cutthroat giants. In his first year of operation the deficit stood at $50,000. The next year, thanks to long hours and drastic cost-cutting, the amount was halved. In the third year, Dick and Jeannie broke even. The prospect of prosperity is remote, but at least the financial monkey is off Dick's back enough that he can have the fun of sharing a brew with the likes of us and tweaking the noses of the Miller and Budweiser juggernauts.

Our glasses are refilled without asking and we are taken on an impromptu tour of the darkened brewery. In contrast to the programmed pap which is customary from the squeaky clean, uniformed tour guides at most large breweries, we are regaled with stories of ornery condensers with whom Dick has waged all-night combat and compressors salvaged from dairies. Each tale is punctuated by the characteristic booming laugh.

Inevitably we wind back to the tap, where Dick waxes philosophic, sharing with us some of his experiences in the early days when he spent entire nights in the brewery trying to keep alive refrigeration equipment which belonged in a museum but still maintained the brewery bloodstream. It was then that he met the legendary ghost of John Geyer, the man who founded the brewery on the Cass River in 1879. It was old John, claims Dick, who would appear to him at the point of despair to provide the courage, advice, and abandon to go on. He is deadly serious as he speaks. No one believes him, he knows, not even Walter Geyer who still oversees brewing operations, but maybe we will. In the semi-twilight the surroundings recall an era when beer had more taste and brewing was still fun as opposed to the calculating profession witnessed earlier this day at Stroh. We nod. We believe.

There are more stories to tell, Dick insists. Why don't we follow him home where he can clean up, grab Jeannie, and take us around to some of the Frankenmuth taverns which do justice to his brew. He grabs his keys and hits the light switch, leaving us momentarily in a dark, malty world of hisses and clanks. There is a sudden noise from upstairs in the brewhouse. The ghost? Dick Brozovic lets the suspense continue for just the right length of time, then dispels the ghost with a booming laugh.

"I find holding the shot glass between first and middle fingers affords greater control."

— DOGBONE BROWN

Boilermakers

The boilermaker is the Friday afternoon drink. It's payday, you've just cashed your check, the weekend stretches endlessly before you, and a little celebration seems in order. If you order a boilermaker, however, what you get and how it is served will depend on where you are.

Wisconsin wins the award for the most creative combinations. In Milwaukee there are no questions asked. You are served a glass of beer with a shot of brandy, probably Coronet. Farther north in Stevens Point we observed beer accompanied by a four-ounce glass of Chablis. In Monroe, where there is a strong Swiss population, a "schnitt" of beer is accompanied by a shot of Appenzell, a bitter, herb liqueur from the homeland. When we inquired about this unusual combination we were informed that the Appenzell is correctly accompanied by a schnitt of Huber Bock beer which is only available seasonally. (Of course the establishment where we observed this, called The Depot, has as its motto the epitaph of a famous engineer genius named—appropriately enough—George Train:

Here lies George Train . . .
The mind of twenty men
Pulling in different directions.

George, it seems, had a little too much Appenzell and Huber.)

In Buffalo a boilermaker will get you beer and peppermint schnapps. In Boston beer and Scotch, unless in South Boston where Irish whiskey will be substituted for the Scotch. Elsewhere, the consensus choice is beer and blended whiskey from the bottom shelf.

The style of consumption varies. Generally the shot is served separately without ice. In some places you sip it, in others you belt it back in a single gulp using the beer as a chaser. A "depth charge" is where the shot glass is dropped, whiskey and all, into the beer vessel, gently settling to the bottom and mixing its contents with each sip. The trick is to finish the drink without having the shot glass chip your teeth.

The Great Beer Trek award for creative drinking style goes to the fraternity crowd in Ann Arbor, Michigan, where both the shot glass and pilsner tumbler are held in the same hand. As the beer glass is tipped toward the mouth, the contents of the shot, held between the first and middle fingers dribble into the beer below. Practice, if you must, this technique with something other than whiskey as the first few attempts are guaranteed to result in a snootful of 86 proof.

A Question of Taste   *Chicago, Illinois*

In Mishawaka, Indiana, just east of South Bend, the brewing complex of the former Kamin & Schellinger Brewing Co. has been lovingly preserved and given new life as a home for trendy shops, restaurants, and offices. Although it is heartening to see such veneration of our Industrial Revolution, one cannot avoid the inevitable twinge of sadness at the disappearance of yet another regional brewing tradition. Nowhere is the loss more acute than in Chicago.

At one time Cincinnati made pretenses of becoming the Queen City of brewing, but the lack of a good natural ice supply dictated that the crown move farther north. Chicago, being the hub of midwestern commerce, was the obvious choice and, indeed, the Windy City wore the brewing crown until the Great Fire incapacitated many of the city's breweries. Chicago's thirst was satisfied by Milwaukee's breweries. Although Chicago never recovered the crown, it regained status as a first-rate brewing center, feeding a burgeoning population of Slavic immigrants.

Chicago's minions are still thirsty, but their beer now comes from St. Louis, Milwaukee, and, especially, La Crosse, Wisconsin. Semi's filled with Old Style stream down Interstate 90 from "God's Country" as daily reminders that Chicago no longer has a single brewery to call her own.

There is no shortage of good beer drinking here. Good taverns are a tradition as any reader of Mike Royko or Studs Terkel knows. This is the "city that works," and beer is the drink of the upwardly mobile blue-collar stiff. Chicagoans brag about their sudsy heritage, then admit sheepishly that the tradition has neither a present nor a future.

For The Great Beer Trek, Chicago was a place to don the business suit and tie. While Chicago is no longer the heart of the brewing industry, it is the home of Siebel Institute, the industry's pre-eminent technological center.

Any doubts about what kind of reception an institution dedicated to the technological aspects would have for a venture whose priorities clearly lay on the softer side of the subject were quickly dispelled. Our host, Ron Siebel, made it clear that the nuances of beer manufacturing must never interfere with the basic goal of producing a beverage which is fun to drink and which tastes good. The traditional side of beer drinking is not taken lightly by the technological side.

We were discussing the Rheinheitsgebot, a 16th century German law affirming the beer drinker's right to pure beer when our conversation was interrupted by a bell, the kind which in many offices heralds the arrival of the coffee-and-Danish vendor. At Siebel, the bell signals time for taste-testing. Ron is a member of the tasting panel and invited me along. We entered a plain room partitioned into separate booths, each of which was occupied by a studious, white-frocked gentleman completely absorbed in

Taste testing at Siebel's

the task at hand, specifically sniffing, swishing, swizzling, and swigging samples from red glasses. After each sample a score sheet was filled out. Ron tasted his brews, then explained the process in more detail.

Breweries around the country use Siebel as an independent consultant to give impartial feedback on their products. Since many brewing problems are cumulative in nature, periodic tastings from an impartial source help keep a brewer honest by providing an independent quality-control checkpoint which might be impossible to achieve in-house where subtle alterations occur too gradually for the resident brewmaster to notice.

The beers to be tested are served under highly controlled conditions. The special red glasses prevent the testers from being influenced by visual factors such as cloudiness. Flavor, body, and odor characteristics are broken down into nearly forty variable categories and then rated numerically according to the degree to which they are present. The results are fed into a computer which generates a composite profile which is returned to the brewer. The tasters never know whose beers they are testing to avoid any possibility of prejudicial evaluation.

Tastings occur up to three times daily, with as many as seven beers in each. Despite the sophistication of the technology available today, no one has developed automated techniques which surpass the human palate for sensitivity. Man's greatest drawback is that he is fallible. Individual tasters have blind spots to certain flavor characteristics which have to be maneuvered around. One taster might be super-sensitive to phenols, a very specific off-flavor, while completely taste-blind to the presence of diacetyls. Man also tends to get tired, to have colds, and to have lapses of attention. The use of multiple tasters in combination with the computer-generated profiling technique should correct for human factors in the rating process.

The taste-testers at the Siebel Institute are workman-like while in progress, but once the evaluation forms have been turned in, the banter becomes lively, not unlike what one might encounter at the local pub. One of the testers, a kind, brewmasterly type with a heavy, appropriate Germanic accent, gave me a sample to taste.

"Vot do you think?" he asked.

I sipped cautiously, trying to imitate the techniques I had just observed and hoping desperately that I would not say something foolish. "Not too good," I ventured. "It has an unpleasant aftertaste which ruins the initial flavor."

My mentor nodded indulgently. "Skunky!" he practically spit the word out. "It's terrible! This beer has been exposed to light. Ve call it light struck. Beer is very fragile, that is vy it is packaged in brown bottles, to protect it from the light. Now try this one."

The second beer was sweeter. Even the red glass could not hide that it was a dark beer. "Nothing bad," I said. "But nothing special either. No distinctive flavor characteristics."

My mentor nodded. "The brewer calls this a 'bock' beer, but all he has done is add food coloring to his regular lager. To be true to the type he should be getting his color and sweetness from the use of roasted malts. But at least," he sighed, "he has not made any other mistakes."

I realized that I was sweating profusely. I did not mind being exposed as a novice, but I did not want to say anything to make myself seem completely ignorant. The gentleman perceived my uneasiness and smiled, "You did very well." No comment could have sent my spirits soaring higher. In a very small way The Great Beer Trek had earned a stripe. We spent a few moments telling everyone about our trip to date. The world of professional brewing was apparently smaller than I realized. Who had I visited? How were they doing? Where were we heading next? "Be sure to visit old so-and-so and tell him I sent you. He's an ornery old cuss, but he knows brewing like no one else in the country." When the gossip and chitchat was finished, our notebooks were loaded with names and places enough to sustain the balance of the trip.

Ron showed us the rest of the operation, including the test brewery, the hospitality lounge, and the classrooms where would-be brewmasters from all over the world come for the eleven-week course which officially qualifies one as a brewmaster.

Ron answered all questions openly and thoroughly. He seemed interested in developments on the home brewing front and grassroots trends in beer consumption which we had observed in our travels. We swapped thoughts on the feasibility of opening a small brewery. He painted a bleak picture of the prospects of survival of such a venture, but he did so in such specific terms that he had obviously given the project a lot of thought. As a counterbalance he painted a glorious portrait of Siebens, a famous Chicago brewery which served its own brews in their restaurant and gardens. Had Ron, I asked, investigated the possibility of opening up his own brewery?

"Oh, I don't think a small brewery makes a lot of sense in this day and age."

But, I persisted, had he at any point considered opening up his own plant?

"Listen," said Ron, glancing furtively about as if to make sure we weren't being overheard, "there is no one in the beer business who doesn't dream of opening up his own brewery someday."

I was glad to have my suspicions confirmed.

There's <u>no one</u> in the beer business
who doesn't dream...

Following our visit to Siebel, a wiser Beer Trek entered onto Eden's Expressway, heading north toward Milwaukee, just in time for evening rush hour. Our spirits were soaring. Ever since the beginning of our trip there had been a sense that the big national brewers were the bad guys and the small brewers the good guys. Will Anderson and Tim Matson had contributed to this feeling, while DeWitt Jones and now Ron Siebel helped dispel it. Now, for the first time, I began to see the need to segregate the people, the businesses, and the beers. Nice people can make bad beer. Conversely, good beer can be made by bastards. In either case the business part is simply an impartial structure for the people and products. A business does not cast judgments about whether a given move—acquiring an ailing brewery, for instance, or cutting back on the hop content in a beer— is "good" or "bad." It follows the path of greatest profitability as determined by its decision-makers.

As for the beer drinker, he really doesn't care. Like the tasters on the Siebel Institute panel, the proof is in the palate. What really matters is what is in the mug. A simple, but crucial, lesson had been learned.

Honey, Cheese, Chocolate, and Beer
On the road in Wisconsin

The drive from Milwaukee to La Crosse can be completed in four hours. For The Great Beer Trek, however, six days proved to be entirely too short a time.

Milwaukee is a town where, for once, all the taverns serve local beers. One need not feel guilty about ordering Miller, Pabst, or Schlitz. The same choices which are bland and unappealing elsewhere, in Milwaukee have character and snap. This is Pittsburgh, but a Pittsburgh scrubbed, detoxed, and sent for a permanent rest cure in the pristine north. The industrial machinery operates at the pace and schedule of a steroid-fed Black Forest hamlet.

Milwaukee rivals Covington, Kentucky, and Baltimore for watering holes per capita. The block is the unit of social organization, and each one has an establishment named for the owner who doubles as bartender and cook. No one argues the merits of Miller, Schlitz, or Pabst. So long as you are drinking Wisconsin, no one cares. Regional foods abound, most testifying to a slavic heritage—blood sausage, summer sausage, bauerwurst, beerwurst, and brats. Fridays are for fish fries. The good places feature native perch or walleye. The rest serve frozen cod. Pool is the favorite recreation, and many bars light the action with elaborate pseudo-Tiffany Schlitz lamps which will someday be collector's items. There is even a word to describe the collective spirit of beer drinking and hospitality— gemütlicheit. If a given brew or tavern passes muster, it can be said to have gemütlicheit.

A Proper Beer Tasting

Cleanse the palate with a solution of baking soda and Perrier. Stimulate the tongue by massaging vigorously with steel wool. Put the blindfold in place, seal the ears with wax, and immerse yourself in a 7 percent saline solution at 98.6°F.

The taste test is a time honored tradition which can be as elaborate as the procedure above or as simple as closing your eyes at the bar and trying to guess whether the first brew handed you is a Heineken or a Bud, knowing that the incorrect answer means you have to pay for the next round. Taste tests have only one thing in common—they prove nothing. Skeptics can review the promotional literature of virtually every brewing company in which a test by a panel of experts has rated their Swillbräu brand as second only to Pilsner Urquell in the taste derby. Unfortunately, an equally distinguished panel in a different tasting has rated Guzzleweiser as the planet's premium brew while bringing up the rear is old friend Swillbräu. Perhaps the height of tasting absurdity was reached in **The Great American Beer Book** (Warner Books, 1980) where a well-meaning panel religiously tasted a number of identically formulated beers from the same brewer and managed to find no two alike.

Tasting takes great practice and concentration. Still there is significant room for error. Even at the Siebel Institute where tastings are held under ideal conditions by professionals, variation is unavoidable. The human palate, while the most sensitive instrument of measuring taste, is one of the most fallible. The experts acknowledge this; your buddy at the bar will not likely be so rational.

Some of the variables which must be controlled to achieve even the most remote approximation of accuracy are:

1. *Temperature of samples—a dark ale served at a lager temperature will not taste right or vice versa.*

2. *Age and handling of samples—if your beers come off the shelf, how do you know if one is brewery fresh while a second has languished in a hot warehouse for the past year?*

3. *Abilities of tasters. Some people are genetically more sensitive to certain tastes, saltiness for instance, while being oblivious to others.*

4. *Prejudices of tasters. If a taster has a predilection toward sweet beers, the first sample with a pronounced hop character is certain to get a low rating, whatever its merits.*

5. *Order of tasting. The ability to concentrate diminishes with each sample and a judge's scoring will be altered accordingly. Whether this works to the advantage or disadvantage of beer #1 is completely arbitrary.*

6. *Reliability of the brewer. McSorley's Ale, as one example, is actually a series of brews under the same name. And who is to say that Pabst from their Georgia plant is identical to that produced in Milwaukee?*

And finally there is the simple fact that the conditions of a taste test are generally alien to the normal manner in which beer is drunk. A proper beer tasting would be to buy a six-pack, bring it to a friend's house, drink it, and tell him what you think. Next night, buy a different six-pack, take it to your friend's house . . .

Taste tests, then, are completely biased and unreliable. Does this mean they are worthless? Absolutely not. Remember, any occasion which gives an excuse to drink beer is a worthwhile event. Just don't spit out the samples.

Milwaukee has had its brewing casualties, although, surprisingly, fewer than other cities. At its busiest, sixteen companies brewed beer here, as compared to five times that number in Chicago. Signs for Gettleman's can still be seen, and the buildings of Blatz are owned and used by Pabst (who owned the company for eleven years during the fifties and sixties until forced to divest by the federal government.)

THE BREWHOUSE

The Milwaukee Dreadnoughts

THE SCHLITZ PALM GARDEN

Historic Milwaukee breweries include Jung ("Jung Beer Serves You Right"), John Graf ("The Best What Gives"), and Milwaukee-Waukesha ("The Imperial Health Beer"). Add to the list since the passage of our van, Schlitz, now owned by Stroh. Even venerable Pabst, whose name is synonymous with Milwaukee is a radically altered version of its former self, having merged with Olympia and simultaneously selling large chunks of itself off to Heileman in a recent Beer Wars' confrontation. The Pabst plant is well worth visiting. Its Tudoresque beer garden puts a 350-year shield between the beer drinker and the twentieth century. Ivy and leaded glass create an environment in which the consumption of beer, particularly on a summer afternoon, is raised to the sublime. Statues of King Gambrinus and Frederick Pabst look on approvingly.

The Pabst brewhouse is the city's second-best, the best (Schlitz's) having recently been closed. The copper and tile sanctuary which places man in proper perspective with the brewing gods, stands idle, a victim of the inexorable movement toward stainless steel and efficiency. The Brown Bottle, Schlitz's legendary hospitality room, is likewise lost to the public. Both the brewhouse and tap room are monuments to the bygone era which holds such great appeal for the nostalgic beer fanatic. The mighty have fallen. The truth is as sad as it is inevitable.

On the opposite side of Wisconsin there is a new challenger to the throne, and a most unlikely one. As majestic as Schlitz and Pabst are, Heileman is a plain Jane. No Gothic spires, no statues of the founder, no inspirational beer gardens. This plant has simply discovered ways to brew, to sell, and, especially, to distribute beer that make the company more adaptable to the contemporary brewing environment. Just as the battleship and dinosaur eventually reached an age where they could no longer survive, so have the brewing dreadnoughts. Meanwhile, Heileman thrives.

In between Milwaukee and La Crosse, there is no shortage of good beer drinking. Wisconsin's beer drinkers rank among the most enthusiastic in the nation on a per capita consumption basis, and they have been rewarded for their efforts by the best beer drinking environment of any state. Choices are abundant, prices are moderate, and freshness is assured. Everyone we met seemed knowledgeable and appreciative of the advantages of living in the heart of America's Bavaria. They all have gemütlicheit.

Each brewer left us with something special, but collectively they left us with even more. Bill Leinenkugel let us participate in one of the blind taste tests he conducts regularly. At first he was embarrassed that he could not distinguish his own light beer from Miller Lite when we could, but then he rationalized that Leinie Light must be pretty good if even he could not distinguish it from the country's best selling light beer.

When he heard that we had just come from Wisconsin's three other independent family brewers (Stevens Point, Huber and Walters), he was filled with questions, specifically about their bock beers. Each of the Wis-

When you're out of Point, you're out of town.

STEVEN'S POINT: WISCONSIN'S SMALLEST BREWERY

consin brewers still produces a seasonal bock in which the firm takes justifiable pride. Bill Leinenkugel's questions were quite pointed, portraying a healthy dose of competitive curiosity. Had we tasted the other bocks? What did we think? Had the other brewers sold out their supplies?

There are too few independent brewers for anyone to wish anyone else ill. None of the small brewer's beers are sold in the other's market, so there is no real competition. Within a context of mutual support, however, each one wants to be the best. Man has an innate need to strive for excellence, and the need finds its finest opportunity for expression in the field of brewing. We answered Bill Leinenkugel's questions as tactfully as possible. Yes, we had tried the bocks, yes, they were all excellent, and yes, it's quite possible that his was the best. He looked pleased at our enthusiasm. Nothing pleases a brewer as much as knowing people enjoy his beer. The statement is as true for the home brewer as for Augie Busch III.

Oktoberfest

Heileman is the success story of the Wisconsin brewers. Not long ago they were the peers of the Walter's and Huber's. Now they own the remnants of Carling, Blatz, Sterling, Fall City, and even parts of Pabst. They have broken the rule that a company needs a flagship brand to be big. Old Style may be a household word in Chicago, but it is unknown in Atlanta and Los Angeles.

Old Style is a good beer, bland and malty in the style customary for the region. It is "fully krauesened," a carbonation process in which young, unfermented brew is added to the aged lager ready for bottling. Beers carbonated in this way claim to be naturally conditioned as opposed to beers where the effervescence is achieved through the injection of carbon dioxide. The term "fully krauesened" also finds use locally in La Crosse as a term to describe anyone who has had a few too many Old Styles.

It is the primary function of The Great Beer Trek, lest we forget, to interpret, whenever feasible, all events by examining related beer drinking phenomena. The quintessential Milwaukee beer drinking experience is, depending on one's orientation, either the Andeker sipped in the shadow of Fred Pabst on a sunny afternoon or the pitcher of Schlitz which accompanies the fried walleye at Ed and Charlene's on Friday night. There is no disputing the ultimate La Crosse beer drinking experience. It occurs on the first weekend of October, when the population of the Midwest funnels into this riverside town for the simple purpose of drinking beer with thousands of like-minded souls.

Our timing was off by several months, so Oktoberfest could not be an official part of The Great Beer Trek. We chanced to meet someone, however, who, for the price of an evening's beer drinking, provided a graphic tour of an event which deserves a place on every beer drinker's calendar.

Jeff is a carpenter who lives outside of Chicago, but where he really lives is La Crosse for one weekend each autumn and periodic vacations. He is a carpenter, but he does not actually work for anyone or even for himself. He gets by, he enjoys himself, and he makes for charming company on a night out in La Crosse. He has not yet bothered to settle down, but there will always be time for that. He is in his mid-thirties, going on seventeen, and he has attended the last eleven Oktoberfests.

To maximize the intensity of the Oktoberfest "high," Jeff transports himself from Chicago to La Crosse by riding the rails. Although the danger and discomfort of the two-day trip make this means of conveyance as illogical as it is romantic, he claims that the journey helps the end to justify the means. The festival grounds were dark and empty when we visited, but with the aid of Jeff's descriptions and enough Old Styles it became easy to imagine what the real thing was like. After all, the only difference was the absence of a few thousand beer drinking revelers.

The foliage is at its peak, and for the sake of artistic perfection, make it a brilliantly sunny day, bright enough to turn the Mississippi the color of new blue jeans. There is a nip in the air, enough to let you know that winter is on the way, but it is offset by the warm sun which reminds you that summer is not long past.

La Crosse is jammed with people, all of them fair-haired with clear blue eyes. Even the blacks and Hispanics fit the description. Their names are Jensen and Gundersen. Their speech is interrupted by "Jah's" and "Geez's" and they call their native state "Wis-skaaann-sin."

By eleven in the morning everyone has cracked their first beer. Old Style is popular, as is Blatz, Special Ex., Schmidt's, Grain Belt, and Hamm's. All are products of Heileman, now. The hordes line the parade route watching an endless stream of local beauty queens and squeaky-clean high school bands. Young and old, male and female watch the spectacle and drink the beer, for this is Oktoberfest.

After the parade the crowd drifts toward the festival grounds—the younger and more raucous choosing the main pavillion downtown and the locals preferring the grounds slightly to the north. A button costing $2 gains one admittance, and many people wear their accumulated buttons from Oktoberfests as a good-humored status indicator. Lunch is a series of brats, knockwursts, corndogs, and assorted junk foods. It's OK. Oktoberfest comes just once a year.

At the main grounds the band is on an elevated platform in an open hall lined with pictures of the presidents. There are a couple of televisions, but only if the Brewers are still in the pennant race. A cryptic sign beneath the bandstand reads, "Please, for the Enjoyment of Others, No Beer Throwing . . . Thank You." You can ponder the meaning as you push to the massive bar staffed by local fraternal organizations peddling plastic cups of Old Style, Special Export, et al. Here is a situation where the logistics of volume beer drinking are well-understood. Kegs on pallets are off-loaded by forklifts and delivered right to the bar. Someone has given careful consideration to the logistics of feeding beer to the masses. If your taste runs to wine, bourbon, or even bottled beer, go somewhere else. You won't find anything here but draft.

To save yourself an extra trip to the bar you get two beers, as does everyone, using as exchange the tickets purchased at a booth by the entrance. Slowly a cry rises from the crowd, nothing sudden or shrill, just a random, animal opening of the vocal chords on a certain pitch which incites a deep-seated species' need to join in. So you do, wondering where it will all lead. The volume grows as does the pitch, the band members run for cover, then you see the beer globules arching upward, a fluid chandelier. The magic is ended when the fluid chandelier lands in a malty splash. It's all in good fun, but now you understand the signs.

No one would dare throw beer at the North Fairgrounds, just two miles up the road. This is the preferred drinking spot of the locals who do not need the spontaneous exuberance of beer throwing to have a good time. The setting has none of the splendor of the Milwaukee breweries, its architectural style being best described as "basic roof." The beer drinker at Oktoberfest needs only to be protected from torrential rain to be happy.

The hall is packed, and progress to the beer lines is as hard won as the turf at Verdun. Between the area that you have staked out with your friends and the bar, you will meet no end of new friends, all of them smiling a beer drinker's grin and babbling a constant, "Hi, howya doin? Jah! Me too!" If you have to ask, "What's the point?" then you've missed the point, because this is what it's all about. For the likes of Jeff, this is when he is most alive. By nine o'clock the mass of humanity sways in unison, and each passing face greets you with a smile. This is the same state of mind following two pints of homebrew which, in *Mountain Brew*, is described as "blissed." In La Crosse the feeling is the same, only the description is different. At Oktoberfest Jeff would describe everyone as "fully krauesened."

Trekker's Guide to
The Beer Belly

Chicago is the "city that works." It is as much a hub for its region as Boston is for New England.

The Beer Belly offers no shortage of great places to drink. Softball fields, VFWs, and fraternities supplement the ever-present local as proper places for the consumption of brew, which is the accepted beverage of the working class hero. Unhappily, too many of these upwardly bound imbibers have had to cope with the withering of the national workplace which has occurred in the last decade.

The beer quality matches the quality of the camaraderie. This is the birthplace of many of the nation's most famous beers, including Schlitz, Pabst, Miller, and Stroh, with a healthy number of regionals to keep things interesting. Although the nation's richest consumption is close at hand, it tends to be the midwesterner who will drive a zillion miles to buy ten cases of Coors, Genesee, or whatever novel brew might stimulate the cultured palate. Ironically, the local brews tend to be long on maltiness and short on the counterbalancing bitterness of hops. The nationals have had to sacrifice regional character to the lowest common denominator, but the smaller breweries like Point and Leinenkugel retain the heartiness of Bavarian ancestry.

The best way to Beer Trek is to blunder through Ohio and Michigan, then to Chicago. Hit the famous spots like Berghoff's and O'Rourke's, then spend at least two days bar-hopping and talking to patrons. You will be amazed at how well-informed the average beer drinker is. Why not? Beer is a way of life in the Beer Belly.

Your apprenticeship is now complete. Proceed directly to Wisconsin, last bastion of Bavaria in the United States. The countryside is beautiful, the people congenial, and the beer ubiquitous. You are not in heaven, you are just as close as you can get in North America.

ILLINOIS

State Beer   Old Style (Heileman)
Breweries
- Carling National Breweries, Inc. (division Heileman), 1201 West "E" St., Belleville, IL 62221
  No tours. No breweriana.
  Brands: see Heileman Brewing Co., La Crosse, WI in this chapter.
- Siebel Institute, 4049 W. Peterson Ave., Chicago, IL 60646
  No tours. No breweriana. No brands.

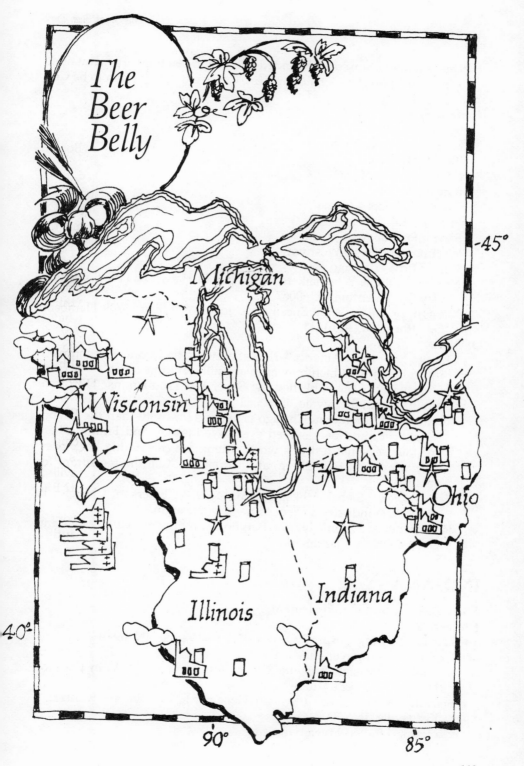

The Beer Belly

Michigan

Wisconsin

Ohio

Illinois

Indiana

-45°

40°

90°

85°

113

This is a fully licensed and bonded five-gallon test brewery maintained by a technological consulting firm. Can legitimately claim to be Chicago's largest.

Kindred Spirits

BCCA Chapters:

Blue Room—Sycamore

Bluff City—Alton

Bullfrog—Lake Zurich

Forest City—Rockford

Heart of Illinois—Peoria

Prison City—Joliet

Sangamor Valley—Decatur

Westmont Stroh's—Westmont

Windy City—Chicago

Northern Illinois Winemakers Guild, c/o Ed Harrison, 1196 So. Brockway St., Palentine, IL 60067

Mississippi Valley Wine Society, c/o John W. Miller, 3709 Flambeau Dr., Rockford, IL 61111

Of Note

Chicago has one of America's richest brewing traditions. For complete information on which breweries are still standing consult: *The Great Chicago Beer Cans* Published by: Silver Fox Productions, 113 Birchwood Lane, Libertyville, IL 60048

Berghoff's in downtown Chicago is famous for more than the halibut sandwiches and beer served every Wednesday and Friday. There are four seasonal festivals worth attending: celebrating bock beer, May wine, Old Heidelberg, and Christmas. Call the restaurant for details.

Brewers Digest, Siebel Publishing Co., 4049 W. Peterson, Chicago, IL 60649. The industry's premier trade publication.

(RIP) Sieben's. Originally, like Berghoff's, a brewery cum restaurant. Once a Chicago landmark.

INDIANA

State Beer   Sterling (Heileman)

Breweries

- Falstaff Brewing Corp., P.O. Box 926, Ft. Wayne, IN 46801

  No tours. No breweriana.

  Brands: see Falstaff Brewing Corp., San Francisco, CA, in the Hop Heaven Trekker's Guide

- Sterling Brewers, Inc., (division Heileman), 1301 Pennsylvania St., Evansville, IN 47707

  No tours. Limited breweriana.

Brands: see Heileman Brewing Co., La Crosse, Wisconsin, in this chapter.

Kindred Spirits

Hoosier Chapter BCCA, South Bend, IN

Three Rivers Chapter BCCA, Ft. Wayne, IN

Hoosier Homebrew, 8621 W. Vernal Pike, Bloomington, IN 47401

Of Note

Indy 500. Memorial Day, Indianapolis. Cars, beer, spring. There is more action off the track than on.

Antique Advertising Show. Indiana State Fairgrounds. March, July, September. Best place to wheel and deal in breweriana.

Mishawaka. Former Kamm & Schellinger complex now houses offices, boutiques, and restaurants, but is a beautifully preserved piece of brewery architecture.

MICHIGAN

State Beer   Stroh

Breweries

- Carling National Breweries, Inc., (division Heileman), 926 So. Main St., Frankenmuth, MI 48734

  Tours and breweriana available. Call for details (516) 652-6161

  Brands: see G. Heileman Brewing Co., La Crosse, WI, in this chapter

- Geyer Brothers Brewing Co., 425 So. Main St., Frankenmuth, MI 48734

  No tours. License plates, mugs, cans sold at the brewery.

  Brands: Geyer's Lager, Bavarian Dark, Bavarian Light

- The Real Ale Co., Inc., 320 North Main St., Chelsea, MI 48118

  Tours by appointment (313) 475-8343. Some breweriana.

  Brands: Chelsea Ale, Porter, Stout, Midwest's first micro-brewery.

- Joseph Schlitz Brewing Co., Headquarters (division Stroh), One Stroh Dr., Detroit, MI 48226

  Brands: Schlitz, Old Milwaukee, Schlitz Malt Liquor, Schlitz Light, Old Milwaukee Light, Erlanger, Primo.

- The Stroh Brewery Co., One Stroh Dr., Detroit, MI 48226

  Tours given. Extensive breweriana available.

  Brands: Stroh, Stroh Light, Goebel Beer, Stroh Signature

Kindred Spirits

BCCA Chapters:

Goebel Gang—Niles

Mid Michigan—Lansing

Patrick Henry—Kalamazoo

Silver Foam—Jackson

Stroh's Fire Brewed—Westland

Of Note
> Frankenmuth Bavaria Festival, 2nd week June, Frankenmuth. A celebration in the Bavarian tradition, held in a town which takes its roots very seriously. Appropriately attended in a Winnebago. A smaller polka festival is held in late August.
> Lindell A/C, corner Michigan & Cass Aves., Detroit. Required attendance after Tiger games. You might even get a stool next to Billy Martin. Lots of beer.

OHIO

State Beer   Hudepohl
Breweries
- Anheuser-Busch, Inc., 700 East Schrock Rd., Columbus, OH 43229
  Tours offered. Extensive breweriana.
  Brands: see Anheuser-Busch, St. Louis, MO, in the Great River Trekker's Guide.
- Hudepohl Brewing Co., 505 Gest St., Cincinnati, OH 45203
  Tours Monday–Friday, 10 A.M.–1 P.M. hourly. Signs, glassware, and clothing offered for sale.
  Brands: Christian Moerlein, Hudepohl, Hudy Delight, Burger, Burger Light, Hudepohl Bock (seasonal), Hudepohl Oktoberfest.
- Christian Schmidt Brewing Co., 9400 Quincy Ave., Cleveland, OH 44106
  No tours. No breweriana.
  Brands: see Christian Schmidt, Philadelphia, PA, in the Colonies Trekker's Guide.
- The Schoenling Brewing Co., 1625 Central Parkway, Cincinnati, OH 45214
  Tours by appointment. Clothing, decals, and other souvenirs offered for sale.
  Brands: Little Kings Cream Ale, Big Jug Beer, Top Hat.

Kindred Spirits
> BCCA Chapters:
> Buckeye—Toledo
> Gambrinus—Columbus
> Johnny Appleseed—Loudonville
> Lake Erie—Cleveland
> Miami Valley—Dayton
> Old Dutch—Lima
> Pioneer—Marietta
> Queen City—Cincinnati
> Wooden Shoe—Minster
> Cleveland Brewers, c/o Pat O'Hara, 435 Broadway, Bedford, OH 44146
> High Grain Drifters, c/o C. Plazo, 331 ⅓ Franklin Ave., Kent, OH 44240

Of Note

Germantown in Columbus is a well-preserved example of a German-American neighborhood dating from the late 19th century. (RIP) August Wagner's Gambrinus Brewery.

Miller has completed a brewery in Trenton, Ohio, but has not yet started production.

WISCONSIN

State Beer   Leinenkugel
Breweries

- G. Heileman Brewing Co., Inc., 100 Harborview Plaza, La Crosse, WI 54601

  Tours Monday–Friday, 10 A.M., 2 P.M., 3 P.M. Extensive breweriana.

  Brands: Eastern division—National Bohemian, National Premium, Black Label, Black Label Light, Colt 45, Kingsbury Near Beer, Mickey's Malt Liquor, Zing, Red Cap Ale, Tuborg, Tuborg Dark, Wiedemann, Wiedemann Light, Blatz, Blatz Light, Blatz Cream Ale, Malt Duck, Sterling, Sterling Light, Pfeiffer, Falls City, Drummond Brothers, Stag, Drewrys.

  Central Division—Old Style, Old Style Light, Special Export, Heileman Light Black Label, Pfeiffer, Kingsburg, Altes, Colt 45, Kingsbury Near Beer, Mickey's Malt Liquor, Zing, Schmidt, Schmidt Light, Schmidt Select, Schmidt Extra Special, Tuborg, Tuborg Dark, Wiedemann, Wiedemann Light, Blatz, Blatz Light, Blatz Cream Ale, Malt Duck, Sterling, Sterling Light, Falls City, Falls City Light, German Brothers, Stag, Stag Light, Red Cap Ale, Drewrys, Red, White & Blue.

  Western Division—Special Export, Rainier, Rainier Light, Kingsbury Near Beer, Mickey's Malt Liquor, Tuborg, Tuborg Dark, Blatz, Blatz Light, Malt Duck, Blitz, Lone Star, Lone Star Light. All Blitz-Weinhard brands.

- Joseph Huber Brewing Co., 1208 14th Ave., Monroe, WI 53566

  No tours, but hospitality room open Monday–Friday, 8 A.M.–4:30 P.M. Extensive breweriana sold.

  Brands: Huber, Hi-Brau, Wisconsin Club, Wisconsin Gold Label, Bavarian Club, Holiday, Potosi, Braumeister, Regal Brau, Augsburger, Augsburger Dark, Gemütlichheit, Huber and Rhinelander Bock Beers.

- Jacob Leinenkugel Brewing Co., 1–3 Jefferson Ave., Chippewa Falls, WI 54729

  Tours Monday–Friday, 10 A.M–3 P.M. (June through August). Extensive breweriana.

Brands: Leinenkugel, Leinenkugel Light, Chippewa Pride, Leinenkugel Bock (seasonal), Bosch.

- Miller Brewing Co., 3939 W. Highland Blvd., Milwaukee, WI 53201
  Tours available. Extensive breweriana available.
  Brands: Miller High Life, Lite, Löwenbräu Special, Löwenbräu Dark Special, Miller Special Reserve, Magnum Malt Liquor, Gettleman's (available in Milwaukee only).
- Pabst Brewing Co., 1000 N. Market St., P.O. Box 766, Milwaukee, WI 53201
  Tours available. Extensive breweriana.
  Brands: Pabst Blue Ribbon, Andeker, Pabst Special Dark, Pabst Extra Light, Pabst Light, Olde English "800" Malt Liquor, Jacob Best Premium Light, Olympia, Hamm's.
- Stevens Point Beverage Co., 2617 Water St., Stevens Point, WI 54481
  Tours available only with advance notice. Breweriana sold on premises.
  Brands: Point Special, Point Bock (seasonal)
- Walter Brewing Co., 318 Elm St., P.O. Box 143, Eau Claire, WI 54701
  Tours, May 15–September 15, Monday–Friday 10 A.M.–2 P.M. Glassware, clothing, coolers, patches, and other items available at brewery.
  Brands: Walter's, Walter's Special, Walter's Light Ale, Breunig's, Bub's, Master Brew, Old Timers.

Kindred Spirits

Badger Bunch BCCA, Statewide
Lakeshore Chapter BCCA, Two Rivers, WI
Packer Chapter BCCA, Green Bay, WI
Bidal Society of Kenosha, c/o Elmer Olep, 8935 3rd Ave., Kenosha, WI 53140
Central Wisconsin Amateur Winemakers Club, c/o William Dehn, 112 West Fifth St., Marshfield, WI 54449
Wisconsin Vintners Association, c/o Charlie Thompson, W188 N8991 Maple Rd., Menomonee Falls, WI 53057
Cream City Homebrew Club, c/o John Hermanson, Life Tools Co-op, 401 N. Clay, Green Bay, WI 54301

Of Note

La Crosse Oktoberfest, the granddaddy, Bavaria by the river. Annually each autumn in La Crosse.
Milwaukee Summerfest. The brewers do it up big each summer. German America at its best.
Wisconsin is filled with brewery corpses (Potosi—1972, West Bent—1972, John Gund—1920, ad infinitum) which make for interesting touring. The best state for a mini-trek.

Breweriana shops: Bear Trap Inn, Box 36
Land O'Lakes, WI 54540

The Mill, Box 45
Woodruff, WI 54568

Beer Drinking in Madison, a guide to Madison taverns, $5.50 plus $1 postage from Warsaw Strohs, P.O. Box 695, Madison, WI 53701

Native Brews of The Beer Belly

ORDER OF THE TREK

Leinenkugel's (Leinenkugel). This beer hardly belongs in the ranks of the elite, but with a name like this, brewed from the waters of Big Eddy Springs in Chippewa Falls, it *has* to be good. In fact it is a pleasant brew with overtones of grain huskiness. Leinie's, quite simply, is fun to drink. (P.S.—Their bock is a genuine sleeper. Stock up each spring.)

Andeker (Pabst). Perhaps the best of America's superpremiums. Smooth and well-balanced. The first always makes you want a second. The bitterness of the hops is just enough to cut the maltiness. The best product from one of America's best brewers.

Schlitz (Schlitz/Stroh). The beer is good again after a dismal period when the efficiency experts overpowered the company brewmasters. Definitely aimed at the lowest common denominator beer drinker, but the one who takes his beer seriously. Welcome back, Schlitz.

Augsburger (Joseph Huber). A terrific beer in the European style. Perceptible taste of Hallertauer hops which the company reportedly flies in from Europe in refrigerated planes. The care shows. One of the few American beers accepted by the snob contingent.

Augsburger Dark (Joseph Huber). Sweeter but with enough hops to carry. A small brewer should not be able to make brews this good, but, thank God, they do. Here's to you, Huber!

WORTHY OF MENTION

Stroh (Stroh). A clean, inoffensive beer, entirely professional. Well-regarded everywhere but Detroit.

Frankenmuth Dark (Frankenmuth). The scientific brewmaster could rip this brew to shreds, but if you have a sense of adventure, it's worth a try.

Christian Moerlein (Hudepohl). Laudable attempt at a European-style premium beer misses the mark but earns points for trying. Unfortunately one needs more than a foil top and hard-to-read graphics to create a superior beer.

Little Kings Cream Ale (Schoenling). More notable for its packaging than its content. The 7-oz. mini-export bottles are ideal for those who want maximum flavor in minimum consumption.

Miller High Life (Miller). People like or hate it based on their opinions of the company, but the brew itself can be faulted only for its total lack of personality. The former Champagne of Lager Beers is now a starlet—nice-looking in a vacuous way.

Löwenbräu Dark (Miller). Miller has taken a lot of flak from connoisseurs for their rip-off of the Löwenbräu name. Without casting judgment on that, their dark has an appealing winey aftertaste which stands up well to repeated drinking. Don't let your opinions of Miller interfere with your enjoyment of their fine brew. The Light Löwenbräu is less distinguished.

Pabst Blue Ribbon (Pabst). An excellent premium lager from a brewery which has a reputation as a brewmaster's company. Unfortunately, seems to vary regionally; perhaps the result of letting brewmasters run the firm.

Pabst Extra Light (Pabst). 60 calories. Almost water, but if you want a light beer, you might as well go all the way.

Old Milwaukee (Schlitz). Consistently one of the worst beers in America. The city of Milwaukee should sue to have the name changed to "Old Fargo, North Dakota." Don't even buy it on sale.

Point Special (Stevens Point). The beer is overrated, but the can is exceptional. Buy it just to show you are glad to be in Stevens Point. Remember, "when you're out of Point, you're out of town."

Old Style (G. Heileman). The best-selling beer in Chicago. You can see the semi's barreling down Interstate 90 to serve the thirsty masses. Bland and malty, it serves midwestern tastes well.

Special Export (G. Heileman). Supposedly the highest expression of G. Heileman's art, it spices its minimal body with a liberal dose of pretension. Stick to Old Style.

6 The Great River

Cold Spring, Minnesota, to New Orleans, Louisiana
55 days, 11,920 miles on the road

Headwaters

Minneapolis, Minnesota

The Great Beer Trek made its first crossing of the Mississippi at La Crosse, Wisconsin. It was another significant passage which provided an occasion to take stock. We had now been gone 40 days and had traveled 8,120 miles. We had visited most of the nation's breweries and had stopped at countless taverns. The attrition of independent breweries which had begun as an abstract statistic was now a harsh reality, brought home by viewing too many riddled hulls of once vital businesses. On the positive side, our ability to taste beer intelligently had improved significantly thanks to mini-lessons from the likes of Ron Siebel and Bill Leinenkugel. Our appreciation for the delicacy of a fragile foodstuff had grown enormously. Good beer can become bad very quickly if the packaging and handling are not equal to the brewing. Not all the pieces were in place, but a perceptible sense of progress could be sensed in the van. Despite some early disappointments, our trip to date was a smashing success and still continuing onward, upward, and beerward.

The Bavarian traditions in Wisconsin continued in Minnesota. Although in strictest racial terms Minnesotans include a variety of populations who migrated from all over northern Europe and Scandinavia, in terms of beer we are talking strictest pedigree. This became apparent after we visited Minnesota's two country breweries.

Cold Spring Brewing Co., in Cold Spring, is not a spectacular looking affair. What made it special for us was the tour provided by brewmaster Jim Schorn who explained in detail the function of every valve and pipe in a Rube Goldberg maze. Cold Spring ships much of its product to the badlands to the west. "And there aren't many people between here and the West Coast," Jim reminded us. Marketing-wise the company can't afford to be too proud, so their beers run the gamut from little known budget brand White Label to super-premium Cold Spring Premium Export. As for the difference between the brands, Schorn answered, "For the most part, the cans."

In addition to providing honest answers to simple questions, Schorn proved to have a sentimental side to counter his technical expertise. He grew misty eyed when describing his previous employer, the Mankato Brewing Co.

"There were 110 different rooms, all on different levels, so you couldn't even use a forklift. She was built on the side of a hill, with lagering caves dug right into the hillside. I knew every pipe and switch. Once, after they turned off the electricity, they had to send me back in the pitch black to find a certain valve to turn off. In some places you couldn't even use a flashlight, and I had to do everything by feel, but I did it.

"There was no way for her to survive, but oh, she was pretty. To see her from the other side of the valley was a sight. I couldn't bear to be there when they finally tore her down."

Later that day, at the August Schell Brewery in New Ulm, Minnesota, we felt that we were reliving Jim Schorn's vision. The brewery is built on a lush hillside with lagering cellars which penetrate the rich earth. The brewery grounds are well-maintained and feature a park with grazing deer and a Victorian mansion for the resident brewery owner. Man, the brewing gods, and the cosmos seem to be in harmony at August Schell.

As had become our custom, we asked at the brewery for the best place locally to sample the company's wares. We were directed to the local Turner Hall. August Schell arrived in New Ulm sponsored by the Turner Colonization Society (Turn Verein), a group which took upon itself the task of properly populating the New World. Its recruits were followers of Father Friedrich Ludwig Jahn who developed a patterned series of exercises for Germans to promote their strength of body, mind, and society. Its recruits were dispatched to remote American outposts where they were charged with starting the German-American equivalent of a Brave New World. Many Wisconsin and Minnesotan towns had as their first substan-

THE OWNER'S "BIG HOUSE" AT

Schell's

SURROUNDED BY THE PARK.

tial structure a hall where the Turners could meet for exercise, followed—not surprisingly—by healthy doses of fraternal beer drinking. Beer was an integral part of the formula, demonstrating the esteem in which the beverage was held by the society of the day. Beer was not a luxury beverage with connotations of wickedness and degeneracy; rather, it was a liquid foodstuff, brewed by a pillar of the community and consumed as a matter of course by its members. A demonstration of the brewers' community status occurred in 1862 when the Sioux of southern Minnesota rose up against the invading white man. New Ulm was pillaged with great loss of life. The Schell family returned to their hillside, expecting ashes and rubble. There were many signs of Indian occupation, but the brewery was intact, a fact the family could attribute only to the universally beneficial role of the brewer. Indians may have hated the white man, but they knew good beer when they tasted it.

After our tours of the country breweries, we visited Minneapolis where we saw another glorious testament to the Bavarian heyday. Of the great meccas of beer consumption—Siebens in Chicago, Trommer's in New York, the Gerst House in Nashville—The Grain Belt Brewing Co. and its drinking garden was reputedly the granddaddy of them all. Now it stands as a champion out to stud. Only this champion is sterile and will bear no

Grain Belt

offspring. At present the Grain Belt plant seems to be merely sleeping, awaiting the return of workers to start the juices flowing and of patrons to enliven the handsome gardens. Once the best families of Minneapolis gathered here to share steins of Grain Belt, good food, good music, and good company on Sunday afternoons.

The patrons would certainly come today, if they could, but the owners would lose money with every glass of beer sold. Grain Belt is a monument to the Gothic excess of Bavarian fancy. Alas, this is an age which requires high-speed functionalism. The whole became worth less than the sum of its parts. A professional liquidator moved in, sold the brands to Heileman, the equipment to whichever South American breweries wanted it, and kept the rapidly increasing real estate which appreciates just as fast whether or not the handsome complex continues to make beer. The magnificent structure and equally magnificent grounds lie fallow, stubbornly awaiting the inevitable wrecker's ball and hoping for a miracle. Only when she is gone will we realize we have lost a treasure.

Beer drinkers everywhere lament the loss of Grain Belt. To have it standing so magnificently, its brick and mortar outliving economic viability, only rubs salt in the wound. Sentimentalities are heard amid elaborate plans for its revival and curses for the hard-hearted liquidator. We stare into our beers and understand the battleship captain whose mastery of the ocean's surface is now irrelevant in light of the capabilities of the submarine and airplane. We try to keep a stiff upper lip, to remember not to cry over spilt beer. A tradition is now past; it is the function of The Great Beer Trek to understand why.

The explanation is deceptively simple.

Grain Belt's downfall was as inevitable as Schaefer's, Ballantine's, or hundreds of other worthy brewers. When the country was growing by leaps and bounds, there was opportunity aplenty for any industrious firm. Brewers grew, expanded capacity, and built monuments such as Grain Belt where the aesthetic considerations superceded the practical. Once the combined industry capacity created more than was necessary to slake the national thirst, the brewers could achieve growth only by taking a portion of a neighbor's market share. Add to the mathematics Prohibition and several decades of war-related anti-German sentiment to negatively affect total national beer consumption, and the stage was set for the attrition and consolidation which, in fact, is still occurring. The excesses of a Grain Belt could no longer be obscured by a burgeoning marketplace. Just as survival of Cold Spring and Schell is remarkable, the downfall of Grain Belt, however lamentable, could not have been prevented.

The Great River Road
Dubuque, Iowa

The Great River Road rides the bluffs on either side of the Mississippi. At the foot of the steep embankments run the railroad tracks, a conduit for the nation's commerce. Between the bluffs, filled with barges, tugs, and water, runs the greatest conduit of all, the mighty Mississippi. We caulked the seams of our van and followed the current, our senses peeled for telltale signs of beer.

By the time we crossed the river at Prairie du Chien, we had already lost count of the number of times the river had passed beneath us. Thunderstorms had been rolling down the valley with us, buffeting us with hail and violent winds. Had we somehow incurred God's wrath?

In Dubuque we stopped to visit the Picketts, family brewers since 1977. Beer runs as thick in the veins of the Picketts as in the Strohs, Coors, or Busches in the country. The Picketts' problem is that their family never owned their own brewery until they purchased the bankrupt Dubuque Star plant in the early seventies. Joe Sr., claims the title of senior brewmaster in the country, having graduated from the first brewmaster class of the Siebel Institute following Prohibition. (Note: One other member of that class is still alive and brewing, Ed Siers of The Lion in Wilkes-Barre, Pennsylvania. Mr. Pickett earns the senior brewmaster award, according to Mr. Siers, on the basis of meritorious service during Prohibition.)

The Picketts' plant is located in a turn of the century industrial park within sight of the river. The area is strangely silent, its best days—in fact, Dubuque's best days—forty years past. On the day The Great Beer Trek

It's the Water

The river which flows past the Rolling Rock brewery had a shopping cart in it when we peeked over the bridge. The river by Genesee foams with multicolored effluents from decades of industrial use. In "God's Country" where Heileman's Old Style is brewed, the Mississippi lives up to its name of the Big Muddy. Clearly, if water has the importance in brewing that some brewers would have us believe, we are in trouble.

How important is water to the brewing process? After asking the question a hundred times of a hundred people, The Great Beer Trek has settled on the answer, "Water is as important to the finished beer as the brewery's marketing department would like us to believe it is." Thus, while the people at Coors have us imagine their cans to be filled with rivulets of melted mountain snow, the city brewers freely admit to obtaining their water from the municipal supply. Because all commercial brewing water must be brought to a chemically neutral point before the brewing process can begin, claim the latter, all waters are created equal in the eyes of the modern scientific brewer.

For the home brewer, however, the character of the original "liquor" (as brewing water is correctly called) is a crucial element in the finished product. The same recipe made from a treated municipal source and an artesian well may vary so much as to be unrecognizable. Ironically, the chemically adulterated one may well be the better tasting. Brewers long ago discovered that certain beer types taste best when brewed from a chalky, oxygenated source. The river Trent in England, wherein comes the liquor which becomes Bass Ale, has long been renowned as the archetypical brewing source. The hardness of these waters is estimated at 1800 ppm (parts per million). The modern brewer scoffs, and claims that with the right filters and additives he can create water which is indistinguishable from that plucked from the Trent.

In fact municipal water supplies average about 100 ppm hardness. United States brewers adjust their water to 400 ppm while German brewers go 50% further to 600 ppm.

The hardness can come in many forms including such delicious items as calcium sulphate, magnesium sulphate, and good old sodium chloride. "It's the water" may be the claim of the marketing department, but the truthful brewer will tell you, "It's the chemist."

Pickett

arrived, the scene was painted with violence. A thunderstorm meeting its first resistance after a thousand miles of prairie turned the sky black, then rent it asunder with lightning and thunder. The hail came in rhythmic waves, an army of tap dancers on the van roof, interrupted by eerie interludes of silence.

In between downpours we dashed from the van to the second-story office of the Pickett Brewing Co., pausing just long enough to ask directions of a man walking his dog, an exotic Hungarian Vizla. Inside we asked the receptionist if Mr. Pickett was available. "Which one?" she asked. Joe Sr., it turned out, was the nice man with the Vizla who had just disappeared into the thunderstorm. Val Pickett was on vacation, but if we did not mind waiting, she was sure that Joe Jr. could be talked into taking some time with us.

The Pickett offices are plain, a few functional desks and straight wooden chairs. The look is neither ugly nor unfriendly, but gives the accurate impression of having been designed by people who have neither time nor money to spend on appearance. They are too busy making beer.

When Joe Jr. finally came out he was sweaty and tired, but not too tired—never too tired—to take a moment to tell anyone interested about the beer his family makes. We talked in the deserted hospitality room, a quaint taproom on the ground floor of the brewery which bears testament to the working class roots of Dubuque and its hometown beer. Joe drew us a beer, and we toasted a hospitality room which glorifies a different side of beer drinking than the Bavarian plastique we had encountered in so many other breweries. Subsequently, we toasted to thunderstorms, to catfish, to Vizlas, to Dubuque, to Chevy Beauville vans, to Pickett's, and to The Great Beer Trek. The beer, brewed exclusively with two-rowed barley, has a roundness which seems to lubricate the throat as it goes down. This beer is as good as any yet encountered in our travels.

Joe Pickett Jr. was well on his way to a promising career in the beer business before his crazy father went and bought this run-down, debt-ridden riverside plant. He worked as a Technical Service Representative for the Siebel Institute, wore a jacket and tie, traveled the United States, drew a good salary, and did not have to get his fingernails dirty. Now his twelve-hour days are followed by evenings of back-slapping and flesh pressing, as he and other family members strive to convince Dubuque that just because a beer comes from the hometown does not mean it cannot be good. He earns half of what he could elsewhere in the industry, and his future is as unsure as the outcome of the Beer Wars. As for the finger-nails . . . well, no one cares much about that in Dubuque. Tonight when he leaves the plant Joe will load a quarter-barrel in his car to deliver to some Good Ol' Boys having a catfish fry. There will be all the fish anyone can eat, cooked over an open fire in an ostrich egg skillet with a six-foot handle, and homemade onion rings—the thick kind—and lots of beer. He is just supposed to drop off the beer, but will probably wind up setting up the tap, eating some fish, and sharing a few brews. It is a night when he might rather be home with the family, but a brewer has responsibilities. Besides, if Joe, his father, and his brother are not out there selling the beer, who will?

Joe Pickett is his own boss. He treats us to definitive explanations on every complex beery situation we can throw at him. The explanations are bold, comprehensive, and unique, the pronouncements of someone who does not have to worry about displeasing superiors. "You wanna know about the Coors' mystique? It all goes back to World War II. Light beers? I'll tell you something about light beers. The whole problem with beer comes down to one thing, drinkability."

We take it all in, and too quickly it is time to move on. Joe locks up Zigi's, as their hospitality room is called, and gives us tips for fishing in Iowa if we get the chance. He swears there are trout spots in this maligned state which have to be seen to be believed. Before Laura and I leave Dubuque, we stop at a take-out joint which advertises fried catfish. Our appetites have been whetted by the Pickett hyperbole. The thunderstorm has passed, we've all survived, and there is even a post-storm sunse. to grace Dubuque.

The Hollywood Connection

Zigi's is a sham. True, it personifies the "shot 'n' a beer" working-man's sanctuary. True, its wood shines with the polish of years and bears the scars of exuberant good times. But the faded paint, beer stains, and worn footrests do not tell a story of good times and hard times but instead a chapter from the annals of Tinseltown.

In 1977 some Hollywood moguls made a movie called "F.I.S.T.," starring Sylvester Stallone, set in post-depression Cleveland. Rather than recreate Cleveland circa 1937, they came to contemporary Dubuque. Certain scenes were set in a working class tavern, and the Pickett hospitality room was selected as the best site. Extensive alterations were required, and the Tinseltown technicians set to work. Within a few days the sawdust had settled, and "Zigi's" was born, a perfect period piece, now a permanent addition to the brewery.

The film career of Pickett's does not end here. Several years later the brewery served as the location for "Take This Job and Shove It," starring Robert Hayes, and Art Carney as Charlie Pickett, the aging master brewer of a family concern struggling to survive in a corporate jungle where quality-consciousness is as rare as the three-day weekend. Sound familiar? The movie climaxes when the brewery is sold from one uncaring owner to an equally insensitive one, whereupon the hero tells his new boss to, you guessed it, "Take this job and shove it."

A glance at the most recent Brewers Digest Brewery Directory reveals that Pickett has now reverted to the Dubuque Star name. Joe Jr. and Val have moved on and Joe Sr. is a part-time consultant to a business which is no longer a family independent, but a division of AGRI Industries, a giant cooperative. It is a story you feel you've heard before.

(P.S.—Pickett has now closed, most likely forever. The reasons include aging equipment, an uncommitted management, an inflexible union, and an apathetic public. It is a story you know you've heard before.)

I drop off Laura to order food, and leave to gas up the van for the miles still to be covered. The attendant asks in what could only be described as a Dubuquan drawl, "What's The Great Beer Trek?"

"My wife and I are making a trip around the country, learning everything we can about beer."

"Oh, yeah? Well, have you tried our local beer?"

"Sure have."

"And what did you think about it?"

"I think it's great. You can't beat it."

He looked genuinely surprised. "You think it's good?"

"Yup, and I've tasted almost all of them."

And it is true, Pickett's has won widespread praise among beer aficionados. Yet, in their own hometown, they have to constantly combat the blank stare of the gas station attendant. I flashed back to our meeting with

Will Anderson when the Beer Trek was barely wet behind the ears. He had predicted we would find beer drinkers thoroughly ignorant of the virtues of their local breweries. "When's the last time you tried some?" I asked.

"Oh, I haven't had any in years," replied the attendant. He paused, his answer sounding a bit flat in light of my enthusiasm. He decided to check again, in case his ears had deceived him the first time, "And you think it's good?"

Pretty Little Things   *St. Louis, Missouri*

St. Louis greeted The Great Beer Trek with temperatures approaching 100 degrees and humidity to match, a climate more commonly associated with primeval rain forsets than the Midwest. The natives took it in stride, having perfected life-styles in which they hop with great facility from air-conditioned car to air-conditioned office, exposing themselves to the elements for only minimal periods. The day was best suited for floating down the river à la Huck Finn, but Huck did not have a Beer Trek to make.

Our attitude toward Budweiser had by this time made a dramatic turnabout. No longer were the people of Anheuser-Busch villains who had mercilessly driven hundreds of colorful local breweries into obsolescence. Instead they had become the most prominent survivors of an era, the success story who through luck, skill, and fate have been in a position to turn the misfortune of others to advantage. And do not for a moment think there is a brewer in the history of America who would not change places with Anheuser-Busch. Their St. Louis brewery alone has an annual capacity of over 12-million barrels of beer, well more than the combined capacity of all the breweries in Pennsylvania. Along with the Pabst plant in Milwaukee this plant is one of the remaining citadels of beerdom, a Gothic masterpiece, a Notre Dame. Someday the scions of Anheuser-Busch will have to cope with the fact that strategically located plants of half the size make the St. Louis plant a dinosaur, but for now they need all the capacity they can get, thus assuring the vitality of this fulfillment of an Industrial Revolution dream.

The self-proclaimed "King of Beers" has been crowned only recently but it wears the crown so easily one would think that Budweiser had been a fixture for generations in America's refrigerators. Prior to the 1950's, lest we forget, there was no such thing as a national beer. Thus, brewers all over America could, and did, refer to themselves as the "King of Beers." Nor was the brand "Budweiser" (derived from the reknowned Budvar brewery in Czechoslavakia) unique. Versions of Budweiser have been served up from concerns as varied as the DuBois Brewing Co. in DuBois, Pennsylvania, Budweiser Brewing Co. in Brooklyn, New York, and even

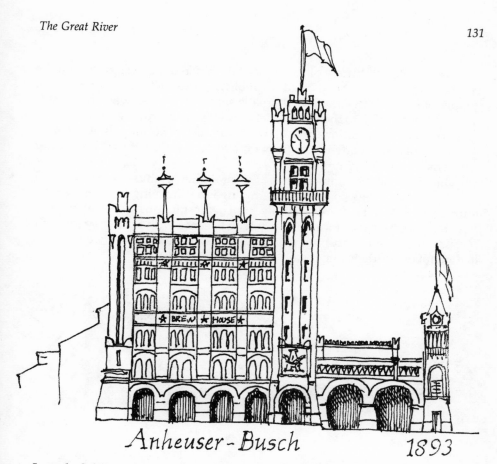

Anheuser-Busch   1893

Joseph Schlitz of Milwaukee. Why did the St. Louis Budweiser succeed where so many others slipped into obscurity?

The contemporary King displays its royal gowns willingly to all who care to see. The first-rate tour features a glimpse of the Clydesdale stables and a view of a brewhouse which, with the closing of Schlitz's Milwaukee plant, is unrivaled as a cathedral for the worship of the brewing gods. Compared to many other tours offered by major brewers, the Budweiser story features a healthy dose of hard information, the technical story being one the company is proud to tell. Within the brewing industry, no one faults Anheuser-Busch for what goes into their beer (more barley and malt and hops per barrel than any other national brewer), for their brewing methods (partial kraeusening and beechwood aging), or even for what they return to the beer drinker (tours and widespread support of related interest events ranging from NASCAR races to offshore powerboat racing). The Budweiser approach is slick, intelligent, and professional. Moreover, the beer is good. If one prefers the type of beer that Budweiser, Michelob, and Busch represent, the argument can be made that no finer or fresher beer can consistently be found in America.

We met with a variety of Anheuser-Busch personnel, ranging from the company historian to their head of publicity, and including more than a couple of guys off the line. No dramatic secret of success was uncovered, beyond a dedication to the basics. Make good beer and run a good business. The formula is revolutionary only in its simplicity. So long as Anheuser-Busch resists the tendency to overcomplicate their business, Budweiser will remain the "King of Beers."

On this steamy summer day a tour of Anheuser-Busch's refrigerated lagering cellars followed by a free sampling is a refreshing prospect for the tourist on a Beer Trek. We happily joined the minions, well-satisfied at how far we had come since our early acquaintance with Budweiser at their Merrimack, New Hampshire, plant. No longer the adversary, we now felt like members of the same team.

AA/Fuel Funny Car, 1981

From a pay phone at Anheuser-Busch we called the first of several local beery leads collected along the way—Bill Henderson, vice-president of the Beer Can Collectors of America. After we explained the purpose of our trip, we never got to the second call. He instructed, nay commanded, us to:

1. Proceed directly to his house.
2. Cancel any plans for dinner.
3. Plan to spend whatever time we had in St. Louis with the can collectors.

Later, we discovered this to be not atypical of the hospitality of can collectors.

Here's the story. You collect toothpaste tubes.

Damned if you know how this whole thing started. As a kid you thought the colorful tubes attractive and once in a while when an unusual tube design was found you threw it in a drawer. Before long the drawer was filled. One ambitious night the tubes were glued to strips of wood and hung prominently around the rec room. Your friends thought you unusual, and you had to agree.

The more tubes collected, the more they were sought. You began writing to toothpaste manufacturers to obtain mint condition tubes which had never been filled. Old dumps were searched for obsolete brands, painstaking hours spent restoring rusty tubes. One day a reporter from the local paper came by to do a small article ridiculing the town nut who collects toothpaste tubes. Then, surprise of surprises, you receive a letter from a man in a nearby state who says that he thought he was the only toothpaste tube collector in the world. He wants to come and see your collection this weekend. The letter is like a salve to your abused subconscious. You are not alone! Someone else appreciates the beauty of an empty tube. There are more calls and letters, and soon there are enough of you to form an organization!

Beer can collectors no longer need to feel alone. To their credit they have maintained the giddy enthusiasm they had on the evening of April 15, 1970, when a group of six met at Denver Wright's house in St. Louis for the purpose of organizing to further the cause of can collecting. Now, more than 24,000 members later, with 93 chapters in the United States and 24 more spread across the globe, whenever they get together they still have a good time.

At the early meetings, members would bring duplicate cans which would be placed on the table for the others to take. Soon the inevitable occurred, and one member swapped his duplicates for a particularly desirable can from someone else's collection. A tradition was born. The BCCA's by-laws reflect the desire on the part of the founders to keep the fun in their hobby. One of the hottest issues currently among can collectors is how to keep the hobby free of creeping commercialism. The damn things have gone and gotten valuable!

Dinner at the Henderson's consisted of pot roast and non-stop beer can stories, no offense intended to Bill's wife Kathy, who is long-accustomed to unannounced visitors and Beer Trekkers.

Bill Henderson once worked in the keg racking room of the Pabst Brewery in Milwaukee, his hometown. This is where the biggest and burliest men were assigned. Bill looks as if he has lifted a few kegs in his day. With red hair, blue eyes, and the build of a defensive end, he looks potentially menacing until he tempers his appearance with a smile. Without a sense of humor this man could be dangerous.

The dinnertime stories invariably have as their butt Bill himself. This is the man who tips over a hand cart of 300 beer cans in the middle of a busy street, risking life and limb to save his empties. This is the man who removes his spare tire to fit more traders in the car for a 1500-mile convention trip, the man who spends a week accumulating cans in Canada only to find out that they will not let him back through customs. Can collectors delight in ignomy. Bill returns to pick up a previously purchased piece of breweriana from a liquor store only to be subjected to the humiliation of hearing the counterman yell to the back room, "Hey, Hymie, where's the sign we got for the fat boy?" Bill roars with laughter at the punchline. In every one of the stories someone is made a fool of. Sometimes it's Bill, sometimes another collector, sometimes the person on the other end of the transaction. No matter, it's all in good fun.

The downstairs of the Henderson's has been surrendered to Bill's treasures. The walls are lined with cans and festooned with colorful electric signs. In the center of the room is a tangled mess of breweriana collected at recent flea markets. In contrast to Will Anderson's where each item is handsomely mounted and displayed, with Bill Henderson the collection clearly rules the man.

As he showed us his collection, Bill Henderson donned his togs, the outfit he wears on the trading floor at the national convention. His costume

Henderson's
VEST OF MANY COLORS

consists of a blue denim vest dappled with the patches of different beers and can-collecting chapters. The effect is not unlike that produced by a Hell's Angel wearing full colors. The specter is imposing in its frivolity.

Soon after the Hendersons moved to St. Louis, they began receiving calls where the caller hung up as soon as the phone was answered. Bill, knowing the experience of some other collectors, made a difficult decision. He took each can in his collection worth more than $20 and sold it, making sure that everyone in the local can world knew what he had done. The phone calls ceased almost immediately. His collection is now worth less, but the fun is back. He collects obscure groups of cans—cans with bottles pictured on them, cans with a history on the back, bock beers. As he leads us through the metal maze, arranged in an order which has meaning only to him, Bill revels in past dealings with other collectors, of being both a BCCA honcho and somewhat of a nut, and in the tall tales and practical jokes which seem to be a part of every gathering of the clan. In his vest of many colors, he is a changed man.

Unintentionally I do something very stupid and cruel. I ask what he does for a living in the real world. He brushes the question aside with a curt, "Oh, I'm just a salesman." What he really is, is a beer can collector. And what he really does is collect cans. In an instant the twinkle has returned to his eye.

"You know," he giggles, "one of the guys was showing his collection to his mother-in-law, and the only thing she could do was keep saying, 'You poor thing, you must not have had any toys when you were young.' "

We continue our slow tour, learning the random circumstances which formed this gathering of cans. An old flat top, blighted by rust, is taken from the shelf to show us the Internal Revenue stamp which once appeared on all cans. We are told the history of the particular brewery, the whys and wherefores of revenue stamps, and the conditions surrounding the acquisition of this can. Bill lectures on the can for ten minutes, stopping not because the topic is exhausted, but because there is so much more to see. He gives the can a last, loving look before returning it to its resting place.

"It's not worth much. It might be if it was in perfect condition, but really none of them are worth anything. You're supposed to use them and throw them away. They're not supposed to be worth anything. It's just . . . they're such pretty little things."

The second Beer Trek day in St. Louis was, like the first, hot and steamy. Also, like the first, it was commandeered by the Beer Can Collectors of America, as we returned to the Henderson household where some of St. Louis's finest were assembled. Any illusions that we had of being beer authorities were quickly shattered, as each new topic brought our appalling ignorance to light. Everyone had a specialty: beer in movies, beer in song, brewery suicides and kidnappings.

Dumping

The fall issue of Beer Can Collectors News Report *was very late. Between arranging conventions, holding full-time jobs, and leading normal lives, the editors had simply not met their deadlines. When the issue finally appeared, chockful as usual with indispensable information for the collector or general beer enthusiast, the normal cover photo had been eliminated in favor of a stark, self-deprecating, typically honest BCCA statement in 72-point type:*

"Yes, This Issue is Very Late."

The good humor which permeates the BCCA, its conventions and publications, has its roots in the fact that what its members are doing is absurd. That established, any degree of fanaticism is accepted, yea, encouraged. No pursuit captures the passion and frivolity of this group so perfectly as dumping—the practice of exhuming abandoned dumps in search of old beer cans. For the serious collector who wants to earn his (or her, the BCCA is definitely a liberated organization) stripes, here are some pearls of wisdom gleaned from recent issues of the News Report:

- *Wear your worst clothes. Your pursuit of the perfect can will bring you in connection with the most foul oozes and excrements known to man. Waders, work gloves, and a fishnet helmet are all advisable apparel.*

- *Hazards to be encountered while dumping include hornets, wasps, poison ivy, snakes, irate landowners, and the law. If you are nabbed, do not bother to explain what you are doing, it's liable to make things worse.*

- *Places to look for cans include old homesites, railway crossings, abandoned cars, drained lakes, hollow logs, and any old place you see a "No Dumping" sign. People to ask about prospective sites include police, firefighters, and anybody old.*

- *Items to bring dumping include spades, machetes, pitch-forks, cardboard boxes, plastic bags, and a cooler of beer.*

- *Dented cans can be undented by dropping a firecracker inside. Lemon juice, oxalic acid, and Naval Jelly are useful in removing rust. A soft-bristled toothbrush is your best cleaning implement. Cleaned cans can be protected with car wax, "Clear Rustoleum," or "Krylon Workable Fixit." If you don't trust yourself send it to a professional beer can restorer:*

> *George Mrugacz*
> *1639 N. Wood St.*
> *Chicago, IL 60662*
>
> *Chuck Foster*
> *5446 White Oak*
> *Hammond, IN 46320*

If you are not yet discouraged, you might have the right stuff to collect beer cans. For the acid test, pack your gear, pack your beer, pick up your buddies and begin the four-hour drive to a reputedly good dumping site. If, at the end of a long day of driving, tramping around, digging, and drinking, you can truly say you've had fun, you have found your calling

The Well Dressed Dumper

HAZARDS
· ANGRY WASPS
· SNAKES
· RATS
· SMALL CREATURES WHO INHABIT GANG.

WARDROBE
· WADERS
· WORK GLOVES
· NET HAT
· BANDANNA

LOCATIONS

NO DUMPING

EQUIPMENT
· PLASTIC BAGS
· BOXES
· SPADE OR PITCHFORK: ALSO REPELS HAZARDS
· BEER COOLER

IGLOO

137

A typical interchange:

BCCA'er: Did you see *Deliverance?* (The movie starring Burt Reynolds.)
GBT: Yes.
BCCA'er: What did you notice?
GBT: What do you mean?
BCCA'er: (expressing disbelief) You know . . . the Lucky Lager scene.
GBT: (completely befuddled) The Lucky Lager scene?
BCCA'er: Yeah, when Burt Reynolds cracks open a beer while they're
canoeing.
GBT: What about it?
BCCA'er: Well, it was a Lucky Lager.
GBT: (utter bafflement; incapable of further response)
BCCA'er: (speaking slowly, as if explaining something elemental to a child):
The river was supposed to be in Georgia, but Lucky Lager is only sold
on the West Coast. Get it? Someone really screwed up.

Another member proudly showed off a scrapbook which featured pho-
tos of dumps and liquor stores which had yielded tremendous stores of
steel and aluminum treasures. The pictures were as dull as a rusty can,
but the stories which accompanied them were entertaining. The evening
passed quickly and often hilariously. Our contribution came in the form
of the beers we brought from our recent journey through the Bavarian
northwoods. Schell's Deer Brand, Bosch's (from Leinenkugel), and Point
Special were religiously bottom-opened (the collector's preferred method)
and consumed. The choice of the natives was eclectic. One person brought
Buckhorn (a budget brew from Olympia), another Miller Lite. Although
can collectors are avid consumers of beer, it is clearly packaging they prefer.
One story tells it all. It is not uncommon for can collectors to schedule trips
to Europe to bolster their collections. Itineraries are carefully planned
around needed cans. Long hours of driving are punctuated by mad dashes
into package stores. Because the collecting rate outstrips the consumption
rate, startled natives have frequently been treated to the sight of mad
Yankee tourists marching from store to curbside where the contents of the
cans (bottom-opened, of course) are summarily poured down the gutter.

The Case Of The Bad Batch   *New Orleans, Louisiana*

Armed with trinkets, stories, and memories, The Great Beer Trek set forth
on a span which was to prove one of the most arduous of the trip. We had
once again entered the Wasteland, although this time we entered drunk
on the sudsy successes of the previous few days. We were unprepared for
the stultifying beerlessness which greeted us in Tennessee, Arkansas, and
Mississippi. The trip was marked with hazards. In addition to heat and

beerlessness, tiny mites called "no-see-ums" invaded our sleeping quarters, keeping us from much-needed rest. And for the first, and only time on our trip, we were apprehended by the law. We were thoroughly guilty of making an illegal left-hand turn, but midway through babbling explanation of the Beer Trek and its nobility of purpose, the officer good-naturedly waved us on.

We reached Louisiana on the upswing, a conclusion reached while sucking the heads of crayfish and sipping on Dixie as a suitably spectacular sunset enveloped the French Quarter. The morrow, we knew, would bring better things, even if it brought simply more of the same—the gustatorial delights of New Orleans and Dixie beer.

New Orleans is not yet a no-beer town, but it teeters on the brink. Falstaff owns a brewery but the plant was inoperative when we visited, the result of a work stoppage by union workers striking for higher wages. When, and even if, the brewery would refill its kettles was unknown. The other riverboat beer whose renown equals Dixie's is Jax. Their attractive white brewery commands the French Quarter as if watching for Napoleon's warships. The only signs of life at the brewery now are the exhaust fans which spin lazily in the wrong direction whenever struck by a puff of wind. Jax is another casualty, another good beer which could not go on. The brand is still available, made by Pearl in San Antonio, but if the present product matches the old Jax, perhaps the demise was just. The beer was one of the most forgettable we had yet encountered.

"There's nothing as New Orleans as Dixie," the saying goes, and only the Mardi Gras Committee or Preservation Hall Jazz Band would quibble. The Great Beer Trek, however, did not receive a rousing welcome at Dixie, because the day of our arrival coincided with the appearance of a bill before the state legislature which would give a tax break to Louisiana's small brewers, i.e., Dixie. The passage of such a bill had important ramifications for the survival of the business, and we willingly took a back seat. This beer, for many years a city fixture, was now struggling to stay afloat, a victim of obsolete equipment, discriminatory competition, and a bad batch of beer which destroyed, in a span of several days, a reputation which had been decades in the making.

The timing could not have been worse—Fourth of July weekend, 1975. All through Louisiana and the adjacent states, beer drinkers were stocked up with local favorite Dixie, primed for a weekend of softball, picnics, and fishing. But something was wrong, drastically wrong, as thousands of Dixie drinkers simultaneously found out as the sun crossed the yardarm on that fateful day.

The trouble was apparent from the first "psscht." The beer was terrible. It was worse than terrible. It had a medicinal taste more akin to Vicks NyQuil than a decent lager. For legions of loyal Dixie drinkers a nightmare had become a reality. It was the ultimate affront: their brew had let them down. For Dixie, a company of limited resources already trying to stave

Trivial Beer

If one attends the annual BCCA or the summertime gathering of the NABA (National Association of Breweriana Advertising) clan, one best be prepared to make proper smalltalk. Certainly the beer will flow like water, and the predominant spirit will be one of conviviality, but what will separate this group from a mere fraternal gathering will be the topics of conversation. These are informal scholars who have directed considerable energy into their pursuits. Individually each one likes nothing better than to strut his stuff verbally in front of the other experts. Below are twenty trivia questions and answers which will help you tread water when the big guns start swapping shots. 1–5 correct means you should stick to diet soda. 6–10 means you will win at least an occasional free beer. 11–15 denotes a certifiable beer nut, and 16–20 means you should have written this book. A true Jedi Master will know all the answers but will quibble with each one so as to show off the full extent of his knowledge.

1. The name of Schlitz's Milwaukee hospitality room?
2. Who is the oldest brewer of lager beer in the United States?
3. Who were the four brewers of Billy Beer?
4. Prior to the opening of New Albion in 1978 who was America's youngest brewer?
5. What brewer used the slogan "The Best What Gives"?
6. How many additives has the FDA approved for use in beer?
7. "MFR" stands for?
8. Two beers referred to as "The Green Death"?
9. The name of Rudy Schaefer's famous yacht?
10. The only female sole owner of a brewery in history?
11. What animal is traditionally associated with Lone Star Beer?
12. How many brew kettles are in the brewhouse of America's largest brewery?
13. Who was John Jenny?
14. Which is the only American brewery known to close for deer season?
15. The first American micro-brewery to open east of the Mississippi?
16. Which city in the United States currently produces the most beer?
17. What brewery currently "gives its soul for rock 'n roll"?
18. What brand of beer compares itself to German Fassbier?
19. Who is the creator of New Amsterdam beer?
20. The name of the "diet beer" brewed by Rheingold?

ANSWERS:

1. The Brown Bottle
2. Schaefer
3. Fall City, F.X. Matt, Cold Spring, Pearl
4. Schoenling Brewing Co., Cincinnati (1937)

5. *John Graf, Milwaukee*
6. *59*
7. *Mountain Fresh Rainier*
8. *Haffenreffer Malt Liquor, Rainier Ale*
9. *America*
10. *Cecelie "Miss Celie" Spoetzl, Shiner Brewing Co.*
11. *The armadillo*
12. *38 (Coors)*
13. *The first known professional brewmaster to arrive in the New World (1623)*
14. *Straub Brewery, St. Mary's Pennsylvania*
15. *William S. Newman Brewing Co., Albany, New York*
16. *Los Angeles*
17. *Dixie*
18. *Altes Golden Lager (Carling/Heileman)*
19. *Dr. Joseph Owades*
20. *Gablinger's*

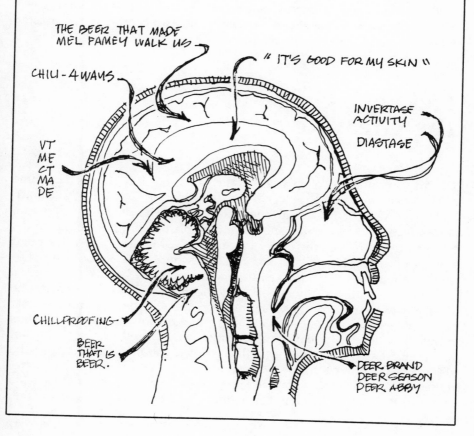

off the onslaught of the nationals, the blow was nearly fatal. In the modern brewing wars, the odds were stacked against the little guy to begin with. His only ace in the hole is the loyalty of his long-time consumers.

It did not matter that the cause of the bad taste was discovered—the beer had picked up flavors from phenol fumes given off by a floor sealant used near the brewhouse—and quickly rectified. The problem now was how could the faith be restored in the consumers who had abandoned Dixie in droves? Word of mouth reputation among beer drinkers spreads fastest when the news is bad, and in Dixie's case the news was catastrophic. How could the brewery convince people that good ol' Dixie was back?

Necessity is, indeed, the mother of invention, and the situation was desperate enough to make Ben Franklins of the dullest of us. The officers of Dixie came up with a suitable plan. They decided to put their money where their mouths were. They would give their beer away, gambling that a taste of the real Dixie would convince the beer drinkers of Louisiana to let bygones be bygones.

The plan worked! Sixty-thousand free six-packs convinced the residents of New Orleans that the South, and Dixie, had risen again. Dixie still walks the fine line between prosperity and extinction, but the Disaster of the Bad Batch has been survived.

Trekker's Guide to The Great River

The Mississippi is the main artery of the heartland. It is bounded by three distinct beer regions (The Beer Belly, the Frontier, and the Wasteland), and its personality is a composite of the three. The river originates as a clear stream, fed by melting snow from the pristine northern hinterlands. You can catch trout in the upper reaches of the Mississippi! At this point it is as pure and blond as a Norwegian towhead. The innocence is lost quickly enough as the waters gather momentum and head south.

The waters are already imposing by the time La Crosse is reached. The river passes several corndog lengths from the Oktoberfest grounds, site of one of beerdom's greatest events each autumn. Flowing south the waters continue to lose their Bavarian pristinity. Rough and tumble riverfront towns like East Dubuque offer a flavor of the Frontier, but don't let the sleaziness discourage you from one of the region's greatest culinary traditions—the catfish fry. If you can't do your own with a six-pack of Pickett's and a driftwood fire, try any place which goes by the proprietor's name, i.e., Mick and Marie's.

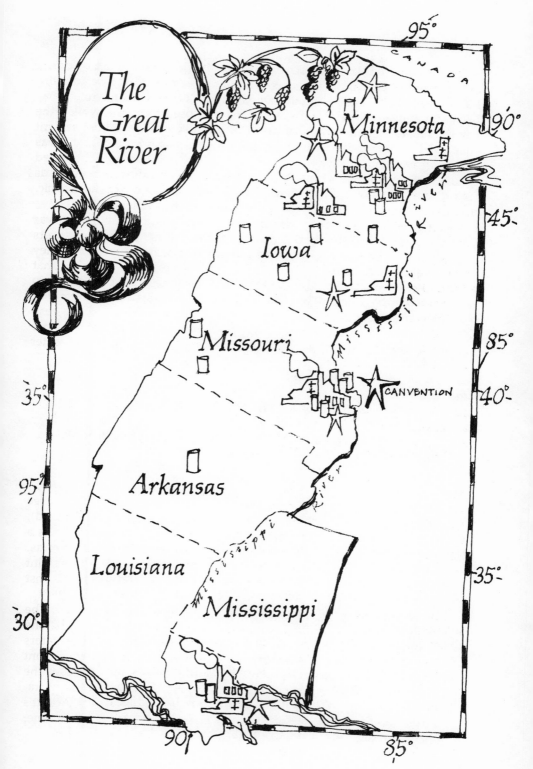

The Great River

Minnesota

Iowa

Missouri

CONVENTION

Arkansas

Louisiana

Mississippi

CANADA

MISSISSIPPI RIVER

95°
90°
45°
85°
40°
35°
35°
95°
30°
90°
85°

143

By the time the Arch is reached, the River (which now must be capi-
talized) is out of control. Forty acres of dissolved farmland are said to pass
St. Louis each hour, and seeing the roiled waters is to believe it. Anheuser-
Busch's immense cathedral provides a last glimpse of Bavaria while the
busy riverboats let you know that the Gulf is but several days float away.
While in St. Louis, don't forget to stop by the Bismarck for a cold one in
the finest tradition.

The voyage from St. Louis to New Orleans may be downstream, but
it is arduous, passing through some of the most depressed parts of America. Arrival at the French Quarter is accompanied by an inevitable feeling
of having achieved destination. There is more trekking to do, but one can
afford the luxury of sitting in the shadow of the defunct Jax brewery and
treating yourself to a six-pack of Dixie and any of a dazzling array of New
Orlean's culinary delights.

For any Beer Trekkers who cannot afford the time or dollars to cover
the entire country, a trip down the Great River provides a microcosm of
what the country offers.

ARKANSAS

State Beer   Razorback (Dixie)
Kindred Spirits
    AR-CAN-SAS Chapter, BCCA, Little Rock, AR
Of Note
    Legendary Brewing Co., Little Rock, promises to bring this state a
    micro-brewery in the near future

IOWA

State Beer   Dubuque Star
Breweries
 • Dubuque Star Brewing Co., East 4th St. Extension, P.O. Box 1248,
    Dubuque, IA 52001
    No tours. T-shirts, hats, glassware available at the brewery.
    Brands: Dubuque Star, Edelweiss, Weber, E & B, Pickett's Premium.
    (Ooops, another "too late," closed Spring '83.)
Kindred Spirits
    Hawkeye Chapter, BCCA, Cedar Rapids, IA
    Pint Size Chapter, BCCA, Rowley, IA
    Central Iowa Winemakers, c/o Paul R. Martin, 6404 Washington, Des
    Moines, IA 50322
    North Central Iowa Wine Club, c/o Laurence Fredrichksen, 1012 Ninth
    Ave., Clear Lake, IA 50428
    Schleswig Wing Club, c/o Larry Gull, Box 293, Schleswig, IA 51461

Of Note
> Amana Village Oktoberfest. Not on the same scale as La Crosse's, but fun enough. Experience Gemeinde Brau. Early October.

LOUISIANA

State Beer   Dixie
Breweries
- Dixie Brewing Co., Inc. 2537 Tulane Ave., New Orleans, LA 70119
No tours. Limited breweriana.
Brands: Dixie, Dixie Light, Jagerwahl das Bockbier, Schwegmann, Schwegmann Light, K & B, K & B Light, Krewes, Fischer, Golden Brau, Golden Brau Light, Razorback, Rock & Roll, Mizzou Brew, Battlin' Bulldogs, and assorted generic brands.

Kindred Spirits
Mardi Gras Chapter, BCCA, New Orleans, LA
Crescent City Homebrewers, c/o Al's Wine Supply, P. O. Box 13986, 8139 Oleander St., New Orleans, LA 70125

Of Note
(RIP) Jackson Brewing Co., New Orleans. Originators of Jax Beer now produced by Pearl in San Antonio, TX. Class riverfront brewery still stands. The idle Falstaff plant is close by.
Mardi Gras. Grand celebration annointed with beer. Starting date varies according to Lent. Bring a costume and leave your valuables and breakables at home.
Dixie Brewing Co., now owned by the Kayes of Coy International fame, operates a hospitality area in an alley behind the brewery which is claimed to be a truly unique New Orleans experience.

MINNESOTA

State Beer   Hamm's
Breweries
- Cold Spring Brewery Co., Inc., 219 North Red River Ave., Cold Spring, MN 56320
No tours, but hospitality room serves beer. Empty cans and beer pitchers available.
Brands: Cold Spring, Cold Spring Light, Cold Spring Export, Fox DeLuxe, Kegle Brau, Western, White Label, Northern, Gemeinde Brau
- August Schell Brewing Co., Inc., Schell's Park, New Ulm, MN 56073
Tours available by arrangement. Deer Park and gardens open at all times. T-shirts, glasses, jackets, and other breweriana sold on premises.

Brands: Schell's, Schell's Lite, Schell's Export, Stein-Haus, Twin-Lager, Fitger.
- Olympia Brewing Co., 707 E. Minnehaha Ave., St. Paul, MN 55165
  No tours. No breweriana.
  Brands: Hamm's, Olympia, Buckhorn, Oly Gold, Lone Star, Hamm's Special Light. Originally a Hamm's brewery, then Olympia, then Pabst, and soon Stroh.
- Jacob Schmidt Brewing Co. (Heileman), 882 W. 7th St., St. Paul, MN 55102
  Tours available by appointment. No breweriana.
  Brands: see G. Heileman, La Crosse, Wisconsin, in The Beer Belly Trekker's Guide.

Kindred Spirits

North Star Chapter, BCCA, Minneapolis, MN

Schell's Border Batch Chapter BCCA, Glenville, MN

Home Foam League, c/o Donald Crenshaw, 3436 Portland Ave., South, Minneapolis, MN 55407

Minnesota Grape Growers Association, c/o Carolyn Barrett, 6133 Oak-lawn, Edina, MN 55425

Purple Foot Wine Club, c/o Lou Barrett, 433 Dogwood Rd., Wyoming, MN 55092

Of Note

(RIP) Standing breweries: Fitger Brewing Co., Duluth (1972). In process of being converted into retail space; John Hauenstein Co., New Ulm (1969); Grain Belt Breweries, Minneapolis (1976). Brand still produced by Heileman. Historic plant still stands.

20 years of American Beers: The 30s and 40s, c/o Reino Ojala, Box 1121, Burnsville, MN 55337 ($8.95 plus $1.50 postage).

Beer Cans of Minnesota, c/o North Star Chapter BCCA, P.O. Box 21378, Columbia Heights, MN 55421 ($4.75 plus 75¢ postage)

MISSISSIPPI

State Beer   Pearl Light

MISSOURI

State Beer   Budweiser

Breweries
- Anheuser-Busch, Inc., One Busch Place, St. Louis, MO 63118
  Tours are available 9A.M.– 4P.M., Monday–Friday, Winter; 9A.M.–4P.M., Monday–Saturday, Summer. Over 2000 items offered in gift shop. Tour includes visit to Clydesdale stables and a glimpse of one of the most inspirational brewhouses left in America. Not to be missed.

Brands: Budweiser, Bud Light, Michelob, Busch, Natural Light, Michelob Light, Michelob Classic Dark (draught only), Wurzburger Hofbrau (imported).

Kindred Spirits

Beer Can Collectors of America, National Headquarters, 747 Merus Ct., Fenton, MO 63026

Gateway Chapter BCCA, St. Louis, MO

K.C.'s Best Chapter BCCA, Kansas City, MO

McDonnell Douglas Chapter BCCA, St. Louis, MO

No Name Homebrewers Club, c/o Suzanne Weatherman, Box 4444, Springfield, MO 65804

Missouri Winemaking Society, c/o Dave Peterson, 12 Medi Dr., Creve Coeur, MO 63141

Of Note

(RIP) Lemp, St. Louis. Standing in the shadow of Anheuser-Busch, a grim reminder of the fate which can befall the industry's fastest rising star. Many other standing casualties in a city which was renowned as "First in booze, first in shoes, and last in the American League."

CANVENTION. The annual gathering of the can-collecting clan each September. Location varies nationally. Contact BCCA for details.

Bacchus & Barleycorn Ltd., 7713 Clayton Rd., St. Louis, MO 63117. Mail-order homebrew suppliers.

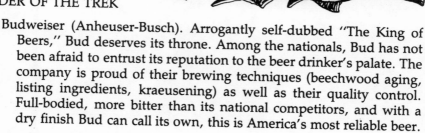

Native Brews of The Great River

ORDER OF THE TREK

Budweiser (Anheuser-Busch). Arrogantly self-dubbed "The King of Beers," Bud deserves its throne. Among the nationals, Bud has not been afraid to entrust its reputation to the beer drinker's palate. The company is proud of their brewing techniques (beechwood aging, listing ingredients, kraeusening) as well as their quality control. Full-bodied, more bitter than its national competitors, and with a dry finish Bud can call its own, this is America's most reliable beer.

Michelob (Anheuser-Busch). Slightly smoother than Budweiser with a filling "eggy" taste which gives the illusion of luxury. On balance a notch below Budweiser, although the exquisite bottle might justify the price premium.

WORTHY OF MENTION

Gemeinde Brau (Cold Spring). Thick, heavy-bodied, reminiscent of what many lager beers tasted like thirty years ago before the trend to lightness took over. Body alone, however, cannot redeem this beer. Available in summertime only.

Dixie (Dixie). Nothing exceptional about Dixie. A house flavor which is not at all unpleasant goes down well with the local cuisine. It is hard to judge Dixie objectively without being influenced by the euphoria of New Orleans.

7 The Frontier

Luckenbach, Texas, to Golden, Colorado
71 days, 14,850 miles on the road

Long Live Long Necks

Luckenbach, Texas

On the Fourth of July, exactly two years after The Great Beer Trek had been conceived in the salty air off Massachusetts Bay, we sipped on Lone Star from long necks in Luckenbach, Texas (population 3, except on nice days like this). There are no signs to Luckenbach; it is not listed on any state map, but it is famous because some cowboy wrote a song about it. Now it is the capital city for Kozmic Kowboys who have infinite capacity for settin', sippin', and pickin'.

To get to Luckenbach, take Route 290 west from Johnson City. A few miles before you reach Fredricksburg take a left. A couple of miles up that road you go down a hill. At the bottom there's a road off to the right, winding through some hardwoods—big trees for Texas. Turn off the engine of your car (ideally you come in a pickup). If it is a nice day and the wind is blowing just right, you will hear the telltale strum. There also might be a little hootin' and hollerin' and surely the sound of bottle caps being removed from long necks.

On this Fourth of July, the scene at Luckenbach was distinctly laid back. Texas heat ain't so bad if you can get out of the sun, and shade is one commodity (along with music and beer) which is never in short supply here. Officially Luckenbach is a rundown post office/general store, a couple of foul outhouses, and however many cowboys have made the trip from Austin or San Anton'. Three native beers are sold: Lone Star, Pearl, and

Shiner (although only the latter truly retains its independence). Each brand has devotees, but all three share the characteristics of the regional taste. These beers are clean and light, but with almost a complete absence of hop bitterness. They share the blandness but not the full-bodied maltiness of the midwestern beers.

The hop is the ingredient in beer which awakens the palate with a scream, demanding respect. Texans make up for any lack of gustatorial muscle by serving their beer crackling cold and without a glass. Beer drunk from the container is intentionally gassy. Brewers inject carbon dioxide immediately prior to packaging. Because it is important for beer to retain a nice head after being poured into glass, beer is overdosed with CO_2 to compensate for gas released during the pouring process. The person who drinks directly from the can or bottle has his taste buds titillated not by the delicacy of the hop, but by the jackhammer stings of a million bubbles exploding on the tongue like the grand finale of a fireworks display. The sensation is made bearable only by the numbing cold.

The cowboy mouth is as well-worn as the muzzle on his horse. There's lots of action that's taken place here. This cavity has been filled by vile forms of weed, chewing tobacco being the most common protective lubricant against drying wind and dust. Smoke is a not-unknown habitue of the oral opening, often from a hemp derivative from south of the border. Chili, barbeque, huevos rancheros, tamales, enchiladas, and other fiery fare sustain the cowboy in his pursuit of the American dream, and burn out his taste buds in the process. By the time he is of legal drinking age, his taste buds are worn as smooth as his saddle, and in need of all the stimulation they can get.

Hondo Crouch is the legendary guru of Luckenbach. Hondo's dead and gone, but for 75 cents you can buy a cold one from his wife. A brew in hand entitles you to go outside and sit on a stump to contemplate life as a truck drivin' man or honkey-tonk angel. If yer lucky mebbe someun' famous will show up—Willie Nelson, Jerry Jeff Walker, David Allen Coe, or even Ol' Waylon—but nonetheless there will be no shortage of beer and music. After a languid afternoon of both, we found ourselves thinking like cowboys.

"There's only one problem with Alabama cowboys," a Luckenbach regular confided in me. "They don't wear their hats low enough." Style is paramount. The jeans and the boots come off only to make love and then sometimes only the jeans. 100-degree heat is never a reason to dress down; better to suffer in silence. There is a cowboy hat, a cowboy belt, a cowboy way to dance, a cowboy way to pick teeth, to spit tobacco juice, to howl at the moon, and to drink beer.

The cowboy way to drink beer is from a long neck, the standard returnable bottle which throughout the rest of the country is known as an "export" or "bar bottle." Speedy Beal, sales manager of the Spoetzl Brewing Co., makers of Shiner beer, offered five reasons why the long neck is the vogue in Texas whereas the rest of the world is phasing it out. Only one rings true:

1. Tradition.
2. The brown bottle is light-proof and protects beer from the harmful effects of the sun.
3. Long necks are better suited to pasteurization than any other container.
4. Long necks ice down well and retain their coldness better than a can.
5. 'Cuz they're tall.

Shiner is a perfect Texas beer, bland and agreeable, the ultimate accompaniment to an outdoor barbeque or a chili cook-out. Herbert, the bartender at the brewery's tiny stand-up bar, serves more than 250 free beers daily to tourists, visitors, and anyone who walks in off the street. A mural of Kosmos Spoetzl dominates the tiny hospitality room which is a pleasant weigh-station for travelers between Houston and San Antonio. Kosmos bought the tidy little brewery on the banks of Boggy Creek after having tried to carve a niche for himself in Egypt, Canada, San Francisco, and his native Bavaria. Southeast Texas has a surprising number of German/Czechoslavakian settlers who came to raise the cattle and to grow the cotton that has made this section of the state nearly as prosperous as the

The Fake Beers

There are obvious similarities between the Good Ol' Boys of Plains, Georgia, and the Kozmic Kowboys of Luckenbach, Texas, but the two mix as well as milk and beer as evidenced by the events of the Fifth (Almost) Annual Luckenbach World's Fair. Someone had the idea of inviting Billy Carter and crew for some spittin' contests, washer pitchin', and general carousing. Hell, they could even watch the feature event, a bare-knuckle fight conducted under the Marquis of Queensbury rules, outlawed since 1917 or so. Billy actually came, but turned heel within 24 hours, according to the local redneck rag, because the local Luckenbachians refused to "kiss his peanut."

Regardless of the authenticity of the story, it demonstrates what it seeks to disprove, i.e., that there is a great deal in common between two groups who are but subspecies of the genus Beer Drinker Americanus.

Just as an anthropologist might compare similar species by studying their patterns of behavior, so does a Beer Trek. Both groups drive pickups, wear jeans and boots, inhabit warm climates, and drink lots of beer. The Georgians favor their brew in cans, while the Texans prefer bottles, but they are otherwise genetically identical.

Both groups have been commemorated by special beers supposedly formulated to the individualized and sophisticated tastes of their namesakes. Billy Beer and Luckenbach Beer are typical of new brews appearing on the American scene. They are formulated and marketed by entrepreneurs who do not have their own brewing facilities, but who contract the actual brewing to professionals. The entrepeneur is thus freed of the capital expense of investing in brewing equipment, while the independent brewer defrays his overhead. The beer drinker benefits in that he has an additional choice of brew, one that is marketed to his specialized taste. Here are some of the "fake" brews to appear on the market in recent years:

Billy Beer—(Falls City, Cold Spring, Pearl, F.X. Matt)—The original "fake." Now defunct, reputedly brewed for Billy's maltier-than-thou taste. Died due to lack of consistency and general lack of interest.

oil regions. Kosmos built his business on the strength of a handshake and a free beer. He was famous for driving a Model A around the countryside, stopping at every homestead to give the farmer in the field a welcome draught of beer from the iced keg he kept in the back seat.

Spoetzl died in 1950, having run the brewery for 35 years. Control passed on to his daughter, Cecelie, who became known throughout the town as simply Miss Celie. Believed to have been the only female sole owner of an American brewery, she furthered the family image established by her father. To this day there is an atmosphere of friendliness in Shiner which hovers somewhere between southern hospitality, gemütlicheit, and "howdy partner." Miss Celie is gone, but if you want to see the brewery,

---

Luckenbach Beer (Pearl)—Supposedly brewed for the tastes of the sidewinders and varmints who hang out in Luckenbach, but mostly capitalizing on the name.

Gilley's (Shiner)—Sold primarily at the world's largest beer drinking joint, mostly to give the tourists something to take home so they don't rip off the ashtrays. Beer is ordinary.

Coy International (Pearl/Dixie)—An ambitious attempt to create a national brand using regional breweries, à la Billy. The Neil Kayes, Jr. and Sr., bring considerable beer business experience to the effort.

Gemeide Brau (Cold Spring)—Brewed and distributed for the Amish communities around Amana, Iowa. Genuinely malty and heavy-bodied, a distinct departure from typical American beers. Distributed only in the summer.

Rock & Roll Beer (Dixie)—Its slogan "I sold my soul for Rock & Roll" was raunchy enough to get it banned from Texas taverns. Any beer which can bill itself as "Too tough for Texas" is just tough enough for a lot of people. "The ultimate party beer" is the brainchild of Joe Edwards, proprietor of the Blueberry Hill Pub and Restaurant in St. Louis.

New Amsterdam (F.X. Matt)—An all-malt, amber, light ale akin to English-style brews which shows that commercial brewers can be versatile if they want to. Distributed mostly at Manhattan's poshest watering holes, this brew is an encouraging, but sad, reminder of the Big Apple's sudsy roots. New Amsterdam is fully krausened and kept refrigerated at all stages in its shelf life, a genuine attempt at brewing a top quality beer domestically.

Tahoe (Leinenkugel)—"Tahoe Beer, Famous as the Lake" has been resurrected by Mark Lang, a concert guitarist turned beer baron. Brewed originally by the Carson Brewing Co., Lang, like many of the "fake" brewers, hopes the success of his brand will lead to a brewery of his own in Nevada.

Some might say that the "fake" beers are the poor man's way to get into the brewing business. Others would say that this is the sane man's way. In any case, the beer drinker sits back and watches the proceedings with bemusement. Anything which results in more and different beers is fine with him.

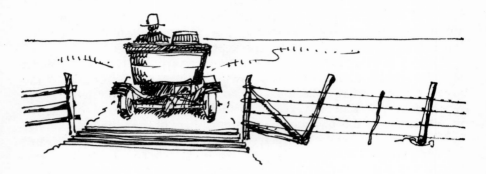

Herbert will be glad to show you around as soon as he has taken care of everyone at the bar. If things are busy, Speedy will take off his sales manager's cap to come over and help out for a while.

The people at Shiner work hard to make friends. No festivity worth going to in this part of the country is not accompanied by kegs of Shiner. Otherwise brewing is big business in Texas. Anheuser-Busch has a Houston plant, Miller one in Ft. Worth (where they brew Löwenbräu), Schlitz in Longview, Falstaff in Galveston (now closed), but it is San Antonio which is the heart of Texas beer country.

The brewery tour at the Pearl Brewery has been eliminated, but the free beer remains. The Jersey Lilly Hospitality Center is a handsome, spacious facility at its best with a loud piano, dancing girls, and a thousand men with foam on their mustaches. The new Jersey Lilly was remodeled in 1970, but a replica of Judge Roy Bean's original in Langtry, Texas, is located right across the street. Pearl also features manicured grounds and gleaming white buildings with a Spanish motif. It is one of the most attractive places where beer is made in the United States.

The ultimate long neck accolade, however, goes to Lone Star, originators of the "Long Live Long Necks" slogan. In Beaumont I asked for Lone Star at a store, only to be told that they carried it only when the motorcycle races were being held nearby. A cowgirl in Lubbock whose life revolved around life at the roadhouse claimed that Lone Star was to be drunk when, and only when, one was in the mood to descend to the true depths of depravity. With such a lusty image we expected Lone Star to flow from a squalid factory. Sanitary conditions would be non-existent, the air clouded with fly swarms. The water would be taken from the San Antonio River just downstream from an asbestos factory. In the hospitality room, gemütlicheit would be reduced to a quart bottle passed from mouth to mouth.

With such expectations we were disappointed to see a gleaming white brewery stack spelling out L-O-N-E S-T-A-R. The brewery sits amid lush surroundings on a favored spot immune from the Texas sun. The visitor facilities are impressive. There are fountains, band shells, and the largest selection of overpriced souvenirs south of Milwaukee. For those who choose to skip the Hall of Antlers and other testaments to man's ability to slaughter, there is a History of Texas wax museum and a brewery tour. The appeal is strictly neo-Disney theme park, and, as such, of little interest to The Great Beer Trek. This was a great place to bring the kids, but hardly the home of the raunchiest beer in Texas. Frankly, we were disappointed.

Lone Star is best experienced not at the brewery, but at any number of Texas roadside joints, late at night when the locals start getting rowdy. The meaning of country music comes into focus just as someone hits you for no apparent reason. You wake up with a fat lip, a beautiful girl whom you've never seen before, and the taste of Lone Star still in your throat.

The White Elephant in the Ft. Worth stockyards, just around the corner from the original Longbranch Saloon, is an excellent place to savor the Lone Star Experience. The house song which everyone sings on Saturday nights is "Let's Get Drunk And Screw." If that is not your style, you might enjoy a few rounds of "Cotton-Eyed Joe"—a song whose resounding "bullshit" chorus accompanies a raucous tribal dance which confirms the cowboy lack of civility. The cow palaces, BillyBob's in Ft. Worth and Gilley's in Houston, mix high-tech urban cowboy style (mechanical bulls and soundproof call-home booths to convince the Old Lady you are still at the

HOME, HOME ON THE RANGE...

office) with the best in low-tech beer drinking. The low-life cowboy experience is infectious, especially when lubricated with enough beer. The outlaw has his own perspective on the world, one with its own rules, morals, and beer drinking style.

I broke down and bought a hat, a raunchy straw affair with a band of exotic bird feathers. Not until we crossed the Oklahoma border, however, did I work up the courage to try it on. The cowboy movement had claimed another convert.

The Beer Wars   *Golden, Colorado*

Late at night, somewhere in the outback of Texas, I awoke Laura to witness an event of cosmic significance—the passing of the century mark on the van's odometer. We whooped and hollered and sprayed a ceremonial Lone Star over the wheels. The jubilation was swallowed, but not diminished, by the blackness.

The pioneers of the West had no idea what would befall them once they left the womb of civilization. Slow, tedious miles were arbitrarily interrupted by panoramic vistas, Indian raids, and violent storms. The thrill of adventure was tempered by the threat of danger, the exhaltation of success counterbalanced by the specter of ignominious defeat.

The Great Beer Trek, cutting a swath northward and westward, was an emotional roller coaster over the nation's flattest terrain. Blessed by a nobility of purpose and annointed with beer, we always seemed to land on our wheels. A madman drove us off the road in Kansas. Rather than robbery and mayhem, however, it turns out he wanted to present us with a jar of bar sausages which he claimed to be the world's best accompaniment to beer. (He was not far from wrong.) The van's muffler fell off in Idaho, but a vacationing mechanic cheerfully spent an hour reassembling it with baling wire. We got stuck in a mud hole while in the middle of a Montana wilderness, miles from the nearest human habitation, only to be quickly rescued by an elderly couple who were exploring the back roads and who happened to have a chain. We dented a good ol' boy's beloved pickup in a Wyoming gas station and received sympathy instead of the expected torrent of abuse. In each case beer bridged the gap between unfortunate circumstance and happy resolution. We freely shared the brightly colored cans from Pottsville, Pennsylvania, and Stevens Pt., Wisconsin, places which grew more exotic with each passing mile. Our liquid tokens successfully broke down whatever communication barriers exist between Scituate, Massachusetts, and Yankton, South Dakota, or Great Bend, Kansas.

At a dusty flea market we traded a number of empty beer cans from eastern breweries for a beautiful, old Falstaff tray. The flea market operator clearly lusted after our remaining cans and proposed the following deal which we could not refuse: two full cans of the local brew for each eastern empty. The deal was immediately struck, the implications as clear as a glacial Rocky Mountain lake. These new cans could be consumed, transported west, traded again two for one, and the process continued. By the time we returned home, if we ever bothered, we would need a trailer for the beer. This Beer Trek could go on forever!

Of the many discoveries made by The Great Beer Trek in the Frontier, a mother lode of breweries was not among them. The occasional skeleton was uncovered. Research often revealed a business that had eked out an arid existence for several decades until the founders simply gave up. The exception is the Adolph Coors Co. in Golden, Colorado, a brewery which claims the distinction of being one of the planet's largest. A look at the success of Coors, especially in light of the company's present plight, illustrates what is best and worst about American business.

First one must comprehend the immensity of the Coors accomplishment.

When the brewmaster at an eastern or midwestern brewery has a problem and needs help fast, he is likely to call up old Gustav, the brewmaster from the rival brewery on the other side of town who graduated with him from the Siebel Institute back in '49. Cooperation between the technical and production branches of competing companies (never sales or marketing) is a tradition in the brewing fraternity. When your brewery is in Golden, Colorado, however, there is no one around to help you. The Coors family realized this very early on and established a self-sufficient brewing operation. From a single plant they produce and distribute beer to the well-spaced population reserves of the West. What is most impressive is that they have accomplished this while making fewer compromises to the considerations of beer quality than any of their brewing peers. If the Coors family encountered problems, they could rely on no one else to solve them. They had to be smarter, they had to be tougher, they had to be more industrious, and they had to be faster on the draw.

Before long the United States' largest brewing plant was located right in tiny Golden, in the foothills of the Rockies. The company is privately held, able to make decisions without the encumberances of a bureaucracy.

A Six-Pack of Ortlieb Light

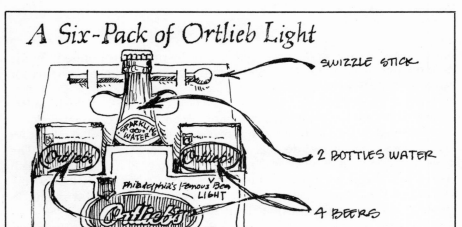

SWIZZLE STICK

SPARKLING GOOD WATER

Ortlieb Ortlieb

Philadelphia's Famous Beer
LIGHT

Ortlieb's

2 BOTTLES WATER

4 BEERS

Light Thoughts on Lite Beer

The brewmaster at one of Wisconsin's small breweries was giving our palates a tour of his company's products. We had just finished sampling his most recent bock, a rich, almost chocolaty brew. He gathered our glasses to rinse in preparation for the next round. Midway through the process he held forth a glass of water with a good-natured offer:

"Care to taste this new Coors Light?"

There is nothing new about light beers. The small beer of the Pilgrims was no more than a watered-down version of the real thing. The English coal miner's "mild" is geared so that his customary five pints after work will still leave him able to walk home. Meister Braü had failed with low-calorie "Lite" before giving Miller a shot at it, as had Rheingold with its Gablinger brand. Small, independent brewers such as Joe Ortlieb and Fred Huber have put the matter into perspective by recommending that consumers create their own light beers by supplementing their normal brews with ice cubes or mineral water.

Michelob Light has 134 calories, 20% less than regular Mich, but almost 200% more than Pearl Light which has one less than Pabst Extra Light and 31% less than regular Pabst Light. Stroh Light and Coors Light claim to be the best tasting of the genre, which is not surprising as both weigh in at over 100 calories, a relatively inconsequential savings over their normal brews. Cold Spring offers perhaps the only truly honest light beer with their Sparkling Mineral Water. Behind closed doors most brewers will admit that they would avoid them if there were not such an unmistakable consumer demand. The American fetish for lightness has infected a wealth of products ranging from potato chips to canned fruit cocktail. It is fashionable for beer connoisseurs to disdain light beers as the lowest achievement of the brewers' craft. In reality, however, the pale nature of light beer exposes brewing flaws just as fair skin does blemishes, and thus is a challenge even to the skilled hand.

There are two ways to make light beers. Some brewers do nothing more than dilute their normal brews (Michelob Light) while others (Miller Lite) employ special enzymes to ferment their beers down to a lower specific gravity. Whichever technique is used, the loss in calories occurs at the expense of flavor and/or alcoholic content. If a more watery brew suits your purposes, don't let the beer snobs intimidate you. But why pay the brewers to do the diluting for you? Try the ice cube/mineral water route. It will raise eyebrows at the local, but it works.

They are well-financed, free of strangulating debt. Furthermore, in its quest for independence, Coors has acquired energy resources (gas, coal, and oil fields) raw materials (barley and hop fields), even packaging capabilities. From the grain to the can, Coors controls the process more than any other American brewer.

What has made Coors' situation even more enviable in recent years has been the unbridled demand for the beer. Coors could limit production to a single brand, eschew fancy graphics and expensive marketing, restrict distribution to eleven western states, establish exacting requirements for its distributors, and still sell out the full capacity of the nations' largest brewery. For years Coors had to be rationed, and the beer world was abuzz with stories of crazy Easterners paying inflated sums for bootlegged Coors.

The Coors Mystique was the industry phenomenon of the early and mid-1970's. The family bypassed opportunities to exploit the demand either by opening up satellite plants or by doing anything which would cause them to lose control of the formula which had brought them so far. Expansion would proceed at its logical pace, and beer drinkers could always be assured that the Coors they drank was just as the family intended. To make a long story short, not many years have passed since those heady days and now Coors finds itself squarely in the world of reality, down there with the regional mortals, struggling not to be caught in the crossfire of the Beer Wars in which the country is involved.

What happened?

Well, everything and nothing. The company still brews a beer that many regard as the ultimate American quaffing experience. Tourists still file through the thirty-eight (thirty-eight!!) kettle brewhouse as if viewing the crown jewels. The company is still profitable, but there are unmistakable signs of weakness. The company which made one beer now makes four (Coors Premium, Coors Light, George Killian Irish Red Ale, and Herman Joseph), all designed for individual market segments. A fifth, Golden Lager, is in the test market stage. Distribution now goes as far east as Florida, and distributors who once regarded carrying Coors as a ticket to a life of leisure now realize they have to hustle to stay afloat. Even with expanded lines and distribution, the company is selling less beer, and having to spend more to do it. The pie keeps being sliced into smaller pieces.

Discussing the rise and (relative) fall of Coors is a favorite industry pastime. Everyone has a pet theory, citing Bill and Joe Coors' well-publicized political conservatism or the charges of discriminatory hiring policies which led to a bitter feud with the unions. The charges and countercharges have been aired in all the national media with no conclusive victor. A Beer Trek, however, tends to avoid explanations which vary very far from the product itself. What really happened to Coors is that all the other brewers got smarter. The company has become a victim of its own revolution.

The early 1970's represented a low point for the American beer drinker in terms of the choices available. Regional brewers were closing at a rapid rate, imported beers were limited in number, and home brewing could potentially land one in the state pen. It was a deprived beer drinker who first heard about a beer brewed in the Rocky Mountains without preservatives or additives, a beer so fresh and lively that it was not pasteurized and was kept refrigerated from the moment it left the brew kettle until it reached his lips . . . A brewer with a genuine commitment to quality was worth getting excited about, maybe even sneaking a few six-packs into your suitcase for your friends in New York.

The novelty did not last much beyond the first six-pack. Certainly the beer was good, but it was extremely light and bland, a disappointment to the beer drinker in search of gusto. "Light" beers appeared on the market as well as beers which advised the beer drinker to "head for the mountains." The word "natural" became the most over-used in the industry. Miller and Bud invaded from the East, spending millions to tout their Coors-like qualities. Olympia pincered in from the West, doing their best to encourage comparison with the original Rocky Mountain High. The subtle advantages of Coors became imperceptible, and the mystique disappeared as inexplicably as it had arrived. The amazing thing is not that it disappeared but that it ever occured in the first place.

The Miracle Dog   *Dillon, Montana*

We rarely took breaks from our travel and beer routines, but the temptation to fish for rainbow trout in Montana proved irresistible. The spot we found proved as spectacular in reality as it looked on the map—a clear, rushing stream backdropped by snow-capped mountains and a blue sky filled with cowboy-sized cumulus billows, accessible only by hiking along the railroad tracks. On the third cast a flash appeared at my muddler minnow and soon dinner was assured. This, the most idyllic of moments, was rudely ripped asunder by the chaos of a freight train carrying bituminous coal from Butte to Detroit or some such. We watched horror-struck as our black pup, Guinness, leaped to her feet from a comfortable resting place between the tracks and tried a futile escape. The hurtling freight, however, was not to be denied. She was hit. For an instant we saw her tumbling beneath the wheels, but then the rumble and blur of the train overwhelmed everything. After several gruesomely deafening minutes we went to clean up the remaining fragments only to discover a dazed, but intact, Guinness lying between the tracks.

We carried her to the van and sped fifty miles to the nearest town, Dillon, where a veterinarian confirmed our fervent but tentative diagnosis—bruised, but otherwise none the worse for her harrowing experience. Back in the van the jubilation became boisterous. We fashioned a special

You Are What You Drink, Part 1

Not a single brewer in the United States admits to brewing an "unnatural" beer. And yet, no one can agree on what "natural" is. The all-grain brewer considers himself more natural than the extract brewer who considers himself more natural than the adjunct brewer. Anheuser-Busch and Miller have waged expensive and protracted war over the definition of natural. A-B accuses Miller of employing microbiological enzymes in the brewing cycle. Miller counter-charges that A-B uses enzymes as well. But, returns A-B, our enzymes are malt-derived and used during the aging, not the fermentation, stage.

As the brewing titans slug it out, tying up the courts and lining the pockets of lawyers with money that could be better spent on malt and hops, the beer drinker interjects a resounding "So what?"

In Germany, beer drinkers are protected by a 15th century purity ruling (the Reinheitsgebot) which defines beer as consisting of barley malt, hops, yeast, and water. That's it. No exceptions, except, ironically, exported beers which have a need for longer shelf life than locally consumed products. The beer drinker who buys German because of the purity standards may in fact be purchasing a more heavily dosed product than anything brewed in the United States.

United States brewers have an FDA approved list of fifty-nine additives that can be used, many of which enhance appearance or stability. Does the use of any of these additives make American beer "unnatural"? Is the domestic product adulterated with chemicals? After visiting scores of breweries, our opinion is no. The brewers we met convinced us of a sincere desire to produce a clean, fresh simple product which will pass the acid test—the palate of the beer drinker. Of the fifty-nine additives, no more than several are used in any given beer and are often used for a specific purpose (to precipitate protein, for instance) and are not present in the final product. Most are organic in nature and, despite scary names, have been exhaustively tested and proven to have no physiological or pathological effect.

Processing methods are of equal importance as ingredients in considering the "natural" question. Pasteurization, a sterilizing procedure in which beer is heated to 145°F for a sustained period, contributes greatly to a brew's shelf life, yet is detrimental to its taste. Nearly all bottled beers are pasteurized; draft beers are not. Coors, which is maintained under refrigerated conditions from brewhouse to retailer, is the most notable exception, the extra care in handling undoubtedly being a major factor in the Coors Cult.

Brewmasters tell a reassuring story about the purity of their beer. The defensive, paranoid posture on the part of the brewing industry which resists open labeling and ingredient listing, however, makes us fear the worst.

cushiony bed for a dog who was by this time receiving demonstrations of affection beyond her dim canine comprehension. Later, when she was comfortably asleep, we went to celebrate in the bars which line Dillon's main street. Like most Montana bars, these feature tables of grizzled cowpokes playing cards, woebegone Indians slumped over their drinks and a sprinkling of smooth-faced neophytes who want nothing more than to have their own visages creased with the scars of elemental human experience which somehow seems closer to the surface in this state than any other. No matter, though. That night we bought beers for any cowboy, Injun or Yahoo in Dillon, Montana, who would listen to our endless repetitions of "Guinness, Miracle Dog of The Great Beer Trek."

There is more to life than beer alone, but beer makes those other things even better.

Trekker's Guide to The Frontier

The distances are great, the terrain and climate extreme. This harsh land comprises most of the continent. For some reason good Americans were content to leave lands of plenty to strike off across deserts and mountains. Among them were brewers for whom there was no opportunity in the

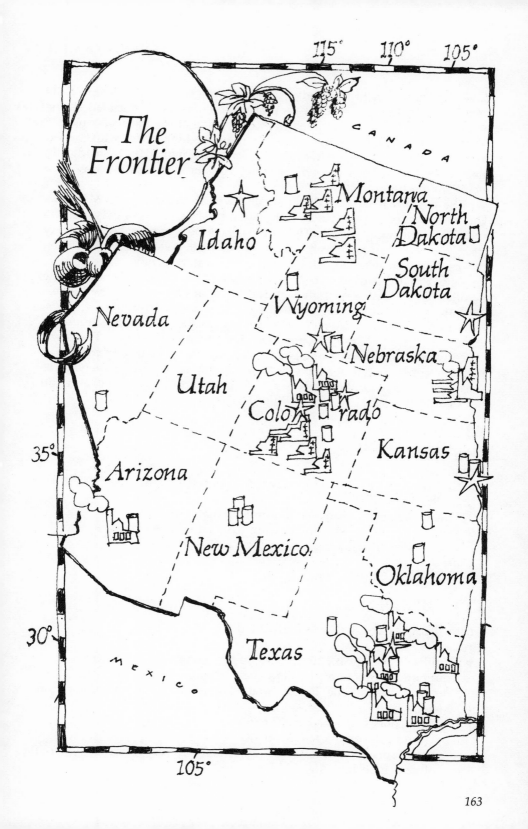

The Frontier

115° 110° 105°

CANADA

Montana

North
Dakota

Idaho

South
Dakota

Nevada

Wyoming

Nebraska

Utah

Colorado

35°

Arizona

Kansas

New Mexico

Oklahoma

30°

Texas

MEXICO

105°

Bavarian Shangri-la of the Midwest. They were hardly the cream of the brewing crop, but the product they produced was as appreciated as the homely, loose women who plied their own trade at the local saloons.

The few native breweries of the Frontier are long gone, with the exception of Coors where the tradition of pioneering mavericks is steadfastly maintained. Their beer is good, and they run the business the way they feel it should be run.

The cowboy bars still exist in small towns from Arizona to Montana. The brands of beer available do not matter much, so long as they are cold and in inexhaustable supply. The cities such as Denver have become every bit as cosmopolitan as Boston or L.A. Imported beers of every pretension can be found at even the simplest Denver watering hole. It is hard to remember that this used to be a cowboy town. That a solid beer drinking tradition exists is demonstrated by the fact that Nevada has the highest per capita consumption in the United States. Boulder, Santa Fe, Taos, Aspen—the names cascade off the jet-setting tongue like a Rocky Mountain torrent in spring. These are not great beer towns, however. The same tastes which can afford a one-bedroom condo for $200,000 or cocaine at $150 a gram cannot be sensitive to a pleasure so basic and inexpensive as a six-pack. Stick with the locals, such as Coors and the Mexicans, and you can't go far wrong.

ARIZONA

State Beer   A-1 (Heileman)
Breweries
- Carling National Breweries, Inc. (division Heileman), 150 S. 12th St., Phoenix, AZ 85034
  Tours available on request. No breweriana.
  Brands: see G. Heileman Brewing Co., La Crosse, Wisconsin in the Great River Trekker's Guide.

Kindred Spirits
A-1 Chapter, BCCA, Phoenix, AZ

COLORADO

State Beer   George Killian's Irish Red Ale
Breweries
- Boulder Brewing Co., 15555 N. 83rd St., Longmont, CO 80501
  Tours by appointment. Limited availability of breweriana.
  Brands: Extra Pale Ale, Porter, Stout, Christmas Ale and other seasonal specialties.
- Adolph Coors Co., Golden, CO 80401
  Tours and breweriana readily available.
  Brands: Coors Premium, Coors Light, Herman Joseph's 1868, George Killian's Irish Red Ale, Golden Lager.

Kindred Spirits
Mile Hi Chapter, BCCA, Denver, CO

Mile High Masterspargers, c/o Brian Milton, 7087 Valmont Dr., P.O. Box 3391, Boulder, CO 80307

American Homebrewers Association, P.O. Box 287, Boulder, CO 80306. National headquarters.

American Breweriana Association, P.O. Box 6082, Colorado Springs, CO 80934

Of Note
Buffalo Bill Days, held annually each summer, Golden, CO. The celebration is midway between Oktoberfest and Wild West, but the beer could not be fresher.

Great American Beer Festival. Late spring, Boulder. Each year the American Homebrewers Association gathers more beers under one roof than ever before. Most of the country's premium beers are represented. This event is the grand finale of the American Homebrewers annual conference.

Microbrewers Resource Directory. Edited by Stuart Harris, published by American Homebrewers Association. An indispensible aid for the would-be commercial brewer. Valuable tips on where to get educated, where to get materials, and how to get legal.

Larimer Square Oktoberfest, Denver. Early October. Drink beer with the chi-chi. Still fun.

(RIP) Standing Colorado breweries: Tivoli Brewing Co., Denver (1967), undergoing renovation; Capital Brewing Co., Denver (1916); Walter Brewing Co., Pueblo, (1975); Phillip Schneider Brewing Co., Trinidad (1957); Telluride Brewing Co., Telluride (1935).

IDAHO

State Beer   Rainier Ale

Of Note
The Politics of Assimilation, c/o Herman Ronnenberg, Box 33, Elk River, ID 83827. A good account of the effects of Prohibition on German-Americans. This book confirms the importance of beer as a political vehicle.

KANSAS

State Beer   Coors

Kindred Spirits
The Amateur Winemakers Association of Topeka, c/o Bob Gilmore, 3824 Doral Ct., Lawrence, KS 66044

Of Note
Bacchus & Barleycorn, 6110 Johnson Dr., Mission, KS 66202. Mail-order homebrew suppliers.

MONTANA

State Beer   Lucky Lager
Kindred Spirits
   Big Sky Chapter BCCA, Missoula, MT
Of Note
   (RIP) Standing breweries: Anaconda Brewing Co., Anaconda (1957);
   Kessler Brewing Co., Helena (1957); Red Lodge Brewing Co., Red
   Lodge (1918); Great Falls Brewing Co., Great Falls (1965).

NEBRASKA

State Beer   Falstaff
Breweries
• Falstaff Brewing Co., 25th & Deer Park Blvd., Omaha, NE 68105
   No tours. Hospitality room sells breweriana.
   Brands: see Falstaff, Corte Madera, CA in the Hop Heaven Trekker's
   Guide.
Kindred Spirits
   Cornhusker Chapter BCCA, Omaha, NE
Of Note
   (RIP) Standing breweries: Storz Brewery, Omaha (1972); Metz Brewing
   Co., Omaha (1961); Jetter Brewing Co., Omaha (1934).

NEVADA

State Beer   Oly Gold
Kindred Spirits
   Sierra Chapter, BCCA, Las Vegas, Nevada
Of Note
   Virginia City Camel Races annually each summer. Climb up to 6000
   feet and leave your civilized side at sea level. Not an event for the
   faint of heart.

NEW MEXICO

State Beer   Tecate
Kindred Spirits
   Sandia Sudz'ers, c/o Roger Minke, 6304 Harper N.E., Albuquerque,
   NM 87109
   New Mexico Wine and Vine Society, c/o Baron Brumley, 6421 Palacio
   S.W., Albuquerque, NM 87105
   Rio Grande Vintners Guild, c/o S.S. Albert, 4115 Marble N.E., Albu-
   querque, NM 87110

NORTH DAKOTA

State Beer   Grain Belt
Kindred Spirits
   Dakota Chapter, BCCA, Valley City, ND

OKLAHOMA

State Beer   Pearl
Kindred Spirits
   Progress Chapter, BCCA, Midwest City, OK
   The Society of Unadulterated Draft Sippers, 2309 Calvert Dr., Ponca
   City, OK 74601

SOUTH DAKOTA

State Beer   Buckhorn
Of Note
   Hop cuttings ($3.29 each) may be obtained from Gurney's Seed &
   Nursery, Yankton, SD 57079

TEXAS

State Beer   Lone Star
Breweries
   • Anheuser-Busch, Inc., 775 Gellhorn Dr., P.O. Box 24297, Houston, TX
     77029
     No tours. No breweriana.
     Brands: see Anheuser-Busch, St. Louis, MO, in the Great River Trek-
     ker's Guide.
   • Lone Star Brewing Co., Inc. (division Heileman), 600 Lone Star Blvd.,
     P.O. Box 2060, San Antonio, TX 78297
     Tours and extensive breweriana available.
     Brands: Lone Star, Lone Star Light, Buckhorn.
   • Miller Brewing Co., 7001 S. Freeway, Ft. Worth, TX 76134
     No tours. No breweriana.
     Brands: see Miller Brewing Co., Milwaukee, WI, in the Beer Belly
     Trekker's Guide.
   • Pearl Brewing Co. (division General), 312 Pearl Parkway, P.O. Box
     1661, San Antonio, TX 78296
     No tours. Breweriana available.
     Brands: Pearl Premium, Pearl Light, Country Club Malt Liquor, Jax,
     Pale Near Beer, Texas Pride, Pilsner Club, Pearl Cream Ale, 900
     Super Premium Malt Liquor

- Joseph Schlitz Brewing Co. (Division Stroh), 1400 W. Cotton St., Longview, TX 75603
  No tours. No breweriana.
  Brands: see Stroh Brewing Co., Detroit, MI, in the Beer Belly Trekker's Guide.
- Spoetzl Brewery, Inc., P.O. Box 368, Shiner, TX 77984
  Tours 10 A.M. & 11 A.M., Monday through Thursday. Wide range of breweriana available.
  Brands: Shiner Premium Beer, Shiner Bock Beer, Gilley's Beer

Kindred Spirits
BCCA Chapters:
Bluebonnet—Dallas/Ft. Worth
Grand Prize—Houston
Lone Star—Austin
Wes-Tex—San Angelo
The Brewers Club, c/o Kindness Israel American Winery and Brewing Supply, 5420 W. Bellfort, Houston, TX 77035
Houston Homebrewers Guild, c/o DeFalco's Home Wine and Beer, 5611 Morningside, Houston, TX 77005

Of Note
The Great (Almost) Annual World's Fair, held some summers in Luckenbach. Sanctioned by no one but not to be missed.
The Adolphus Hotel, Dallas. Built by Adolphus Busch. Now a museum of breweriana both for its architecture and contents.
Micro-brewery planned in Plano, TX, by Don Thompson, American Homebrewer of the Year, 1982.

UTAH

State Beer   Near Beer
Of Note
The former brew kettle of the Walter Brewing Co., Pueblo, CO, is now a tree planter at the Murray Mall, Murray, UT. How the mighty have fallen.

WYOMING

State Beer   Coors Light
Kindred Spirits
Cowboy Chapter, BCCA, Cheyenne, WY
Wyoming Brewers, c/o Todd Cedarholm, Box 3406, Jackson, WY 83001
Of Note
Frontier Days, held annually each summer in Cheyenne. Hot and dusty conditions ideal for prolonged beer consumption.
(RIP) Sheridan Brewing Co., Sheridan, WY (1953)

*Native Brews of
The Frontier*

ORDER OF THE TREK

Coors Premium (Coors). The flagship brand of the nation's largest brewing plant is bound to be good. Its lack of body and bittering characteristics bring condemnation from beer drinkers who resent its lightness, but rather than being criticized for what it is not, Coors should be praised for what it is—America's premium pale pilsner. No one can knock the way Coors brews, packages or handles beer.

WORTHY OF MENTION

Herman Joseph's 1868 (Coors)

George Killian's Irish Red Ale (Coors)
Both brands are noteworthy in that they represent an acknowledgment by a major brewery that its consumership includes beer drinkers who want the opposite of lightness and blandness.

Boulder Extra Pale Ale (Boulder). This top-fermented gutsy brew has not yet hit its stride owing to the brewery's newness, but will continue to improve in coming years. With the demanding standards of the Boulder community, Boulder products have to be good. Their porter and stout are equally welcome balms to variety-starved beer drinkers' palates.

Lone Star Beer (Lone Star). An average tasting lager, but surrounded by enough style to make it special. Seems like you get into trouble after a few Lone Stars.

Shiner Premium Beer (Spoetzl). The lone remaining product of Texas' Bavarian tradition. That's right, Bavarian tradition. A bland, malty, but flavorful beer, it would be more in place in Wisconsin, but Texans don't complain. At least it is available in long necks to douse the flames of chili and barbeque.

8
Hop
Heaven

Phoenix, Arizona, to Yakima, Washington
87 days, 18,220 miles on the road

A Desert Crossing

The southern part of the Frontier is a wasteland in its own right, equal parts blue sky, relentless sun, and sand. Shade and beer are precious commodities, and the two almost always co-exist.

From Golden we headed due south. In Pueblo we stopped at the Walter Brewing Co. which closed on New Year's Day in 1975. This firm was started by one of the brewing Walters whose family plant in Eau Claire, Wisconsin, still survives. At one time, Walters' was the best known Colorado beer, distributed over a twenty-state area.

Four Walter brothers emigrated from Germany in the mid-19th century following the well-worn path of industrious predecessors. They continued west until they found places with no breweries. Three Walters stopped in Wisconsin, but the last, Martin, went on to Pueblo. After seven struggling decades, the brewery fell into the hands of General Brewing Co., the company owned by the same people who control Falstaff, Pearl, and Narragansett. Their specialty is distressed concerns, and the ruthless bottom-line orientation often means that a brewery is worth more liquidated than

170

operating unprofitably. The Walter plant provides a familiar tableau, albeit with a southwestern flair, of a scene witnessed too many times on this Beer Trek. The carcass shows the ravages of repeated predators, its bones bleached by the Colorado sun. White bricks glisten, making you squint into the gaping holes ripped in the walls to facilitate the removal of storage tanks. The brewery is off the main drag in a silent setting which features snow-capped mountains on one horizon, plains on the other. The silence brings home what it took for Martin Walter to launch the enterprise. The

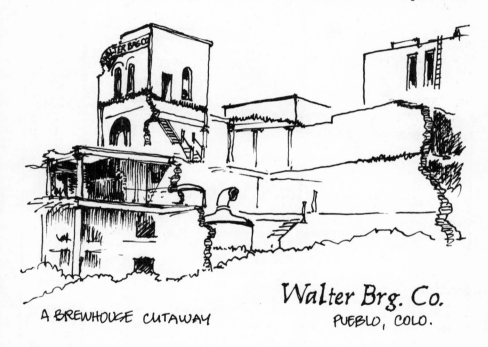

A BREWHOUSE CUTAWAY

Walter Brg. Co.
PUEBLO, COLO.

stores in Pueblo still sell cans with his name, but the beer is really Falstaff from the Omaha plant. We are touched by the stillness and the majesty. Even though we have experienced this same feeling from New Haven to Potosi and now to Pueblo, one is always touched by the death of a friend.

The culture changes dramatically south of Pueblo, the landscape and society reflecting a Spanish heritage from South of the Border. Mexican beers accompany the native cuisine and provide welcome variety after a diet accustomed to the blandness of Coors.

Phoenix proved to be another beer wasteland. Old people, and young people trying to make money off the old people.

We topped off the radiator with the thermometer tipping a Trek-record 114 degrees. A perfect day for a desert crossing. We stopped at a diner for a final dose of air conditioning before setting out. The van managed the heat quite well, the participants somewhat worse. It was a toss-up as to who was more affected, Guinness with her mat of black fur or Laura, now in her fifth month of pregnancy. Both lay in the back panting as I lowered the windows and put the hammer down to try to make the desert pass beneath us.

Mexican Beer

The gutsy character of Mexican beers contradicts theories that attribute quality beer making to a genetic trait shared by Celts and Huns. It also blasts to smithereens theories associating the bland uniformity of American brews with the North American climate. Weak, highly carbonated beers, the brewers claim, are the only types the American consumer will tolerate. Someone has forgotten to tell this to all the people buying Dos Equis, now the second-leading import in the western states. Similar explanations were once given for the popularity of Sunbeam bread. The American consumer, it seems, is not as sheepish as the brewers once thought.

Dos Equis is a caramel colored, English-style brew, not as highly hopped as Bass Ale, but the swarthiest brew west of Yuengling Porter. Interestingly, it has its roots firmly in Bavaria. The Cerveceria Moctezuma which, in addition to Dos Equis, manufactures Mexico's leading brand, Superior, and a special dark holiday brew called Noche Buena, was founded in the late 19th century by a German immigrant, Wilhelm Haase.

Other popular Mexican beers include Carta Blanca, Bohemia, and Tecate, commonly served with a salted rim and a wedge of lemon or lime. All three derive from the Cerveceria Cuahtemoc, S.A., headquartered in Monterey. Mexico's brewing tradition is North America's oldest, dating back to 1544 when Spanish conquistador Alonso de Herrera introduced European-style beer to a native population accustomed to pulque, a concoction fermented from the juice of the maguey plant.

Despite the long history, Mexican beers have only recently become available in the United States. Their popularity in the Badlands has been skyrocketing in the last decade. Coors and Lucky may be fine for the dusty throat, but when it comes to standing up to the fire of chilis rellenos, the serious quaffer looks to the south.

The desert, and man's changing relationship to it, illustrates how compacted our 20th century lives have become. One can fly over the desert in an hour, the drive takes about six hours on Interstate 10, and it is nearly impossible for the prudent traveler to expire. And yet, the desert still holds the same foreboding threat that it did for the early pioneers. As man and Beer Treks move from East to West, the desert is the last and hardest barrier to success. The thought of crossing it on foot is inconceivable.

Most of the breweries were now behind us. Moreover, the tradition of English beer brought to our shores by the Pilgrims and that of Bavarian-style lager which dominates the Midwest were now dim memories at the backs of our throats. For us, as for the Oakies or any American who has set out to Hollywood in hopes of becoming a star, the West Coast held the promise of riches as enticing as they were unknown.

After four grueling hours of hot-wind driving, we reached the Colorado River. The wet, warm, brown ribbon is a poor excuse for the remnants of Rocky Mountain snow, but we were drawn to it as if magnetized—man, woman, and dog plunging into its waters alongside scores of like-minded desert crossers. The experience is as gratifying as it is humbling. Simple pleasures often are. But survival was assured. Several sweltering hours later, the lights of L.A. spread before us. The Pacific was in the air, a balm to parched skins. We treated ourselves to a night of air-conditioned comfort at a Motel 6, even springing for the extra $1.50 to unlock the T.V. The choices on the eight zillion channels included such appropriate fare as *Holocaust* and *The Towering Inferno*. We opted instead for mind fodder. Laura took a cool shower while I went to get a bagful of Mexican fast-food and the usual selection of local brews, forgettable fare including Burgermeister, Brew 102, Lucky Bock, and Eastside.

The beers were as bland and faceless as the television programs. We stared, munched, and sipped, grateful for survival but wondering why we had ventured forth. The tone was sadly transient—a cheap motel, greasy food, and forgettable beer. Stripped of make-up and bathed in fluorescent

light, we stared into the mirror and saw ourselves at our lowest ebb. The hardest barrier, the desert, was behind us, but the Secret of the Suds was still not within our grasp. Time and beer were running out.

The next morning was, by desert standards, cool and dewy. As the rest of the crew slept, I strapped on the trusty Adidases and went for a four-mile jog through the neighborhood. The haze burned off just as I worked up a sweat. Back at the Motel 6 the van was packed and, save for my shower, ready to go. Moments later we were on the road again, in search of more wisdom. There was a cold Burgie-Light in the cooler, a brew which the night before had been judged to be afflicted with terminal anorexia nervosa. What the hell. I cracked it. Morning beer was against the rules, but this was L.A., almost Hollywood, where the rules are permanently suspended. Maybe Burgie-Light will never win any prizes in taste tests, but on that day it provided enough hue to the morning light to make life worth living again.

Morning Beer

Is morning a proper time to drink beer? Perhaps no pastime is as stigmatized as drinking before the sun crosses the yardarm. The tests for alcoholism that appear in women's magazines and Sunday newspapers invariably ask a question about drinking in the morning, the positive answer to which automatically insures a reserve spot in the alkie ward. While there is ample historical evidence of prominent Britishers starting off the day with a pot or two of ale, the morning imbiber is generally regarded as being only a small cut above the child molester. The occasional morning beer is a mildly degenerate pleasure which has its well-defined time and place.

Beer was invented as a food, an important element in the diet of the common man. As such, morning consumption has always been considered normal except in societies such as ours where beer has been "elevated" to the status of a luxury beverage. The tradition, however obscured, is not lost. The following case histories illustrate:

> *Case #1—The Calgary Red. Also known as a Red Eye, this drink sounds horrible but in the right setting tastes great. The morning is gray and damp. You are far enough into the wilderness to be slightly scared. No one else is awake. The campfire is built, but coffee is still twenty minutes off. As you contemplate a way to outwit a trout, mix one small can of V-8 or tomato juice with an equal part of beer. Drink the remaining beer solo at the end to wash out the godawful taste of tomato. Grab your fly rod and attack the stream. (P.S. I tried this drink in a suburban home and nearly threw up.)*

> *Case #2—You are vacationing in St. Maartens, an arid Caribbean island which is duty-free and Dutch-affiliated. Tap water tastes like brine, and a bottle of Heineken costs less than thirty cents. The temperature varies no more than ten degrees off 75, and sunrises are so spectacular as to be required viewing. From the casino you watch the sun rise over the jagged peaks of distant St. Barts. After a long walk on the beach where fisherman haul in sacks of tiny, jewel fish, you return to your seaside bungalow. It is nine A.M.—the time*

you normally go to work. Instead you breakfast on buttered croissants and Heinekens, then move the chaise lounge so you can nap in the sun.

Case #3—The Orange Plus. This is for early morning joggers, tennis players, golfers—anyone who believes in rigorous exercise before breakfast. Into a twenty-ounce mug pour 12 oz. of beer. Note: The low-calorie, tasteless beers like Lite, Anheuser-Busch Natural, Olympia Gold (particularly), and Pearl Light are best. Top off with fresh squeezed orange juice. Drink this and read the morning paper until the rest of the family wakes up. They will think you crazy, but this drink will replenish your body with nutritious fluids more effectively than anything available commercially.

Case #4—The Hair of the Dog. The party was terrific, but you drank too much and fell asleep before being able to fortify yourself with Alka Seltzer. Start the water for coffee, but even before that, check the refrigerator for a cold one to pop. By balancing your chemicals skillfully you might even feel normal by the time you get to work.

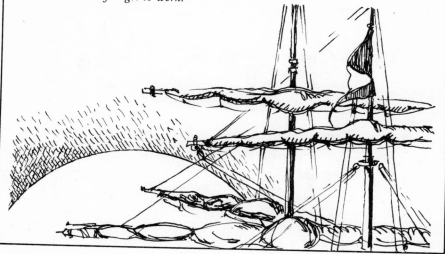

With three operating brewers (Miller, Schlitz, Bud), L.A. can legitimately claim to be one of the nation's largest, if least interesting, brewing cities. The beers of Southern California are not unlike its residents. Everyone comes originally from somewhere else. After several days of touring the breweries and following up leads for various taverns, The Great Beer Trek found itself, not for the first time on its journey, confused. The problem was hardly a lack of variety; in fact, the watering holes featured selections from the antipodes, an average hostelry presenting a more diversified choice of Oriental beers than the collective beer list of the Holiday Inn chain. But the novelty appeared to be an end in itself. Throughout our journey beer had provided a window to the regional soul. Here we found windows, but with views that gazed into endless space. Instead we looked inward.

Prior to Prohibition, it was common for brewers to tout the healthful qualities of the products. Marketers today must scrupulously avoid any suggestion that consumption of malt beverages might be beneficial for anything more than your social life. Beer is portrayed as one of life's little luxuries, reserved for weekends or after work, whenever reality can be temporarily suspended. Constricted by such artifices, the marketers' con-

West Coast Living

cerns inevitably take precedence over the brewmasters'. The clarity of the beer becomes more important than the vitamin B content, and the ability to maintain a stiff, white head supercedes the medicinal benefits of diluted alcohol consumption. Appearance, packaging, convenience, and image are fair weapons for selling beer, issues of content are not. In other words, if you can brew a beer that looks like Farrah Fawcett, you've got a winner regardless of taste.

Brewer's yeast, sold in so many health food stores as a nutritive supplement and a natural by-product of the brewing process, is filtered out of the finished commercial product due to its negative impact on appearance and stability. In our zeal to protect ourselves from false advertising, we are denied access to the truth. Tragically, our prophecies fulfill themselves. Beer has become the leisure beverage it is portrayed as. Its consumption at other times carries stigma. As a nation we live for weekends. We overindulge, then we overcompensate. We counterbalance our pizza with Alka-Seltzer. We drink Lite which is "less filling" so we can "drink more of it." This, we think, is the American way. And if Los Angeles stands for anything, it is the American way.

Fervent Fermenters

San Francisco, California

The Pacific Ocean is probably very nice. It is one of the many prominent features of the American landscape—the Grand Canyon, Mt. Rushmore, and Niagara Falls among others—that we did not see on The Great Beer Trek. In most cases the omission was intentional. Our fermentedly defined schedule left little time for sightseeing. In the case of the Pacific, we drove within a stone's throw of the water for the better part of one thousand miles and never saw more than a grey blur over our left shoulders. The countryside, we understand, is beautiful. We saw only the beer, and have no regrets.

Our inland forays were exercises in pure clarity. We discovered the revolution that we had been seeking, and we learned the Secret of the Suds. And most importantly, we feel confident in stating that beer is alive and well in America, its future in good hands.

The personality parade started innocently enough by looking up the friend-of-a-friend who worked at the famous Anchor Brewing Co. on Mariposa Street. He broke from his multiple duties in the small brewery long enough to say "hi" and to suggest the next person who could add another piece to the mosaic portrait of beer in America. We progressed from referral to referral. By now our black book of contacts overflowethed. The common language was always beer. No one failed to find time to break from active schedules to spend time with an often unannounced Beer Trek. What made the journey even more fun is that there was scarcely a stop we made where we were not offered a beer. When we finally crossed the finish line, we were surrounded by the hop fields of Yakima, heading east, with our journey officially complete. But first, the exception which proved the rule.

PAUL KALMANOVITZ

The Beer Trek was welcomed with open arms almost everywhere, but occasionally our request for an audience fell on deaf ears. Back in New Jersey a call to the Eastern Brewing Co. to ask if we might stop by was met by a firm "no." When we pressed to find if there might be a more convenient day, the response was, "No, not today, not tomorrow, not the next day, not any day after that," followed by a resounding click. Similarly, our attempts to talk to Paul Kalmanovitz, whose signature and personal statements adorn Falstaff cans, were frustrated by stonewalling employees of General Brewing. Although hardly the personification of gemütlicheit, this man's role in shaping the course of beer in America is significant, and no Beer Trek can ignore his maverick influence. His reputation is that of a jackal who preys off the carrion of family concerns, and yet his surgical approach to business has resulted in many fine brands remaining on the market. Overall, his contributions enrich the American beer drinking scene, and we wished he had shared his perspective with us.

FRITZ MAYTAG

The savior of Anchor Steam Beer. Steam breweries historically produced the West Coast equivalent of lager without the use of ice. The steam moniker has been explained in any number of ways, from the beer being invented by a man named Harlie Steam to the hissing foam which bellows

---

You Are What You Drink, Part 2

"Beer is fattening," goes the adage.
"Only if you drink it," answers the sage.
Many non-beer drinkers give as their primary reason for such behavior beer's contribution to the waistline. Prior to Prohibition many brewers made proud claims for the caloric content of their product. In a contemporary society where one can never be too rich or too thin, it is important to reiterate some basic nutritional facts about beer.
Beer is not fattening. No food is fattening except in relation to the individual's total caloric intake.
Calories are a unit measurement that tells how much energy foods provide when oxidized, i.e., burned, by the body. The term "empty calories" is misleading; calories provided by alcohol and the other constituents of beer are just as easily utilized by the body as those deriving from any other food source. "Fattening" describes a relative concept. If more calories are taken in than the body requires, whether in the form of hot fudge sundaes or celery sticks, they will be stored as fat. Examine the following comparison of foods to judge whether or not beer is "fattening":
Put butter and jam on your English muffin and you are up to three beer's worth of calories. A bacon, lettuce and tomato sandwich with mayonnaise, washed down with a glass of milk has about as many calories as a six-pack.
There are as many misconceptions about the positive qualities of beer as about the negative. Beer is low in protein, lipids, and salt. It is high in carbohydrates. Unpasteurized and unfiltered beers such as homebrew contain an abundance of living organisms which nourish the body in physical and spiritual ways. Any homebrewer, having consumed two pints of his favorite, will expound at length on the beneficial qualities of his libation. Whether or not you believe him will depend on whether or not you are sharing his drink.

forth when a keg is tapped. At one time there were twenty-seven steam breweries in San Francisco. Fritz Maytag bought the last one on the day before it was scheduled to close its doors forever. Now he has resuscitated it, and in the process become the symbolic patriarch of America's beer renaissance.

The demise of steam beers came about as a result of the increasing preference for lager, which was regarded as more of a genteel drink than the rock 'em, sock 'em steam beer. Tastewise they were originally similar but the domestic lager has steadily become more bland and tasteless, while Maytag's steam product has retained its original formulation. The workingman's drink has now come full circle and is the elite of San Francisco quaffers. Mr. Maytag's hard-wrought success with the unique, tiny brewery has made him, at an early age, an unofficial spokesman for the enterprising small brewers of the country. With an annual capacity of twenty-five-thousand barrels, he stands as a giant among contemporary

---

In summation, beer is not the all-encompassing nutrition source that a diehard suds-swiller would have you believe. Compared to the utter lack of nutritional value in soft drinks, however, beer has a good story to tell. The question, "Is beer good for you?" has no answer. The question, "Is beer better for you than diet Fresca?" does. The answer is "Yes."

Product	Amount	Calories
Beer	12 oz.	145
Beer (light)	12 oz.	96
Beer (extra light)	12 oz.	70
cola	12 oz.	160
whole milk	12 oz.	249
orange juice	12 oz.	195
prune juice	12 oz.	426
apple	1	120
banana	1	121
fried eggs	2	200
ice cream	1 scoop	185
bacon	3 strips	146
butter	1 tbsp.	100
Swiss cheese	1 oz.	105
bread	2 slices	150
doughnut	1 sugared	151
English muffin	1	180
honey	1 Tbsp.	62
jelly	1 Tbsp.	60
mayonnaise	1 Tbsp.	109
peanut butter	2 Tbsp.	180
sugar, refined	1 Tbsp.	50
yogurt, plain	1 cup	166

micro-brewers. It is more than coincidental that the micro-brewing revival has as its focus neither the top-fermented ales nor Bavarian lagers, but rather this varietal hybrid whose origin is uniquely American.

STEVE NORRIS

Owner/proprietor of The Home Brew Shop, the first retail store to cater solely to the beer maker and one of many Californians to be earning a living from the burgeoning homebrew trade. Over several smooth and creamy Irish-style stouts (his own), Steve, a transplanted New Englander, confessed he knew nothing about beer until he got a part-time job working for a wine- and beer-making supply shop. He never even liked beer until he experienced the delights of his own. Now he services the homebrew clubs in the Bay area: The Maltose Falcons, The Yeast Bay Brewers, and The San Andreas Malts, groups whose approach to brewing is as fractured as their names would suggest. Best of all, his store is a good place to gossip about the who's, why's, and wherefore's of the micro-brewing scene. There is a conspiratorial feeling to the talk, but, even more importantly, a feeling of being on the forefront of the movement. The homebrewers of the West Coast are not back-to-the-land mountain men like Tim Matson in Vermont, but rather yesterday's winemakers, anxious to place English and German beers in a reinterpreted perspective. If Californians can teach the French about making wine and the Peruvians about growing dope, they won't be intimidated by the brewing establishment. Everyone seemingly has plans for a brewery, perhaps in the same way as did the German immigrants of the mid-19th century.

BREWHOUSE

"PART SCAVENGER, PART FOOL..."

—JACK McAULIFFE

New Albion

EQUIPMENT STOCKPILE

JACK McAULIFFE

While others dreamed and schemed, he did it. He opened the first ground-up brewing venture in America since the post-Prohibition era. An ex-Navy man who developed a love for Scottish-style top-fermented ales while in the service, McAuliffe's New Albion Brewery is located in a ramshackle plywood barn in Sonoma, California. With two partners and some part-time help, they turn out four barrels of their ales and stout weekly. The beers look and taste like homebrew with just a little touch of class. (A commercial brewmaster described New Albion to us as "awful, just awful." Later, however, the same brewer admitted that his own bland product could not be given away in England or Germany.)

Because this brewery is so small, there was no suitable equipment available commercially. Jack had to engineer everything himself. When something is not working right, wrenches fly and the air is filled with language that does justice to any ex-Navy man. When asked the brewmaster's most important skills, McAuliffe rapidly ticks off, "Welding, plumbing, scavenging. . . . Stubborness and low initial intelligence don't hurt either." Assistant Suzie Stern wears hip boots and smiles wryly as she starts up the steam hose, "Somehow this is not exactly what I imagined growing up." The future for New Albion is as cloudy as their beers, but their place in American brewing history is assured.

ALAN KORNHAESER

One of the original employees at Anchor Steam, Alan is typical of a new generation who are fascinated by the technical aspects of the brewing process and who apply their expertise with a fanaticism not normally associated with the food processing industry. These are sculptors whose medium is malt and hops. Alan wanted so desperately to learn his trade he paid his own way to brewmaster's school in Scotland. He is professional enough to appreciate the technical superiority of American brewers. One may not like the beer, but one must admire the way it is made. He had visited almost as many breweries as The Great Beer Trek, and one summer made a bike tour of the small breweries in the Midwest.

GUSTAV CHYBA

Brewmaster of the Anheuser-Busch complex in Fairchild, just up the road (but light years away) from Stern and McAuliffe at New Albion. An articulate and gracious spokesman who can make even a subject like liquid chromatography seem simple, he describes the biggest challenge in his brewing career as explaining to the press how his plant could produce thousands of gallons of Budweiser daily back when San Franciscans were rationed to a single toilet flushing per day. His brewing pedigree goes back to his native Austria, but his methods are strictly contemporary Anheuser-Busch. His opinion of New Albion? He wishes them well, but he would prefer Michelob, thank you.

JACK DANIEL

Brewmaster of Blitz-Weinhard Brewing Co., Portland, Oregon. He smiles indulgently when we make the required joke about the brewmaster with the name of a sippin' whiskey. He has seen his company change ownership several times without losing his focus on the requirements of making excellent beer. His calling card will always be Henry Weinhard Private Reserve, a brew he created in response to an assignment from management to create the best beer possible without regard to expense or saleability. His reputation now rests firmly with the dry, hoppy taste of "Henry," a brew which typifies commercial brewing's recognition of the growing sophistication of the American consumer.

ROBBIE SCHMIDT, Jr.

Robbie Schmidt, Jr. of Olympia Brewing Co. is a direct descendent of Leopold Schmidt and the rare executive who breaks the corporate mold. While most people in the beer business serve their product out of a carefully rinsed glass, Robbie tosses you a can. Then he'll follow up with the offer of a chew of tobacco from his pouch. Clearly, he takes the contemporary shoot-outs among the beer industry heavyweights very seriously, but one senses he would have been more at home with the two-fisted style of his great grandfather Leopold who started the family brewing business in Butte, Montana.

CAROL DWOSKIN

Carol is not a brewster (female brewer) or corporate giant. She is something more important—someone who has not forgotten that beer drinking is about having fun. As Director of Public Relations at Rainier Brewing Co., one of the nation's free-swinging breweries, she knows that imagination can sell beer as well as malt and hops. The approach of Rainier is as refreshing as a breeze off Puget Sound. Having fun can be good business.

The brews were as varied as the personalities, sometimes revealing surprising alter egos. Robbie Schmidt's Olympia was delicate and light, bordering on the dainty, while Carol Dwoskin's Rainier Ale lived up to its rock 'em, sock 'em reputation as The Green Death. Gustav Chyba's Budweiser and Fritz Maytag's Anchor Porter share a certain confidence which accompanies the mantle of leadership. The homebrews of the Bay Area brewers are fearless in name and spirit, reflecting the pioneering spirits of their creators. And while brewmaster Daniel raved about his "Henry," we found his everyday Blitz beer to be one of the trip's unsung heroes.

A subtle change had occurred. The West Coast beer fanatics, fervent fermenters all, were not content to simply drink good beer. They had to unlock its secrets and demystify it by plunging into the mechanics of its creation. New frontiers, unlimited horizons, everybody's a star. The process for these brewers holds as much fascination as the product. By mastering the former, they know they can create a new richer world of the latter.

The trip north was as schizophrenic as it was frantic. Blue jeans at one stop, blue business suit at the next. The Great Beer Trek was equally comfortable swapping gossip with the movers and shakers of the microbrewery world, speculating on the next moves by the juggernauts of the Beer Wars, or discussing with runners the merits of light beer as fluid replenishment. Different worlds, different settings, different subjects, different people, but common ground. And the common language was beer.

What to do if you sight an MFR

1. Here are two artist's drawings of authenticated MFR beer shapes. Did the object you observed most resemble (circle one):

A   **B**

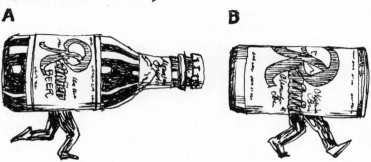

The Wild Rainiers

On the rare clear day that the Seattle resident looks at Mt. Rainier, the second highest peak in the continental United States, for comfort and security, chances are he looks directly through the rising steam of the Rainier Brewing Co.

At one time the Rainier Brewing Co. offered the ultimate brewing tour—free beer, lunch for a nickel, and you didn't even have to tour the plant to qualify. Before long word had spread throughout the rummy population of the Northwest, and the brewery was home to more bums than anyplace west of the Bowery. Such a mistake on behalf of the beer drinker is not atypical of Rainier Brewing Co., a plant which has proved that a loss of independent ownership does not have to mean a loss of individuality.

No beer boasts of its origins as proudly, or as innovatively, as Rainier. Their theme is "Mountain Fresh," but here the logic ends. This is the brewery that puts out sheets to help witnesses document the sighting of a MFR (Mountain Fresh Rainier). They dress adults in giant plastic beer bottles and unloose them on the streets of Seattle in an annual Running of the Rainiers. They stage keg-putting contests and jeep rodeos, brown bag concerts and "Freshtivals." The mainstay Rainier product is a lager beer which comes in both light and dark versions. At one time the company tried to tailor their brews to different drinkerships by putting out a "Light," a "Light-light," and a "Not-so-light." Despite the beerworthy ambitions, the execution was too cute for the lumberjacks, ferryboat pilots, and even the boutique owners of Washington. Chalk up another one.

Rainier Ale has a loyal following which extends from teenagers to beer aficionados. This brew commits the mortal sin of being darker than ginger ale, with more body than Phyllis Diller and more kick than a mule. This is the original "Green Death," and more Washingtonians have first gotten sick on this brew than any other. Every brewery needs one product with a slightly grizzly reputation, and in the Green Death, the people at Rainier have one of the best.

In 1977 Rainier became a member of G. Heileman's stable of regional brewers. Acquisition has not been synonymous with loss of identity. At Rainier regionality is a way of life. Their silly but lovable Rainiers stomp the mountains and moonscapes of Washington State from Snoqualmie to Puyallup each summer, adding sparkle and life to the Northwestern summer. The chest-beating seems to have paid off; at last glance Rainier was number one in sales in Washington.

The Secret of the Suds

Yakima Valley, Washington

If there was a single pivotal moment in the history of beer making, it was when someone cut the bland heartiness of malt and water with the medicinal spice of *Humulus lupulus*—hops. Although the moment is unrecorded, it can safely be attributed to King Gambrinus, the legendary patron saint of brewers. Hops have literally been a fixture in beer ever since, as the distinction between "ale" and "beer" in traditional brewing lore has been simply the absence or presence of this herb. (Ironically, in modern jargon the definition has been reversed, with "ale" describing a more highly hopped beverage.)

Many herbs and spices can be, and have been, used to flavor and preserve brew; in colonial America substitutes included oak boughs, coriander, wormwood, nettles, and horehound. It is probable that the substitutes only compensated for the unavailability of the cone-like flowers of the hop vine. While the others supply flavoring or bitterness, hops supply magic. It's that simple.

Humulus Lupulus

The Great Beer Trek stopped to speak with an official of the Washington State Lab and Hop Division who provided us with a wealth of information about hops, including the following:

- More than one-fifth of the world's hops are grown in the Yakima Valley, accounting for two-thirds of the total domestic production.

- Other commercial hop-growing states include California, Idaho, and Oregon. Other prominent hop-growing countries include England, Germany, and South Africa.
- Hops are perennials which will thrive anywhere between the 40th and 50th parallels. There are multitudes of wild forms and it is not uncommon to find cultivated hops growing alongside colonial farmsites throughout the Northeast.
- Commercial hop vines will grow as long as 30 feet. As with marijuana, male plants must be removed from the crop to prevent fertilization. There is no biological connection between hops and marijuana.
- Commercially grown hops are hybridized to attain specific characteristics such as resistance to mildew and fungus in addition to flavoring elements. Other important bred-in hop qualities: yield bittering value, aroma, durability.
- Most commercial brewers use hops in processed form (extract or pellets), as they lack the proper storage of the delicate flowers. Notable exceptions are Budweiser, Coors, and Pabst.
- Big brewers use a blend of hops (supposedly fifteen varieties in the Budweiser formula) to protect themselves from regional crop failures which could cause annual variations in the taste of their brews.
- The hopping rate of a commercial brewer is approximately one-fourth of what the home brewer or micro-brewer will use. After decades of reducing hop content, there is some evidence that brewers are now increasing hopping rates in response to consumer demand for more flavorful beers.
- The entire 50-million-dollar crop is controlled by five international dealers. If you have illusions of becoming an independent hop farmer or merchant, forget it.
- Home brewers love hops. They will pay outrageous prices for dried-up products, then use them at a rate that would gag the Miller brewmaster. The resulting brew will leave the teeth coated with a bitter aftertaste and will be poisonous to all but the original brewmaster who will consume it with the enthusiasm of a camel at the oasis. Eastern home brewers accuse their western counterparts of overindulgence as far as hops are concerned. And so it goes.

In addition to their flavoring and aroma contributions, hops assist in the clarification and preservation of beer, as well as improving head retention. Moreover, according to folklore, hops will do everything from toning the liver to reducing fever. The one characteristic of hops which is widely accepted scientifically are its soporific qualities, that is, the ability to make you sleep. Two Anchor Steams before bedtime, any beer drinker will tell you, can accomplish more than a fistful of Sominex.

Whenever the first magic moment of hops being added to liquid bread occurred is irrelevant. What is important is that the moment keeps occurring around the world. Although technological improvements in processing have made a range of consistent hop pellets and extracts available, no brewmaster worth his malt, whether at Anheuser-Busch or in his own basement, can resist the sensuous pleasure of working with whole hop flowers.

The Finish Line

The Roadside, eastbound,
Yakima, Washington

The distance runner trains long and hard for his race. The race itself can be an exercise in tedium as the runner fights to maintain his pace within the context of an unwilling body. Then there is the sprint to the finish line followed by the overwhelming sensation of the event having taken a very short time. The long and agonizing miles become compacted into a sense of accomplishment which instantly justifies whatever months of pain and sacrifice have preceded.

On either side of the road in Yakima, Washington, the hop vines absorbed the midsummer sun and transformed its energy into the magical spice which gives beer its allure and mystery. The setting was one of silence and serenity. Harvest time and the influx of machinery and migrant workers were still several weeks off. For the time being, the hops rested in the quiet sunshine to perform their conversion magic. We were tinged with sadness, because for the first time since our sudsy travels started we were heading east. And for the first time there were no new breweries left to trek to. How quick it all seemed!

Any sadness was tempered with a sense of accomplishment, the same feeling of the runner having crossed the finish line. The final leg of our journey, a clockwise semi-oblong beginning in Golden, Colorado, and ending in Yakima, Washington, had taken us over mountains, across deserts, and along the Pacific coast. Most importantly, it had altered our perception of beer in the United States in an inspirational way. Even during our brief moment's respite in the hop fields, the dazzling melange of people, places, and tastes began to take on shape and form. By the time we returned home, we knew the entire experience would have sorted itself out.

Our itinerary completed, we sat in the van awaiting the surge of inspiration that would bring with it the revelation of the Secret of the Suds. It was so quiet one could almost hear the vines grow.

The van was in "park," but our mental wheels were still spinning with the maelstrom of the previous weeks' trekking. The specter of brewery decimation had been saved by the two-out, ninth inning, pinch-hit home run by the West Coast micro-brewers. If but a fraction of them follow through on their plans to start breweries, Mendocino County will someday offer more sudsy variety than 1970-era America.

Moreover, with the proliferation of imports and the diversification of product from the commercial brewing giants, the prospects for the beer drinker are exciting. No wonder the ranks of stalwart beer drinkers have swelled to include health fanatics, gourmets, dieters, and lots of women.

Still . . . no Secret of the Suds. I opened a bottle of Blitz, hoping the imbuement of taste buds in malt and hops might bring forth visible bells or a chorus of angels' voices.

Nothing. Just the sun, the beer, and the hops. But for the miracle of irrigation we would be sitting in a desert. I realized I was stalling.

"So . . . ," I said to Laura, First Lady of the Van and by now a full partner in the quest, if not the consumption, of beer. "What's the Secret of the Suds?"

Her response was a slight shrug. Finally she mustered tentatively, "Maybe beer is too simple to have a secret."

"You mean we made this entire trip, and there is no Secret of the Suds?" The tone of my voice carried the desperation of one whose foundation has started to crumble. Her reply was carried in a slight tightening of the lips and an imperceptible nod.

"Damn," I exclaimed, slapping the dash, hitting the ignition, jerking the transmission into gear and turning eastward onto the road. "Sure was a good excuse to drink lots of beer!" But I was not worried. Although the Secret defied immediate expression, both of us knew it had been revealed long before.

Back in Los Angeles, after our desert crossing, minds and psyches at a low and parched ebb, we had made all the required research stops, had discovered ample evidence of beer consumption, but had experienced none. Whatever laid-back gemütlicheit the city possesses had thoroughly escaped us.

On our last night in town we went for a long walk on the beach. Right at sunset, still feeling somewhat lonely and displaced, we stopped at a tiny neighborhood bar, clearly a local.

Furnishings were spare, as they are wont to be whenever the priorities are people, conversation, and beer. The place could hold no more than a dozen; luckily the collective demeanor was receptive to passing strangers. I asked the person behind the bar, a young woman in her mid-twenties with the blond streaks of an ex-surfer, to serve me a brew which in her opinion represented the best local beer experience to be had. She brought a can of Tecate with salted rim and wedge of lemon. I accepted and consumed graciously, but by the end of the can, once I had explained the purpose of our travels, confessed that the salt/lemon custom aborted the traditional taste of a pretty decent beer.

"I guess you're right," she replied, flipping back her blond locks in a way which would arouse any beach boy. "But we're not much on tradition here."

"Why?" I asked, but I needn't have, as the answer became self-evident after a few minutes of conversation with locals. Jerry, a flight instructor, hails from Madison, Wisconsin. While sipping on a Michelob, he filled us with stories about attending Oktoberfest in La Crosse each autumn of his youth. Mary prefers Miller Lite and is making a fortune in real estate after escaping Nashville and two bad marriages. Her brothers used to take her to the Gerst House, and she remembers fondly the surly competence of the waitresses. Ed spends a lot of time keeping fit. He rides motocross on weekends and has a Ph. D. from NYU where one favorite professor held court with wide-eyed students at McSorley's Ale House. He was glad to hear that McSorley's was alive and well, with crust on the mustard and bite to the beer. He couldn't remember what the beer tasted like, only that it was good. At present his favorite is Dos Equis, but that will change before long. Even the surfer-girl waitress was an immigrant from St. Louis where she and her high school friends used to tour the Budweiser brewery every Friday afternoon for the freebies. She came to L.A. for college and hopes of getting into show biz. So far the closest she has come has been delivering singing balloon-a-grams. But she is not complaining. She's a stalwart on the neighborhood volleyball team, her days are free, and life at the local is casual enough that she felt comfortable joining us for a beer. She drinks Molsons, Schlitz, whatever. One of these days, she confided, she's sure to get a break.

The California lack of tradition revealed itself to be simply the presence of all other traditions. This was certainly food, or should I say "beer," for thought. I asked the bartender for another recommendation. She offered a choice of Tsing-Tao from China or Beck's. "It's great on the rocks with a twist," she added.

We left feeling good about new friends (whom we would never see again), but also about Los Angeles and humankind in general. The world, thanks to the addition of a little water, grain, yeast, and hops, looked a bit cheerier. Good beer, bad beer, brown beer, warm beer . . . what is important is not so much what is in the beer, but what is in the Man. The bottom of the mug is a porthole, and beer, being a fluid subject, provides the lubricant to wipe aside the grime and mire of everyday life. The view, however blurred, streaky, and temporary, is directly into another's soul. That's the Secret.

Trekker's Guide to Hop Heaven

There is no working class on the West Coast, only those who have not yet achieved stardom. Thus, there are few places where one can find an unemployed steelworker staring into his Iron City. The West Coast denizen, be he a biker, runner, cultist, or dope farmer, has invariably managed to include beer in his rituals. Beer is even accepted fare for hot tubs.

Brewery-wise the West Coast is in reasonable shape. All of the nationals have branches there (L.A. is now the highest-volume brewing city in the country), and there is enough regional activity to at least insure different colored cans on the shelf. Add to this the plethora of imports, the rapid evolution of the micro-brewery movement and the popularity of home brewing, and you have a beer drinking scene as rich as any in America.

The mobile West Coast life-style is not conducive to the existence of the reliable, proprietor-owned local tavern, an exception being Hoffman's Grill in San Francisco. The best beer drinking occurs in the home or in the great outdoors. The absence of obvious gemütlicheit is disconcerting at first, but soon diminishes as one becomes more comfortable with the prevalent hedonistic outlook. Go with the flow. Find one of the beer specialty bars which offers a choice of more than 100 different brews and start in one by one. Once finished, eliminate the two you liked least and then begin again. The Truth of Life will discover you by the fifth time around.

ALASKA

State Beer   Olympia
Of Note
    (RIP) Prinz Bräu, Anchorage. A somewhat weird and abortive attempt to create a German brewing tradition, Alaskan-style.

CALIFORNIA

State Beer   Anchor Steam
Breweries
- Anchor Brewing Co., 1705 Mariposa St., San Francisco, CA 94107
  Tours Monday–Friday by advance appointment. Extensive and exquisite breweriana sold on premises.
  Brands: Anchor Steam Beer, Anchor Porter, Christmas Ale (seasonal), Liberty Ale.
- Anheuser-Busch, Inc., 3101 Busch Dr., P.O. Box A.B., Fairchild, CA 94533 and 15800 Roscoe Blvd., Los Angeles, CA 91406

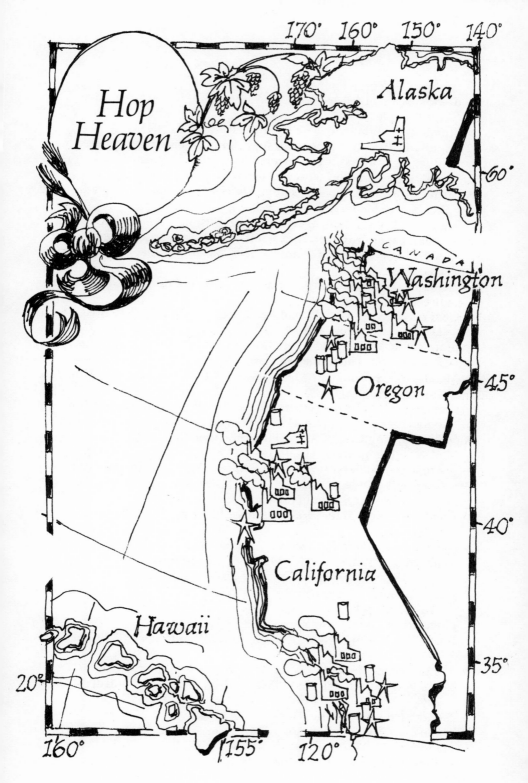

Hop
Heaven

Alaska

170° 160° 150° 140°

60°

CANADA

Washington

45°

Oregon

California

40°

Hawaii

35°

20°

160° 155° 120°

191

No tours. No breweriana.

Brands: see Anheuser-Busch, St. Louis, MO, in the Great River Trekker's Guide.

- Buffalo Bill's Brewery, 1082 B. St., Hayward, CA 94541

  Brands: Buffalo Bill's lager (draught only). Served along with many other fine brews in Bill Owens' brewpub, California's first (or second, depending on who you listen to).

- Falstaff Brewing Corp., Executive Offices, 21 Tamal Vista Blvd., Suite 115, Corte Madera, CA 95925

  Brands: Falstaff, Narragansett, Krueger Pilsner, Krueger Beer, Haffenreffer Lager, Krueger Ale, Croft Ale, Narragansett Ale, Pickwick Ale, Hanley Pilsner, Ballantine Beer, Ballantine Ale, Ballantine India Pale Ale.

  (Separate corporate entity, but common ownership with General Brewing Co.)

- General Brewing Co., Executive Offices, 21 Tamal Vista Blvd., Suite 115, Corte Madera, CA 94925

  Brands: Lucky Lager, Fisher, Lucky Genuine Draft Beer, Brew 102, Regal Select, Ballantine, Falstaff.

- Mendocino Brewing Co., 13351 Hwy. 101 S. P.O. Box 400, Hopland, CA 95449

  Brands: Red Tail Ale, Peregrine Pale Ale, Black Hawk Stout (draught only) Brewpub is open 11 A.M.–11 P.M., 7 days a week

- Miller Brewing Co., 15801 E. First St., Irwindale, CA 91706

  No tours. No breweriana.

  Brands: see Miller Brewing Co., Milwaukee, WI, in the Beer Belly Trekker's Guide.

- Palo Alto Brewery, Mountain View, CA

  Brands: London Bitter (draught only). Catering to the Bay area British ex-patriot.

- River City Brewing Co., 3508 LaGrande Blvd., Sacramento, CA 95823

  Tours by appointment (916) 392-1908. Some breweriana.

  Brands: River City Gold, River City Dark, River City Bock.

- Joseph Schlitz (division Stroh), 7521 Woodman Ave., P.O. Box 32, Van Nuys, CA 91408

  No tours. No breweriana.

  Brands: see Stroh Brewing Co., Detroit, MI, in the Beer Belly Trekker's Guide.

- Sierra Nevada Brewing Co., 2539 Gilman Way, Chico, CA 95926

  Tours by appointment (916) 343-3520. T-shirts, mirrors sold at the brewery.

  Brands: Pale Ale, Porter, Stout, Celebration Ale.

- Thousand Oaks Brewing Co., 444 Vassar Ave., Berkeley, CA 94708

  No tours. No breweriana.

  Brands: Thousand Oaks Premium Lager.

Kindred Spirits

BCCA Chapters:

Road Runner—Ivanhoe

49'er—David

Aztec—San Diego

Golden State—Los Angeles

Humbrewers Guild of Humboldt County, Rt. 1, Box 315E, Arcata, CA 95521

Anza Brewers and Connoisseurs, contact Al Andrews, 5740 Via Sotelo, Riverside, CA 92506

The Maltose Falcons, contact John Fitzgerald, P.O. Box 1073, Thousand Oaks, CA 91360

Of Note

Californians are not steeped in Bavarian traditions but rather tend to create their own happenings and events. The homebrew clubs are particularly active, and each one tends to sponsor some sort of annual extravaganza.

KQED, a San Francisco television station, sponsors an International Beer Festival in the summer. For information call (415) 553-2230.

Composite of California Beer Cans, available from Fred Wolpe, 82060 Tahquitz, Indio, CA 92201 ($7.50 postpaid)

WHB Manufacturing Inc., Tustin, CA. William H. Boam invented "Nude Beer" with the scratchable label and the removable bikini.

Hop root-cuttings (as well as other homebrew supplies) available from Great Fermentations, 87 Larkspur St., San Rafael, CA 94901 ($2.49 postpaid)

Mail-order homebrew supplies from: Wine and the People, 907 University Ave., Berkely, CA 94710

(RIP) New Albion Brewing Co., 20330 8th St. E., Sonoma, CA 95476. The original micro-brewery survived a scant five years, long enough to spawn a gaggle of successors. May yet be revived. Other micro-casualties: DeBakker Brewing Co., Novato (1981); Franklin Brewing Co., Emeryville (1980).

HAWAII

State Beer   Primo

OREGON

State Beer   Blitz (Blitz-Weinhard)
Breweries

● Blitz-Weinhard Co., Inc. (division Heileman), 133 W. Burnside St., Portland, OR 97209

Tours available. Breweriana sold.

Brands: Blitz-Weinhard, Henry Weinhard. (Other Heileman products brewed here). Oldest continually operating brewery west of the Mississippi.

Kindred Spirits

Cascade Chapter BCCA, Portland, OR

Cascade Brewers Society, c/o Don Shankle, 595 Warrenton Ave., Eugene, OR 97404

Heart of the Valley Homebrewers, c/o Steve McGeehan, Rt. 1, Box 10-A6, Philomath, OR 97370

Oregon Brew Crew, 4033 S.E. Belmont, Portland, OR 97214. c/o Joe Bartell, 1411 S.E. 31st St., Portland, OR 97214.

Of Note

(RIP) Cartwright Brewing Co., 617 S.E. Main St., Portland, OR (1981) is distinguished both as one of the first micro's to live and then to die. A worthwhile stop only for the most diehard of beer trekkers.

The Willamette Valley, south of Portland, is the second largest hop growing region in the United States. Many of the small valley communities have summer festivals where beer, quite naturally, is the featured fare.

St. Paul Rodeo, late August, St. Paul. A final blast just prior to the harvest.

WASHINGTON

State Beer   Rainier

Breweries

- General Brewing Co., 615 Columbia St., Vancouver, WA 98660

  No tours. No breweriana.

  Brands: see General Brewing Co., Corte Madera, CA in this chapter.

- Olympia Brewing Co. (division Pabst), P.O. Box 947, Olympia, WA 98507

  Tours 8 A.M.–4:30 P.M. daily. Extensive breweriana available.

  Brands: Olympia, Hamm's, Olympia Gold, Lone Star, Hamm's Light, Lone Star Light, Buckhorn, Pabst Blue Ribbon.

- Rainier Brewing Co. (division Heileman), 3100 Airport Way South, Seattle, WA 98124

  Tours Monday–Friday (except holidays), 1–6 P.M. Extensive breweriana selection.

  Brands: see G. Heileman Brewing, La Crosse, WI in the Beer Belly Trekker's Guide.

- Redhook Ale Brewery, 4620 Leary Way Northeast, Seattle, WA 98107

  Tours by appointment (206) 784-0800. Some breweriana. Brands: Redhook Ale, Blackhook Ale (both draught only).

- Yakima Brewing & Malting Co., Inc., 25 N. Front St., Yakima, WA 98901

  Tours by appointment (509) 575-1900. Limited breweriana.

  Brands: (draught only) Grant's Scottish Ale, Light American Stout,

Grant's Christmas Ale, Russian Imperial Stout, Grant's India Pale
Ale.

Kindred Spirits

Rainier Chapter BCCA, Seattle, WA

The Brews Brothers (home brewers), c/o Vince Cottone, 1123 Palatino
N., Seattle, WA 98133

Of Note

Running of the Rainiers. One of the many promotional events sponsored by this active company. Contact the brewery for a complete
roster.

Merchant Du Vin, 214 University St., Seattle, WA 98101. These people
have brought the panache of the wine world to beer. Their publication, *Beerons*, is an urbane look at the sophisticated side of suds.
More importantly, they have made some of the world's most exotic
brews available to the American quaffer.

(RIP) Carling National Brewery, Tacoma (1978)

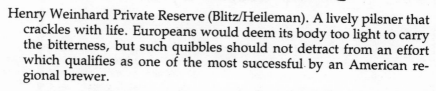

Native Beers of Hop Heaven

ORDER OF THE TREK

Henry Weinhard Private Reserve (Blitz/Heileman). A lively pilsner that
crackles with life. Europeans would deem its body too light to carry
the bitterness, but such quibbles should not detract from an effort
which qualifies as one of the most successful by an American regional brewer.

Anchor Steam (Anchor). Deserves the accolade for the inspiration it
has provided the emerging class of American micro-brewers. The
beer itself carries its points of body and bitterness to an extreme to
make a point well-worth making, i.e., how far contemporary American lagers have strayed.

All products of the micro-breweries. Any beer drinker has to love and
support what these folks are doing. If you're in town, don't miss
the opportunity to sample what might be the future of American
specialty brewing: Washington—Seattle (Red Hook); Yakima (Yakima Brewing & Malting); California—Chico (Sierra-Nevada); Sacramento (River City); San Francisco (Thousand Oaks).

WORTHY OF MENTION

Blitz (Blitz/Heileman). The house brand of this northwestern brewery
is surprisingly underrated. Malty, fruity, lively, and beery, Blitz

lacks the glitzy reputation of West Coast glamour brands. This is a solid brew, the closest to a working-man's special as can be found in this region.

Rainier Ale (Rainier/Heileman). Its amber color hints at its punch. Hard to explain, but this ale is fun to drink.

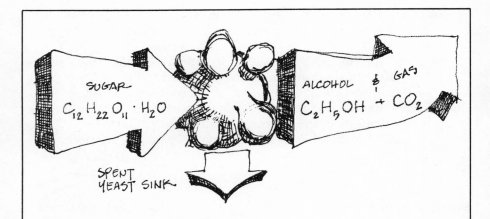

SUGAR
$C_{12}H_{22}O_{11} \cdot H_2O$

ALCOHOL & GAS
$C_2H_5OH + CO_2$

SPENT YEAST SINK

The Secret Of Beer?

Beer yeast, when dispersed in water, breaks down into an infinite number of small spheres. If these spheres are transferred to an aqueous solution of sugar they develop into small animals. They are endowed with a sort of suction trunk with which they gulp up the sugar from the solution. Digestion is immediately and clearly recognizable because of the discharge of excrements. These animals evacuate ethyl alcohol from their bowels and carbon dioxide from their urinary organs. Thus one can observe how a specifically lighter fluid is exuded from the anus and rises vertically whereas a stream of carbon dioxide is ejected at very short intervals from their enormously large genitals.

—By Friedrich Woehler and Justus von Liebig.
Published in the Annals of Chemistry, *Volume 29, 1839*
Suggested by the Siebel Institute of Technology, Chicago, Illinois.

9
The
Flip
Flop

Yakima, Washington, to West Brookfield, Vermont
Many days, many miles

The Case of the Seven Rings

Not long after the completion of The Great Beer Trek, we shared our experiences with some old friends—over beer, naturally. The setting was in the revived harbor district of Portland at $3 Dewey's, an establishment that features exotic brews from every crevice of the planet, served within an unpretentious context which detracts neither from the taste buds nor the conversation. Still overwhelmed with the stimulation of our recent travels, I gushed forth with the wonders to be discovered within the world of suds. One of the crew was sipping at a pint of Guinness Stout which at $3 Dewey's is served in the strict Irish tradition, in a straight glass (a "pounder") and carbonated with nitrogen, as opposed to carbon dioxide.

My friends were considerate enough to let my enthusiasm run its course as I babbled through a litany of newly acquired beer knowledge. The onyx color of Guinness gave me opportunity to tell about the ingredients of beer, how black patent malt is the source both of the color and the richly burnt flavor. This discourse evolved into "beer types," providing an opportunity to decry the lack of variety in America while simultaneously

197

applauding the indomitable spirit of the beer drinker which has led to the resurgence of the small, independent brewery as well as the enrichment of the current beer drinking scene. After a discourse on the demise of the local brewer, I turned to the strengths of American beers, specifically the cleanliness and consistency of the product. No way, I pointed out, could Miller claim to be "good for you" as Guinness does in their advertising. First of all, the federal agencies would not allow it, and secondly, a pasteurized product does not contain the living yeast cells as does a naturally conditioned one such as the Guinness that my friend was now halfway through.

My friends, I think, are more polite and indulgent than I am fascinating, even on a subject as rich as beer, for they let me continue. The creamy head on a good stout could reveal many things, ranging from the malt content of the brew to the cleanliness of the glass. The glassware at $3 Dewey's was obviously flawless, you see, because the foamy head clung to the sides, leaving a ring with each sip. When all factors—glassware, carbonation, temperature, company, and environment—are in harmony, it is said that an empty pint of Guinness will have seven distinct rings. I related this bit of sudsy lore just as my friend pointed his glass skyward for the final sip. When he returned the glass to the table, we counted. One, two, three, four, five, six, SEVEN—a perfect seven! I thanked the beer gods and bought the next round.

The "flip flop" is a trucker term for the return trip. An eastbound driver will check out road conditions with his westbound counterpart, and promises to return the favor, although not literally, to "catch you on the flip-flop." While our westbound segment had taken more than thirteen weeks, we drove home in five days, pulling into the driveway in Scituate ninety-nine days and twenty-thousand miles after embarkation.

Our loosely defined mission had been accomplished. We had been to all the breweries, tasted all the beers, met enough people, and seen enough places to feel that we had developed a much more complete understanding of the land in which we lived. The starting point of a Beer Trek, however, is more distinct than the end point, as there is always another beer to sample, a new tavern to check out, a new recipe to try.

The days of boring highway driving let us consolidate our experiences. As a documentation of the contemporary state of beer, however, The Great Beer Trek was quickly obsolete. Even before we arrived home, one of the breweries we had visited threw in the towel and closed their doors. Since then, many other breweries have merged and recombined. Micro-breweries have opened on the heels of New Albion's boldness, and before long even some of these had closed. New brands have appeared, others disappeared, still others have been reformulated. Beer is, after all, a fluid subject. The same changes which have made our journey obsolete have firmly and uniquely fixed its place in time, history, and beerdom.

Our optimism for the future for the American beer drinker was marred by one looming cloud—the specter of consolidation. No brewing concern, in fact no business, willingly sacrifices its independence. The family brewers we met were united in their commitment to pass along the businesses to sons and daughters. Conditions must be close to ideal for the smaller brewer to survive. Management must be strong, finances secure, and the beer good. Only firms with substantial means can comply with dictates of a government which regulates everything from the label on your bottle to the nationalities of your work force. Only firms with substantial means can afford the investments in advertising and packaging which the consumer has been conditioned to need. Of the money spent for a six-pack, a discouragingly tiny proportion actually goes for the beer. While the local brewers scratch and claw, the Buds and Millers of the beer world continue to gain market share.

Consolidation is visible on the distribution level as well. Distributors in one region can sell in truckload quantities to chain stores, taking lower margins and counting on increased volume to make up the difference. Local retailers and distributors cannot complete and are forced to discount products and services. For the local brewer the economics of scale are clearly working against him. Eventually he will have no way to sell his product. He must either become big enough to play the game or to get out of the way. This, too, is the American way.

In the short run, the beer drinker benefits from consolidation in the form of lower prices, but he will eventually be left with a small number of huge breweries who, faced with little competition, may offer less variety of an inferior product at inflated prices. Budweiser will be General Motors, Miller will be Ford, and all the rest will be rolled into Chrysler. For the beer drinker inclined toward doomsday scenarios, consolidation provides the bogeyman.

Our personal observations contradicted this bleak outlook, instead portraying a future for the American beer drinker brighter now than at any time since the 1840's when the English brewing style of the early colonists was enriched by the first wave of Bavarian immigrants bringing their lager beer traditions. Evidence can be found in the growing interest in, and availability of, imported beers, the birth of the micro-brewers, the legalization of home brewing and its subsequent popularity, and finally the belated response to the beer drinker's need for variety by the commercial brewing industry. The existence of a product such as George Killian Irish Red would have been thought dubious several years ago. That it would be introduced by Coors would be unthinkable. As the sophistication of the beer drinker has grown, so has the beer market. More people drinking more beer is something that any industry loves, and the American brewers have learned that they will sell more beer if their product line is not marketed exclusively toward the stereotyped Joe Six-Pack who swills his lager in front of the T.V. set. Perhaps the vision of a future where the brews available range from Bud in red cans to Miller in green is real, but the consumer of fermented grain beverages, referred to on these pages as "the beer drinker," has historically shown his willingness to fight. As the English brewers learned from CAMRA, the aroused beer drinker is better appeased than fought.

The big picture, then, is a good one. We sensed this immediately upon putting the van into gear in Yakima, and used the tedium of the interstates to formulate our thoughts more coherently. Laura combed through accumulated notes and souvenirs so that we could begin to establish orderliness to the previous weeks. Everything fell neatly into two major categories—the People and the Beers.

Five sudsy subcultures opened their ranks to The Great Beer Trek and contributed greatly to our understanding.

The Outlaws. This group includes renegade beer drinkers and amateur home brewers. Together they lend about 1% of the knowledge and 99% of the color to beer drinking. Their interest in beer revolves around what happens when people get together to drink it.

The Zymurgists. The upper-echelon home brewer and commercial micro-brewer comprise a group whose members freely cross boundaries. Their focus is on the process of brewing. Their knowledge is encyclopedic, their adherence to the traditions of brewing total. If they have a drawback it is that they cannot tolerate second-rate beer.

The Establishment. This includes all those in the business of manufacturing and selling beer, ranging from the food-processing expert to the market researcher. Their jobs dictate a devotion to the art of selling rather than experiencing the pleasure of consumption. Happily, the two pursuits can and do co-exist.

The Observers. These are principally the can collectors (zealots who treasure intrinsically worthless objects) and the breweriana collectors (zealots who treasure genuinely beautiful expressions of commercial art). Both groups are perversely interested in the companies that spawn the objects of their passion. Both groups practice scholarship in its purest form without hope for profit. And both groups could not be more different in character. The brewerianiacs are patricians, civilized and polite. The can collectors are rough around the edges and proud of it.

The Rank and File. Anyone who meets on the common ground of enjoying brew is eligible. The steelworker who thinks I.C. Light is the greatest thing to come along since Terry Bradshaw, the college student who bets his Dad he can tell the difference between Michelob and Old Milwaukee . . . these are the final judges of the product and the process. Their opinions count.

Then there are the brews. The most frequently asked question encountered in our travels was, "Which beer is best?" Our competitive national character always wants to condense an experience such as our trip to a one-word summary. The correct answer, alas, is as unsatisfying as a warm, flat Lite. Nearly all beers are good, some are a little better, and each brew has its time and place. Iron City seems to cut the grit of the steel mill in a way that Budweiser never could. Lone Star in long necks is completely at home at a barbeque where Anchor Steam would be hopelessly out of place. Yuengling Porter is terrific, but it is as different from Coors as Pottsville, Pennsylvania, is from Golden, Colorado. Comparison is impossible.

We have tried in our Order of the Trek Awards to spotlight exceptional expressions of the brewers' art. We hope that we have made the point that you, the beer drinker, are the ultimate judge. Our goal is simply to increase awareness of what is available.

Ten years ago, even with more breweries in the United States, it would have been frivolous to classify beer types. Here, one final time, the beers of the nation pass in review.

THE STALWARTS

The national brands have achieved levels of quality and consistency which make distinction close to impossible. From Bud to Black Label, the formulations are aimed directly at the paunch of Middle America. As for the new generation of light beers, the blandness is intensified. Some would say you can't go wrong with any of these products; others would say you can't go right.

American beer is often maligned for its blandness and rarely praised for its many virtues. The domestic brew is clean (free of off-flavors), consistent, conveniently packaged, inexpensive, and relatively unaltered by chemical additives. On this last subject the American brewer has a better story to tell than is commonly believed. The post-Watergate public is quick to assume that its institutions—government or business—are foisting inferior swill on the consumer. The Great Beer Trek went into scores of brewhouses, all of which were scrupulously clean, and talked to brewmasters from Schlitz to Shiner. We are not chemists, but if there was a rat to smell, we missed it. The 20th century brewmaster is not above using 20th century technology to prepare his beer, but there is more attention paid to the simple traditions of brewing than a jaded public would susr. In terms of its impact on one's health, we emerged from our travels confident that, in moderation, the consumption of beer is more than any other available beverage, including mineral water.

The Notables: Bud, Schlitz, Stroh, Coors . . . and the behind.

The Family Gallery

THE SUPERS

Just as the hop was about to disappear from the American palate, it has made a dramatic comeback in the form of the "super-premium" beers which the commercial brewers have developed to offer the consumer an alternative to the full-bodied and flavorful imports. In reality the Supers approximate the formulations of lagers before the trend toward lightness began. By creating light beers (less ingredients but premium pricing), the

brewers have successfully elevated price structures without affecting their flagship brands. No matter, though, the beer drinker now has available a variety of well-brewed products which collectively are the best sudsy development since home brewing was legalized.

The Notables: Andeker (Pabst), Augsburger Dark (Huber), Black Horse Ale (Champale version), Henry Weinhard Special Reserve (Blitz/Heileman), Michelob (Anheuser-Busch).

ZYMURGISTS' DELIGHTS

It is unfair to rate these beers, as all of the producers are new enough that their products are still evolving. Freshness is a key ingredient in the taste of these local products so it is unlikely that one could ever achieve a truly fair taste comparison. What is important, though, is not which of these beers is superior to another, but rather that an entirely new world of beer tastes is being brought to our shores. The communities and companies:

California
    Chico—Sierra-Nevada
    Hayward—Buffalo Bill's
    Hopland—Mendocino Brewing Co.
    Mountain View—Palo Alto Brewing Co.
    Sacramento—River City
    San Francisco (Berkeley)—Thousand Oaks

Michigan
    Ann Arbor—Chelsea Real Ale Co.

New York
    Albany—Wm. Newman Brewing Co.

Washington
    Seattle—Red Hook Ale Co.
    Yakima—Yakima Brewing & Malting

Notables: Anchor Steam (Anchor), Anchor Porter (Anchor), Sierra-Nevada Pale Ale (Sierra-Nevada), Newman's Pale Ale (Wm. S. Newman), River City Gold.

SEASONALS

Modern technology, specifically the advent of refrigeration, caused the brewing world to turn its back on its climatically determined seasonal traditions. Having eliminated the need for seasonal brews, the beer drinker missed the stimulating effect craved by his palate. As with many aspects of modern life, we are discovering that many physical needs are paralleled by spiritual ones. The suburbanite computer programmer may live a life completely insulated from the harvest or the rites of spring, but somewhere within the animal the primal need to acknowledge the seasons still exists.

Bock beers are making a strong comeback. Brewers as large as Stroh and as small as River City are reviving the seasonal tradition in a serious way. Leinenkugel, Huber, and Dixie have introduced new beers which are fast becoming annual classics. Anchor, Newman's, and several of the micros are producing strong ales designed for wintertime contemplation. Harvest beers cannot be far behind, as well as summertime weiss brews in which wheat substitutes for barley. As long as the business environment remains competitive, brewers will be motivated to attack the specialty markets, to the delight of the adventurous beer drinker.

Notables: Christian Moerlein Bock (Hudepohl), Leinenkugel Bock (Leinenkugel), Augsburger Bock (Huber), Anchor Christmas Ale, Frankenmuth Oktoberfest.

FAKE BEERS

A misnomer, as these beers are as real as the motivation of their entrepreneurial inventors. Some are undoubtedly quick-buck specialties, hoping to strike a responsive chord in consumers through the name alone (Luckenbach, Gilley's, Rock 'n Roll), but others (New Amsterdam) represent genuine attempts by individuals to get into the brewing business without having to build a brewery. With the industry's current excess capacity, this approach to beer making has enormous potential to fill in gaps in the national palate.

Notables: New Amsterdam (brewed at F.X. Matt under the auspices of Old New York Brewing Co.).

LAST OF THE REGIONALS

The survivors in this category have carved more solid niches in recent years, but their futures are still tenuous. The locally owned, limited-distribution brewer is a dying breed and he knows it. The current generation, displaying a sudsy survival instinct, never wants to be the one to abandon a family tradition. These concerns should be preserved for better or worse as are all endangered species. It falls to the beer drinker to support them with his beer drinking dollar. Memorize the names and locations so that when in Rome you can do your beer drinkerly duty:

Dixie Brewing Co., Inc.—New Orleans, Louisiana
Geyer Brothers Brewing Co.—Frankenmuth, Michigan
Cold Spring Brewing Co., Inc.—Cold Spring, Minnesota
August Schell Brewing Co., Inc.—New Ulm, Minnesota
Eastern Brewing Co., Inc.—Hammonton, New Jersey
Champale, Inc.—Trenton, New Jersey
Fred Koch Brewery, Inc.—Dunkirk, New York
Genesee Brewing Co., Inc.—Rochester, New York
F.X. Matt Brewing Co., Inc.—Utica, New York
Hudepohl Brewing Co., Inc.—Cincinnati, Ohio
Schoenling Brewing Co.—Cincinnati, Ohio
Latrobe Brewing Co.—Latrobe, Pennsylvania

Christian Schmidt Brewing Co.—Philadelphia, Pennsylvania
Pittsburgh Brewing Co.—Pittsburgh, Pennsylvania
D.G. Yuengling & Son, Inc.—Pottsville, Pennsylvania
Straub Brewery—St. Mary's, Pennsylvania
Jones Brewing Co.—Smithton, Pennsylvania
The Lion, Inc.—Wilkes-Barre, Pennsylvania
Spoetzl Brewery, Inc.—Shiner, Texas
Jacob Leinenkugel Brewing Co.—Chippewa Falls, Wisconsin
Walter Brewing Co.—Eau Claire, Wisconsin
Joseph Huber Brewing Co.—Monroe, Wisconsin
Stevens Point Brewery—Stevens Point, Wisconsin

The Dogbone Brewing Co.   *West Brookfield, Vermont*

Times goes on and a Great Beer Trek—anyone's Great Beer Trek—becomes
a page in a date book. Tim Matson still lives in Vermont, but he no longer
brews with the conviction and zeal which originally attracted him to the
pastime. Will Anderson's collection of breweriana is being sold. Bill Henderson is no longer a member of the Beer Can Collectors of America, and
Joe Pickett's beer is now no more.

For each sad passage, there are offsetting positive developments. Jack
McAuliffe's New Albion Brewing Co. has met its maker, but the flag has
been picked up and carried forward by a dozen new concerns. The American Homebrewers Association, originally a collection of felons and free
spirits, is now an active and respectable organization whose numbers continue to grow as rapidly as the number of exotic beers offered at their
annual festival in Boulder, Colorado. George Killian, Christian Moerlein,
and Henry Weinhard are becoming familiar names to beer drinkers who
continue to demand higher standards of quality in their libations. Specialty
beers, such as seasonal bocks, are being created by the national brewers,
following the paths of success blazed by the Bill Leinenkugels of the beer
world.

But for the most part, life in the beer world simply goes on, much as
it did before the Beer Trek. Miller sues Bud; Bud sues Miller; Stroh acquires
Schaefer; Pabst acquires Blitz; Pabst merges with Olympia; Heileman buys
part of Pabst . . . to make a long story short, the Beer Wars continue without change or effect which is immediately apparent to the beer drinker.
In La Crosse, Wisconsin, Jeff still religiously attends Oktoberfest. In Dunkirk, New York, and Frankenmuth, Michigan, John Koch and Dick Brozovic fight their respective battles for survival and seem to be maintaining
free-board. Schlitz has revived the "gusto" theme in its advertising, and

at McSorley's Ale House professors are impressing their students with their wisdom as well as their worldliness on the subject of malt beverages.

Our days as full-time trekkers were brought to a screeching halt by economic realities intensified by the arrival of a new beer drinker (circa 1996) named Jake. Eventually we packed our belongings into the van and moved north to Vermont, not far from where we first discussed Mountain Brew with Tim Matson. This time we called not as pilgrims on a quest to learn the Secret of the Suds, but as working blokes.

We reassimilated to life, but not life as we had known it in pre-Trek times. This was life enriched by the presence of malt beverages beyond the ken of the average man. Our new acquaintances in Vermont led existences in which relative self-sufficiency was an expected way of life. Heating with wood, gardening, and animal husbandry were universal. Our introduction of home brewing was readily accepted by the locals, and before long the Cram Hill Brewers were born. Moreover, in my new job I had acquaintances whose routines include frequent travel around the country. My standing requests for local brews served both to enrich their travels and to create a beer larder for the Cram Hill Brewers more varied than any north of the Brickskeller. Beer had become a way of life.

The State Championship

From the moment that the Burlington-based Vermont Homebrewers Association heard about the existence of an upstart, rival group to the South, the Cram Hill Brewers, a showdown was inevitable. The challenge was initially issued to take place on the neutral state fairgrounds, but as seems to happen when homebrew and bureaucracy mix, the establishment found the competition vaguely threatening and withdrew their sanction at the eleventh hour. A humble, but hospitable, sanctuary was found in the country valley of West Brookfield.

The beers are delivered from all over the state the day before Labor Day, when the judging takes place. The problems of identifying, marking, and cooling the brews have been worked out by now, leaving the participants free to do a bit of pre-sampling. The next morning the sun is required to shine brightly. The athletically inclined participate in a running race which modestly bills itself as The Classic, and the judging begins soon thereafter. The standard American Homebrewers evaluation form is used, but the judges are so thoroughly amateur that a pre-competition pep talk is required. Finalists from each category—including "sleazo," a regional favorite in Northern New England—are chosen and then everyone breaks for lunch, which is traditionally barbequed lamb and a boggling array of salads from the plentiful gardens. The vanquished homebrews from the morning session are served up with lunch, giving the onlookers an opportunity to taste beers which range from heavenly to swillacious but that capture the good-natured personalities of their creators.

VERMONT
HOMEBREW CHAMPIONSHIP
Category SLEAZO   Entry # 3
Judged by Hadley

APPEARANCE
Air space
Clarity
Head retention   14

BOUQUET/AROMA   3
Bouquet: hops. Aroma: Malt   8
                                         5
TASTE   5
Hop/malt/grain Taste balance
Aftertaste
Bubbles (Carbonation in mouth)
Body.

OVERALL IMPRESSION   10
After-tasting memorableness,   45
drinkability.

TOTAL
COMMENTS   I HATE
SLEAZO -H.

*Following lunch the top beers from each category are evaluated by the more ex-
perienced judges who have selflessly kept themselves sober for the moment. The results
are tabulated, the winners declared, the prizes awarded, the acceptance speeches made.
The entire ceremony is conducted with a maximum lack of decorum. Catcalls and
banter fill the air. People who arrive not knowing each other leave exchanging phone
numbers and promising to stay in touch. The remainder of the afternoon is devoted
to combat—horseshoes, volleyball, darts, and joke-telling. The scene is not unlike a
Löwenbräu commercial, except that the actors have big noses, warts, pimples and gaps
between their teeth. Much beer is consumed, but inebriation is kept at bay by the
frenetic pace of the activity. By the time the afternoon is unmistakably transcending
to evening, the diehards pitch in and clean up, all the while finding new brews to
sample. When the site has been restored to its original condition, the trash bags twisted
tight, the empties rinsed and packed in their cases, there is a sense of nothing having
happened. After all, a lot of people got together, padded around an eight-mile course,*

consumed vast quantities of food and drink, knocked a ball back and forth over a net and made a few nonsensical speeches. The skin is tight from sweat and sun, the muscles have a pleasant soreness, yet nothing tangible remains. A few trinkets have simply changed hands. Is this what beer drinking is all about?

The question, posed to the diehards who have now pledged to kill the final keg, brings a resounding consensus, "You bet your sweet ass it is!" Someone suggests two-on-two volleyball. It's getting dark. The keg still swishes when shook. Seems like a decent idea. You guys don't stand a chance.

The van still runs, but Vermont winters have taken their toll, and the slam of a door is often followed by the dull tinkle of falling rust. The bumper stickers have faded and peeled, but a close examination reveals an abbreviated version of our itinerary, "Schultz and Dooley Love New

York," "Long Live Long Necks," "If you ain't been to Luckenbach, you ain't shit," "Relax— Don't Worry, Have a Homebrew," and "Forever Beer." The poor beast has hauled hay and sheep and garbage to the dump, and one would never know unless told that this noble steed at one time visited all the nation's breweries. The same can be said for the black dog who lies by the sugar maple in the front yard. From looking at her you would never guess that one day in Montana she was run over by a freight train.

Inside the house a beer drinker sits midway between "blissed" and "fully krauesened." He opens a brew (his current favorite is a coppery mixture of Schlitz and his homebrew batch #81 called "Tooferbusher" for

NO TV

NO JUKEBOX

POTBELLIED STOVE

SAWDUST

MUSTARD

McDogbone's Old Ale House

THE TAPROOM AT DOGBONE BREWING

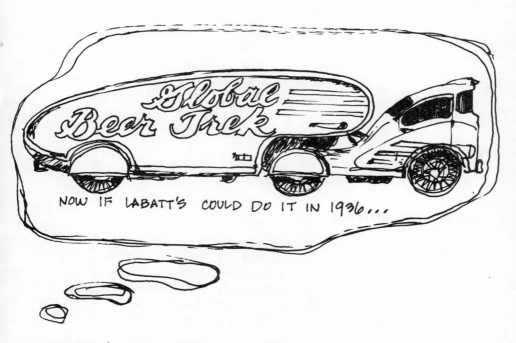

NOW IF LABATT'S COULD DO IT IN 1936...

reasons too obscure to mention), pours it into his favorite mug, and doodles in a spiral bound notebook filled with descriptions, statements, and plans for such exotica as the Dogbone Brewing Company and The Great Global Beer Trek. In the Dogbone section of the notebook are diagrams and schematics, lists of materials, charts and figures. Brands will include Bolt Upright, Dirtball Lager, and Dogbone Ale. The Great Global Beer Trek segment features many crude drawings of yachts, airplanes, railroad cars, and assorted land cruisers, each customized to provide conveyance to the corners of the earth in appropriate comfort and style. On a page marked "Budget" is written simply "a zillion dollars." And on a page entitled "participants" is the line:

"Reservations are now being accepted."

ABOUT THE AUTHOR

STEPHEN MORRIS'S professional career extends beyond the world of beer, touching areas as diverse as rock and roll, baseball, and advertising. At present he is sales manager for a Vermont manufacturer of cast iron wood stoves, claiming that hauling wood and ashes is as intellectually stimulating as drinking beer. He lives in a rural Vermont hamlet with his wife, Laura, and two sons, Jake and Patrick. The van still runs.

ABOUT THE ILLUSTRATOR

VANCE SMITH has been known to drink a beer or two, although her real passion is wood stoves. She's illustrated two books on solid fuel burning (1976 and 1982), runs a design business, belongs to Cram Hill Brewers, and plans to continue brewing beer. Raised in Pasadena, she graduated from Wellesley College in 1970, took her Master of Architecture from Harvard University in 1974, and lives in Vermont.